Wolves for the Blue Soldiers

Wolves
for the Blue Soldiers

Indian Scouts and
Auxiliaries with
the United States
Army, 1860–90

Thomas W. Dunlay

University of Nebraska Press
Lincoln and London

First Bison Book printing: 1987
Most recent printing indicated by the first digit below:
1   2   3   4   5   6   7   8   9   10

Library of Congress Cataloging in Publication Data

Dunlay, Thomas W., 1944–
Wolves for the blue soldiers.

Bibliography: p.
Includes index.
1. Indians of North America—West (U.S.)—Wars,
1866–1895.   2. Indians of North America—West (U.S.)—
Wars—1862–1865.   3. United States Army—Indians.
4. Scouts and scouting—West (U.S.)—History—
19th century.   5. West (U.S)—History—1848–1950.   I. Title
E83.866.D86   978'.02   81–16326
ISBN 0-8032-1658-0   AACR2
ISBN 0-8032-6573-5 (pbk.)

For my mother
and in memory of
my father

Errata

p. 22, line 4: *for* Major Earl Van Dorn *read* Captain Earl Van Dorn

p. 38, lines 37–38: *for* over half of the Fort Phil Kearny garrison
perished *read* eighty-one of the Fort Phil Kearny garrison
perished

p. 163, line 26: *for* 1880s *read* 1800s

p. 220, line 11: *for* vol. 33, pt. 2, pp. 200–203 *read* vol. 34, pt. 3,
pp. 200–206; vol. 50, pt. 2, pp. 1238–39, 1247, 1282–83

Contents

Acknowledgments

First of all I must thank Professor Frederick Luebke, Department of History, University of Nebraska–Lincoln, for a thorough and ruthless job of editing, and for innumerable kinds of assistance and encouragement. Similar thanks are due Professors Peter Maslowski and Ralph Vigil of the same department, and to Professor David Wishart of the Department of Geography, UN-L. Professor Edward Homze of the History Department helped me to acquire a Sheldon Foundation grant, which made possible a research trip to Tucson, Arizona.

The staff of the Nebraska State Historical Society, Lincoln, particularly Ann Diffendahl, are due thanks for indispensable help. I also owe much to the Interlibrary Loan Service at Love Library, UN-L, especially Kitty McGinnis and Shirley Rockel, for their help and for tolerating my frequent appearances. The library and archival staff at the Arizona Historical Society, Tucson, were of great assistance.

Robert M. Utley provided very thorough and constructive criticism and information. I also thank Merrill G. Burlingame, Bozeman, Montana, and Don Rickey, Jr., Colorado, for providing documents. Robert Rhein provided financial and other assistance to make a research trip possible. Colleen Rhein suggested a point that had not previously occurred to me, and Terence Lindell made an interesting and useful piece of information available to me.

The Center for Great Plains Studies, UN-L, granted leave for research in Washington, and Professor Gary Moulton provided useful advice for a country boy in the big city.

Wolves for the Blue Soldiers

*. . . these Crows, who were going to be
Wolves for the blue soldiers . . .*
Frank B. Linderman, *Pretty Shield*

Scout. *Make sign for* Wolf
W. P. Clark, *The Indian Sign Language*

Introduction

In the period following the Civil War, the principal task of the United States Army was to fight, subdue, and control the Indians of the trans-Mississippi West. In carrying out this mission, the military encountered special problems, some of them unique to the frontier, others merely intensifications of problems encountered in more conventional warfare. One method of coping with these problems was a reversion to a practice followed by European armies in North America for centuries: the employment of American Indians as scouts and auxiliaries against other Indians. As time went on, these Indian allies became increasingly important, both in their reconnaissance and in their combat roles.

Two basic questions must be answered. First, why did the army become dependent on Indians to carry out its operations, and how did the allies serve these needs? Second, why did the Indians choose to serve those who sought to dispossess and dominate their own people?

The service of native allies with the military is a significant feature of Indian-white contact and conflict in the American West. For many Indians it was an important form of interaction with white American culture and society—their first major encounter with the whites' way of thinking and doing things. For the Indian scouts it was a way of taking part of the white culture, a part more appealing to them than having the whole thing thrust upon them at once, as the civil authorities intended. Indeed, some military men were thinking of assimilation as the long-term result when they advocated the use of Indian auxiliaries.

The service of the Indian scouts is therefore a phase of both American military and Indian history. One may readily assess the military value of these Indian allies, because many army officers explained in detail why they were needed and how they were employed. But it is more difficult to determine the motives of the Indian scouts themselves, for they looked at life from a different cultural perspective. Moreover, few could speak English and thus have their ideas recorded. For the same reason it is difficult to determine the effects of military service on the scouts and their societies. If the history of the American Indians and their relations with the whites is to be understood, this aspect of that history should be examined.

The subject has not been entirely neglected. Historians have surveyed the period of the Indian wars, examined single Indian campaigns, and written studies of particular Indian tribes. In none of these cases could they make the Indian scouts their main focus of attention.

The historian Robert Berkhofer, writing about the difficulties of treating Indian history, has noted that the diversity of tribal and regional histories renders it difficult to produce a history that is not overgeneralized and that does not give a false impression of uniformity. Yet if the history of a particular tribe or region is to be transcended, the historian must seek some factor or experience that provided uniformity over a broad area or time period. Because of the diversity of Indian cultures and tribal histories, such a uniform factor or experience is usually one provided by whites; the need for reliable written sources reinforces this choice.[1]

The Indian scout phenomenon provides such a unifying experience. Indian scouts cooperated with whites in virtually every Indian-white conflict in the trans-Mississippi West, as they had in earlier conflicts since the beginning of European colonization. The universality of this form of Indian-white cooperation suggests that certain uniformities existed, in spite of variations of time, place, and culture. We may attempt to identify the uniformities, without ignoring the diversities.

The post–Civil War period is especially convenient for this purpose, for several reasons. The reorganization of the army in 1866 regularized the status of Indian allies by providing for their enlistment as soldiers for short terms; what had been an intermittent and haphazard practice became somewhat regularized.

In addition, the conquest of the trans-Mississippi West proceeded rapidly in comparison with the experience in the East. At the same time, however, there were antecedents of the 1866 regularization in the pre–Civil War period and especially during the war itself.

The purpose of this work, therefore, is to survey the entire subject of Indian military cooperation with the whites in the period 1860–90, in an attempt to discern patterns of action and motivation. My intention is less to provide new information about particular scout units—although a number of points made here have not been examined in print before—than to discover the broader meaning of episodes and personalities that have previously been viewed in isolation or in passing.

While the formal scout units formed after 1866 are important in themselves, they are only one of the varied forms of cooperation and interaction between the army and the western Indians. They influenced each other in a variety of ways beyond the dramatic conflicts that have drawn so much historical attention. Despite enormous disparities in population and resources and the Indians' supposed lack of military sophistication, they inflicted numerous tactical defeats on the army. Even more significant, they forced the army to adopt at least some of their characteristics and methods, and to rely heavily on other unsophisticated "primitives" to facilitate their conquest. Sometimes army-Indian cooperation in the West more nearly resembled the alliances of near-equal partners of the colonial period than the limited role envisioned by the authors of the Army Act of 1866.

Europeans could hardly have settled North America, the historian Francis Jennings has argued, without Indian assistance and instruction. It seems obvious that Indian allies greatly facilitated military conquest of the West, and in doing so may have prevented more truly genocidal wars than those that actually were fought.[2]

That Indians served as allies of whites against other Indians has seemed incongruous to many observers. The media of popular culture have rarely treated the matter. Only a few historians have given the subject the prominence it deserves. Indeed, the trans-Mississippi Indian wars have traditionally been the province of amateur and popular historians to a far greater extent than the conflicts east of the Mississippi. Whereas the Indians of the East were involved in conflicts between European powers and the struggles between the United States and Great Britain, the western conflicts were viewed as purely Indian-white struggles, in which the victor was never in danger of losing. Even at the height of popularity of Frederick Jackson Turner's frontier thesis, the focus was on white society, with the Indians as a menace in the background. The western Indian wars were too closely identified with the less admired forms of popular literature and entertainment, and in the eyes of the most influential schools of historical thought, military conflicts were less important than economic factors. The most significant studies of these conflicts in the first half of this century came not from academic historians, but from anthropologists and amateurs of varying degrees of competence. Some of these writers recorded the reminiscences of aging Indians and whites; whatever the limitations of their material, they performed research that cannot now be duplicated.

This earlier neglect has changed because of increased interest in the history of minority groups and a troubled conscience about the treatment of such groups in the United States. The theme of such history, however, has been the simple Indian-white conflict and the destruction of Indian lives and cultures by whites. No one is likely to deny the importance of such a theme, or its tragic implications. But in their diversity Indians and whites did not always react to each other in the same way.

Nineteenth-century whites generally perceived "the Indian" as a monolithic entity; moreover, many whites saw Indians as essentially irrational and generally incapable of adapting to changes brought about in their world by the white presence. They were thought to be savage and uncivilized, and since "civilization" was by definition good, there must be something lacking in Indians. Whites who denied this idea in the interests of humanitarian and democratic ideals thought that they could disprove this immutable deficiency by making whole tribes over into copies of white yeoman farmers. Subsequent failures seemed to support the contention that the Indians were doomed to disappearance by their obstinate failure to change.

Contemporary historians usually condemn both the humanitarian assimilationists and the "racist" Indian haters. Ironically, emphasis on the tragedy of the destruction of Indian culture or on the wrongheadedness of whites who expected sudden, drastic acculturation under trying conditions tends to reinforce the stereotype of the Indian as incapable of change and adaptation. Some historians, in their sympathy for the Indians, describe those Indians who strove to adapt, particularly those who served the whites militarily, as renegades, traitors, and mercenaries. Such interpretations obscure the fact that Indians responded to white pressures in a variety of ways, both individually and as groups.

To present Indian history in terms of Indian-white conflict tends to create the impression that white contact was the only factor of importance impinging on the history of a particular group. Yet the Indians were never simply acted upon by whites. They acted upon the whites as well; furthermore, individual Indians and groups acted on each other. Thus whites play a less prominent part in Indian reminiscences, even in war stories, than one might expect. Indians' reasons for cooperating with whites were more complex than conscious betrayal and self-aggrandizement. Some tribes saw the whites as useful allies against a strong Indian enemy; if they also saw such cooperation as a means of accommodation to the stronger power, they did not conceive of their actions as betrayal of any group to whom they owed loyalty. Indian history reveals innumerable tribal alliances, and changes of alliance, for reasons not dissimilar to those that move supposedly more sophisticated nations. When Indians fought against other Indians of the same language and culture, they did so for varied reasons, some based on self-interest and some on loyalties they considered of the first importance.

It may be that the focus on Indian-white conflict perpetuates the stereotype of Indians as bloodthirsty savages, interested only in war and death and with no broader human dimension; even if we grant the emphasis on martial glory observable in some Indian cultures, such a one-dimensional, cultureless people could hardly exist. The Indian "warrior" was involved in social and political life, participated in religious ceremonies and vitally necessary hunting and other provisioning, and had a family to love and care for. A study that concentrates on Indian military activity is open to the charge that it ignores these aspects of human life and reverts to the one-dimensional "warrior" image. Yet these conflicts were a significant part of the history of many western tribes: those that fought against the whites, those that fought for them, and those that did both as changing circumstances seemed to require. The term "warrior" is not inappropriate for the men of many western tribes, for they did indeed view warfare as one of the most important male activities, and military glory as necessary to full status as a respected male member of the community. Generally speaking, the whites gave over such activities, after 1865 at least, to a small number of full-time professionals, rather than requiring them of every active adult male. The Indians could well have viewed the blue-coats as the true one-dimensional men, although in fact they often accorded the soldiers a degree of respect they did not give other whites. Ethnocentrism was in no way exclusive to whites; to Indian-fighting men the white military were at least engaged in activity that was worthy of men, although they often seemed to go about it in a remarkably inept fashion. Such an attitude facilitated the enlistment of many Indian scouts.

Thanks to the popular interest in such conflicts, a remarkable amount of primary published material is available, however varied in quality. The original authors and collectors were seldom interested in the subjects of most direct interest to this study; in fact, being interested primarily in either Indian life or Indian-white conflict, they were generally not concerned with Indian scouts as such. The exceptions are the Crow and Arikara scouts who served with George Armstrong Custer in the disastrous campaign on the Little Bighorn; these men were repeatedly interviewed, though the interviewers were primarily concerned with finding out what caused the army's defeat at the hands of the Sioux. The Apache scouts have received considerable attention, in part because they feature prominently in some of the best-written reminiscences of the Indian wars, and because of controversies over their loyalties. The Pawnee scouts were the object of George Bird Grinnell's attention; he wrote both as a scholar and as one with personal knowledge of the frontier and the people involved. Grinnell relied heavily on the recollections of Luther North, a personal friend whose memories were necessarily influenced by age and his personal relationship with the scouts and their leader, Frank North. Indeed, Luther North is necessarily the principal source of information on this important and long-serving scout unit; nonetheless, some other information is available by which his accounts can be checked and their value enhanced.[3]

Official records, both published and in archives, reveal aspects of the Indian scouts' role not otherwise available. They tell little enough about the Indians' views and motivations, but often give insight into those of the white military. They show the degree of understanding the military commanders had into the problems of Indian campaigning and Indian-white relations, and the limitations of that understanding. They reveal the conflicts of opinion over the role Indian auxiliaries should play in these campaigns, and the importance the field commanders generally attached to such allies. The records provide a sometimes amusing view of the different perceptions of the army's mission by the administrators in Washington and the commanders in the West. One can observe how often the men in the field adapted to circumstances in ways not provided for in orthodox military theory, regulations, or general orders—how often the restrictions imposed by these orders and regulations had to be avoided or ignored. In the process one becomes aware that the opinions and responses of the frontier army varied from conventional stereotypes, favorable and unfavorable, nearly as much as those of the Indians.

For many years, many Indian groups were more intimately involved with the army than with any other white group of comparable size. Ultimately the influence of settlers, missionaries, traders, and the Bureau of Indian Affairs might be greater and of longer duration. Yet the Indians and the army were often locked into interrelationship and interaction, hostile or friendly and often both, during a crucial period of transition. The effects on the Indians were undoubtedly greater, for good or ill, but the army did not wholly escape being influenced. It is worth noting that the memories on both sides were not always bad.

Historians have modified their treatment of another major form of Indian-white interaction, the fur trade, in recent years. This activity has traditionally been regarded as a process of exploitation by which Indians were given nothing but whiskey and worthless trinkets in return for their labors. Recent studies have argued that this was by no means the Indian view of the trade; whiskey played a less significant part in the trade with many tribes than has been imagined, and the Indians received articles of use to them, which raised their standard of living, in exchange for easily obtained animal skins. Of all the relationships between Indians and whites, the fur trade may have been the most advantageous to the Indians. If it was harmful to them in the long run, as most historians maintain, the harm was not readily apparent to the participants on either side.[4]

The service of Indians with the army was another aspect of Indian-white contact, conflict, and interaction. It offered certain rewards to both Indians and whites, however one-sided these rewards might appear from a later view. That Indians could usually be found to scout and fight for the army indicates that they perceived benefits of some sort to be gained through this activity.

A few terms need clarification. To many people the term "Indian scout" refers to any man who scouted for the army during the Indian wars, regardless of his ancestry or cultural background. Indeed, for many persons the term "old scout" always evokes the stereotype of the buckskinned, bewhiskered white man. In this work the term will refer specifically to army scouts who were largely or wholly Indian in ancestry, and who adhered to their ancestral culture. This definition risks some difficulties; for example, the brothers Robert and William Jackson were one-quarter Blackfoot and three-quarters white in ancestry, but they enlisted with the Arikara scouts in the Sioux wars and were officially "Indians."[5] Similarly, the Seminole-Negro scouts were of mixed ancestry, as their collective name indicates, and their culture was similarly mixed. They considered themselves to be Baptists, but some still wore buffalo-horn war bonnets in the field. They enlisted as Indian scouts, however, and the army valued their services for the same abilities as those of Indians. Their example simply exposes the inadequacy of our ethnocultural terminology.[6]

A somewhat arbitrary though useful distinction is made here between scouts and auxiliaries. Scouts are defined as persons whose duties were those of reconnaissance—discovering and following the enemy's trail, locating the enemy and determining his strength, determining the tribal affiliation of unknown Indians, and all other duties connected with military intelligence. Auxiliaries are defined as those Indians who were expected to engage in actual combat with the enemy in company with, or instead of, regular troops. There was a school of thought that held that a scout's duty did not include fighting.[7] In practice, however, Indian scouts frequently engaged in combat; indeed, they were frequently the only U.S. soldiers actually to fight with the enemy. Hence the distinction between scouts and auxiliaries, however useful for conceptualization of the problems of the topic, only partially reflects reality.[8] The frequently used term "allies" accurately reflects the perception of many Indian groups, who saw their cooperation with the whites as a mutually advantageous partnership into which both parties entered of their own choice.

The terms "guide" and "interpreter" also frequently occur in the literature of the Indian wars; to a great extent they are self-explanatory. The guide's job was to find the way in little-known territory; the interpreter was to ensure communication between white soldiers and Indians. These jobs were generally held by white men or men of mixed ancestry who were in theory well acquainted with the country and the Indians. In practice the duties of guides, scouts, and interpreters, though supposedly distinct, tended to overlap. Indeed, a scout of whatever ancestry was considerably handicapped if he lacked knowledge either of the country or of other languages.

The use of the term "Indian" in this context is subject to many objections, but the use of "Native American" presents difficulties of its own, for a rather large population of persons of Old World ancestry consider themselves to be native to the continent. In any case, the latter term is not universally acceptable to Indians. The terms "Amerindian" and "Euramerican" have been avoided as offenses against the English language.[9]

Many of the army officers referred to in this work held both permanent and brevet rank, the latter often several grades higher than the former. A brevet was an honorary rank, awarded for distinguished service; Civil War veterans, in particular, had often received several. Except under special circumstances, such rank had no force; an officer's authority and status was that of his permanent, lower rank. As a matter of courtesy, however, it was common to refer to an officer by his brevet rank in conversation, in reminiscent accounts, and even in official correspondence. This practice has proved to be a frequent source of confusion to later scholars. The favorite example, of course, is Brevet Major General George A. Custer, a lieutenant colonel of cavalry at the time of his well-remembered demise but invariably remembered as General Custer. In referring to officers I shall use their permanent ranks unless special circumstances require mention of a brevet rank—as when Lieutenant Colonel George Crook took command of the Department of Arizona in 1871 by virtue of orders that brought his brevet rank of major general into force.

Chapter One

Indian Allies: A Long History

The Indian scout units of the post–Civil War era were the final heirs of a long tradition. From the time Europeans first came to the New World, American Indians were, willy-nilly, the pawns or the instruments of white men's conquests and white men's policies. Hernán Cortés's conquest of the Aztec empire was due as much to the fact that the Aztecs had created hosts of enemies among their neighbors as to any other factor. The 500-odd conquistadors marched with a far larger army of native allies who believed that the new regime had to be better than the old. In the long wars with the nomadic tribes of northern Mexico, the Spanish again relied on Indian allies and pacified tribes in their campaigns against those still hostile. When the Spanish attempted peaceful approaches, the friendly tribes were of great service as intermediaries. It was the "reduced" Indians—those Christianized and to a degree Europeanized—that provided the rank and file of colonizing ventures to the north, along with the increasing mestizo population. The Spanish of purely European blood were always "thin on the ground" in the Americas.[1]

The pattern persisted in those portions of New Spain that are now within the United States and the immediately contiguous areas of modern Mexico, a region that experienced frontier conditions and endemic Indian warfare for three centuries. The Pueblo people of what is now New Mexico became allies of the Spanish against the nomadic raiders of the border—Apaches, Navajos, and Comanches. In the course of the eighteenth century, the Pueblos gradually gave way as allies to nomads who, because of military defeat or diplomacy, chose to make peace with the Europeans. Thus Juan Bautista de Anza, governor of the

Kingdom of New Mexico (1778–87), defeated the Comanches repeatedly with regular cavalry and Pueblo auxiliaries, causing them to seek peace with New Mexico, if not with the other Spanish provinces. Anza then required the Comanches, as proof of good faith, to furnish warriors for campaigns against the Navajos. The Navajos, seeking better relations with the Spanish colony, furnished a contingent to aid Spanish and Comanches against the Western Apaches.[2]

In these Spanish practices one can see certain patterns that repeat themselves, though in modified form, on the United States frontier in the nineteenth century. The similarities are more striking in view of the differences in society, duration, and government between the two frontiers—that is, between a relatively static Spanish provincial frontier of centuries' duration and a dynamic, expanding United States frontier that lasted little more than a century. These parallels suggest that conditions on the U.S. frontier called for responses much like those evoked by the circumstances in New Spain. Administrators and professional military men of basically European heritage in both New Spain and the United States may have held similar attitudes and opinions.[3]

Among the parallels that seem important we find an initial tendency to enlist the aid of the more sedentary tribes against the more nomadic; the rapid incorporation of the formerly hostile Indians into the white military organization; the arming of Indian auxiliaries with the white army's military equipment; the subsidizing of Indian groups in return for their military services; the promise of loot after victory; the granting of official rank to Indian chiefs (though the United States offered much lower rank than Spain); the use of friendly Indians as informers and spies; military protection of villages of "friendlies" against their enemies; the use of friendly Indians as intermediaries and negotiators; the use of exclusively Indian parties to harass the hostiles; and the greater rapport between Indians and the military than between Indians and the civil and religious authorities. In most instances of such parallels, the United States' example is on a smaller scale, less systematic in application, and less a consistent official policy than in the Spanish case.[4]

However striking the Spanish-U.S. parallels in this aspect of frontier expansion, it is questionable how much one colonizing power directly influenced the other. The heritage of the British colonial tradition and its own earlier wars with Indians influenced the U.S. Army more deeply than a Spanish-Mexican tradition of which American officers were largely ignorant and generally contemptuous.[5] The only place where one can see a clear continuity between Spanish-Mexican and U.S. military practice is in New Mexico Territory, where Pueblo auxiliaries accompanied American expeditions soon after the U.S. conquest and annexation.[6]

Other European powers that sought to colonize America turned to Indian allies as they felt the need, or as they were able to induce the natives to serve them. When the New England colonies went to war against the Pequots in 1637, their forces included the Narragansetts and, significantly, the Mohegans, who split off from the Pequots. Apparently the Narragansetts found English methods of warfare too brutal and indiscriminate for their tastes.[7] In the bloody King Philip's War (1675–76) Indian allies were almost always associated with the colonial New England troops.[8] The historian Francis Jennings, who makes no excuses or allowances for the Puritan conquerors, observes that "European desire to make use of Indians was matched by the readiness of many Indians to be made use of."[9]

When the colonial powers warred with each other for control of North America, they did not hesitate to use their Indian allies to augment the scanty numbers of white troops. They encouraged Indians to harass frontier settlements, even when the mother countries were formally at peace. By the mid-seventeenth century they had established a pattern that would endure until the Civil War.[10]

To the British colonists, of course, the colonial wars were the "French and Indian" wars. No feature of them did the English so vividly remember, or so condemn, as the French encouragement of Indian hostility against the English colonies. Yet the British government and the colonies made great efforts to win over the woodland tribes, even if less successfully than their enemies, who represented a lesser menace to the Indians' way of life. The powerful Iroquois League had a long-standing hostility to the French, and so remained, for the most part, faithful allies of the English. Under the leadership of Britain's astute Indian agent, Sir William Johnson, they played a decisive part in various wilderness campaigns. Young George Washington led Delaware Indians as well as Virginia militia when he launched the last of these wars with an ambush of French troops; it was after the Indians deserted him that he was besieged and forced to surrender.[11]

Americans long remembered how Edward Braddock's army of British regulars met defeat, with over half the troops lost, from a smaller force of Indians and Canadians who knew how to use the terrain advantageously. Historians have explained the defeat in various ways, but if Braddock had not alienated his original contingent of Indians, he might at least have had advance notice of the impending encounter with the enemy.[12]

When the colonies revolted against Britain, the British exploited that same fear of settlers' encroachments to inspire years of bitter warfare along most of the frontier. In 1776 Thomas Jefferson, cataloguing George III's crimes in the Declaration of Independence, denounced the sovereign for having unleashed the "merciless Indian savages" on his subjects. Yet the Continental Congress, in that same year, authorized Washington to recruit 2,000 Indians. The resulting conflict of loyalties tore apart the 200-year-old Iroquois confederation, as official agents and missionaries representing both sides exerted whatever influence they could to win the support of the Six Nations. Britain's recognition of American independence in 1783, however unavoidable, meant the abandonment of its allies—allies whose activities had forced Washington to make major diversions of troops and expenditure from the effort against Britain's regular forces.[13]

Meeting the opposition of the Indians of the Northwest Territory after the Revolution, the undersized U.S. Army found itself in need of Indian aid. General Anthony Wayne valued his Choctaw and Chickasaw scouts, southern Indians who were ready to serve against the northern tribes; they were his insurance against surprise, which had brought disaster to his predecessor, General Arthur St. Clair. The Northwest tribes were receiving encouragement from British agents, but Britain was not prepared to go to war for the Indians' sake. When challenged by the United States in 1812, Britain was quick to enlist the aid of discontented and desperate Indians, north and south. The Shawnee leader Tecumseh, a passionate advocate of Indian unity, was largely responsible for the British capture of Detroit; at the Battle of the Thames, where Tecumseh died, the Indians resisted long after their British comrades had surrendered or fled.[14]

The Creek nation of Alabama split over the war; "Red Stick" and "White Stick" Creeks battled each other in all-Indian battles and in others in which U.S. troops were involved. Choctaws and Cherokees cooperated with white troops in their campaigns against the Creeks, culminating in Andrew Jackson's victory at Horseshoe Bend. The Cherokees were organized as a regiment, with Indian and mixed-blood officers. A few months later a Choctaw contingent covered the left flank of Jackson's battle line at New Orleans.[15]

After 1815, Indian involvement in white men's wars with each other was of less crucial importance. European powers no longer found it in their interest to gain Indian allegiance, for they were no longer engaged in major conflicts in North America. Mexico and the Republic of Texas made some use of Indians against each other. The Indians of Taos Pueblo became involved in the New Mexican resistance to United States conquest in 1847. In 1861 the services of Indians were again of some interest to contending whites. The "Civilized Tribes" of Indian Territory, partially assimilated southern tribes deported from the East, split into Union and Confederate parties; the splits were generally along the lines of long-standing feuds and factions. Union and Confederate Indian regiments formed, officers being generally white or of mixed ancestry, and fought both as guerrillas and in conventional battles. The mixed-blood Cherokee Stand Watie became a Confederate brigadier general and the last Confederate general to surrender. The consequences of Indian involvement in this white man's war were consistent with the history of such involvements: death, devastation, and dispossession.[16]

In conflicts between the United States and Indian tribes acting solely in their own interest, the whites continued to find Indians valuable allies. The most serious of such conflicts in the period after 1815 was the Second Seminole War (1835–42). The army found it necessary to call on the Creeks and various other tribes that, ironically, were on the verge of removal to Indian Territory. The end of this war virtually closed the long history of Indian-white warfare east of the Mississippi.[17]

The Louisiana Purchase gave the United States a paper sovereignty over a huge area west of the Mississippi; yet for over forty years the army's role in the trans-Mississippi West remained tentative and peripheral. The army established military posts on the eastern edge of the Great Plains: Fort Atkinson, Nebraska; Fort Leavenworth, Kansas; Fort Smith, Arkansas; Fort Gibson, Indian Territory. From these posts soldiers penetrated the West a number of times, but not in ways that would exercise great or lasting influence, to say nothing of control. There were various exploring expeditions; on a few occasions military escorts accompanied Sante Fe caravans; and a few sizable columns marched as far as the Rockies for purposes of reconnaissance and to establish relations with the Plains tribes.[18]

In 1823 an expedition from Fort Atkinson labored up the Missouri River under Colonel Henry Leavenworth; its purpose was to punish the Arikaras in what is now South Dakota for an attack on fur traders and to ensure that the river remained open for the trade. Leavenworth thought it expedient to ally himself with the Sioux, long-standing enemies of the sedentary Arikaras. The Sioux killed a number of Arikaras, but the army commander feared to risk an assault on the enemy's fortified village. The Arikaras eventually abandoned the place, but their state of mind made them even more of a menace to trappers than before. Leavenworth thought the Sioux undisciplined and uncooperative. The Sioux had acquired a poor opinion of the army's fighting ability, which they would hold for years. The army abandoned Fort Atkinson in 1827; it lay so far beyond actual areas of settlement that it served no useful purpose.[19]

In the Indian Territory a complex situation existed, created by the relocation of partially assimilated eastern tribes in close proximity to long-resident farming Indians and buffalo-hunting nomads. In its efforts to police the region and promote peace among the tribes, the army naturally found the services of Indian scouts, interpreters, and intermediaries indispensable. Such immigrant tribes as the Delawares and Kickapoos ably coped with the nomads, and the whites viewed them as a useful buffer to keep the "wild tribes" away from white settlements.[20]

During this period federal officials assumed that the Plains would prove useless to white farmers and could therefore be established as a permanent Indian territory. White settlement was still well east of the Plains, and hence the army's concern with the region did not require large-scale military operations on a regular basis. This situation changed radically in 1848, when the Treaty of Guadalupe Hidalgo extended American authority to the Pacific. Innumerable tribes of Indians, whose notions of sovereignty were not readily compatible with those of the whites, were now under nominal U.S. control.

In the period between the peace with Mexico and the Civil War, the army's highest authorized strength was 18,000. These men were supposed to assert control and keep peace over an Indian population then estimated at over 400,000, scattered over an area of over a million square miles. The army's conflicts with Indians in this period were sporadic affairs, and in most cases were indecisive; further trouble was to come in later years. Conflicts were most serious in areas where whites infringed most seriously on Indian hunting grounds. In California the influx of Forty-niners brought disaster to many small, weak tribes. The army was often in the position of protecting Indians from whites, or protecting whites whom the soldiers regarded as the real cause of trouble. In New Mexico Territory there was a long-standing conflict between the Hispanic settlements and the Pueblos, on the one hand, and the nomadic Navajos and Apaches, on the other. The United States troops had hardly arrived in the region when they became involved in these battles. The new state of Texas was also on hostile terms with various tribes, the most formidable being the Comanches—the "Lords of the South Plains"—and their allies, the Kiowas. In the Pacific Northwest an influx of settlers produced conflict with the various seminomadic tribes of the Columbia Plateau in the late 1850s, culminating in a series of pitched battles.[21]

The Plateau tribes of the Northwest suffered decisive defeat and remained quiet for many years. The California wars were generally decisive, for white violence and disease virtually wiped out many of the tribes. Elsewhere, the Indian-white conflicts remained to be settled in a later period. The army was seldom strong or effective enough to force the Indians to accept the requirements the whites wished to impose on them. It was hampered by its small size; by logistical difficulties in a vast, little-known, and largely roadless country; by tactics and strategy that did not meet the demands of the situation; and by what the historian Robert Utley calls a "compromise of military and civil half-measures."[22]

As a result of these difficulties, the Navajo wars, for instance, were a series of destructive incursions into Indian territory, each followed by an ineffective "treaty," mutual provocations by Navajos and New Mexicans, and another military expedition. In Texas the army pursued for some years a defensive strategy, based on a double line of posts that were supposed to hold off the raiding nomads; they were largely ineffective. Elsewhere, conflict with the Plains tribes was only beginning, for only in the 1850s did the traffic on the various western trails begin to affect seriously the general welfare of the Plains tribes, destroying game, spreading disease, and producing friction and violence. Outbreaks of trouble with the Sioux and Cheyennes led to military retaliation, but attempts at diplomatic settlement were inconclusive.[23]

In these campaigns the army relied chiefly on troops whose organization and training—such as they were—were for conventional, European-style warfare. There was little official, standardized doctrine on frontier service or Indian warfare, aside from the general awareness that cavalry, rather than infantry, was needed to cope with the nomadic tribes. Extensive campaigns against the Plains tribes seldom occurred, while lessons learned in campaigns against the forest tribes in the East were only partially applicable. During this period the record on the use of Indian allies is mixed. In the vast stretches of unknown country the services of experienced guides were indispensable; members of the displaced eastern tribes frequently served as guides and scouts. As partially assimilated persons, Delawares, Shawnees, Potawotamis, and Kickapoos had retained their "Indian" skills and added (so whites judged) some elements of the white society's organization and discipline. The Delawares were particularly esteemed, by both white trappers and the army. The Delaware leader Black Beaver guided several exploring expeditions, engaged in trapping in the Rockies, led an Indian company for a brief period during the Mexican War, and had his home in Indian Territory burned by Confederates because he had guided Union troops in 1861.[24]

Indian allies served frequently in the wars in the Pacific

Northwest. Significantly, it was Governor Isaac Stevens of Washington Territory that recruited them first, rather than the regular army; this pattern repeated itself frequently in the Indian conflicts through the Civil War. Most prominent among the groups that adhered to the whites was the Nez Perce tribe. Although the Nez Perces were divided on the issue, at this period perhaps a majority preferred to be on good terms with the whites, moved by both practical considerations and the influence of Protestant and Catholic missionaries. In 1858 Colonel Edward Steptoe's command found itself surrounded and in danger of being wiped out by a coalition of Plateau tribes in eastern Washington. The Nez Perce leader Timothy guided the soldiers safely past the hostiles by night, and part of the tribe saw the command across the Snake River to safety.[25]

In New Mexico Territory the newly arrived military and civil authorities had inherited an especially complex set of interrelationships. The Spanish-Mexican culture of the Rio Grande was a long-established variant of Western European civilization, though what most often impressed the "Anglos" were the differences between it and their own culture. Perhaps inevitably, the new government undertook to defend the "civilized" people against the "savages." In this endeavor the army seems to have inherited the pattern of alliances established in Spanish times. At an early date, Pueblo guides and allies accompanied military expeditions against the Navajos. In 1849 New Mexico's Indian superintendent James Calhoun recommended the recruitment of at least 200 Pueblos for mounted service as auxiliaries with the army. Colonel George McCall, reporting to the secretary of war the following year, also favored the Pueblos as auxiliaries. Colonel Joseph Mansfield, however, in a similar inspection report in 1853, judged these Indians to be of no military use. The experienced frontier dragoon Lieutenant Colonel Philip St. George Cooke did not agree with Mansfield; campaigning against the Jicarilla Apaches in the mountains of northern New Mexico and southern Colorado in 1854, he recruited a "spy company" of Taos Pueblo men and New Mexicans, and found them notably effective. The army quickly took up an alliance established by the last Spanish governors with a secessionist Navajo band. This group, whom the Navajos themselves called "enemy Navajo," also accompanied military expeditions into the Navajo country.

Later the Utes of southern Colorado, traditional enemies of the Navajos, received encouragement to make war on the latter, even without white supervision.[26]

Texas offers especially interesting and suggestive examples of Indian-white military cooperation in the pre–Civil War period. The common historical stereotype of Texas during the republican era and in its early years as a state is of implacable hostility between the Anglo-American settlers and the Indians. The Texas Rangers are generally viewed as the cutting edge of Texas's battle against the enemy in an unequivocal racial war. Whether historians have praised or condemned Texas and the Rangers, they generally have assumed an impassable barrier between red and white. This stereotype has a large element of truth. Texas was a frontier state, its outer settlements exposed to the raids of the superlatively mobile "wild tribes." Few Texans were prepared to admit that they offered any provocation to Indian hostility, and they most commonly viewed the hostile Indian as a dangerous animal with wholly vicious motives. Yet the lines of this racial war often became blurred, and this phenomenon raises some questions about simplistic views of Texans and frontiersmen in general.[27]

An examination of the actual conflicts between Texans and Indians reveals that from an early date the Anglos sought Indian allies to help them cope with the Plains nomads. The numerous small tribes, generally on bad terms with the overpowering Comanches and Kiowas, were intermittent allies with the Rangers; some of them, to be sure, were also intermittent enemies. In 1839 Colonel John H. Moore led a force of 63 white volunteers and 16 Lipan Apaches, headed by Chief Castro, in an attack on a Comanche camp. Moore mishandled the affair and allowed the enemy a chance to rally; once the Comanches were mounted, they stampeded the Texans' horses, drove off the attackers, and nearly inflicted complete disaster. The muzzle-loading rifles of the day were barely adequate to hold off the fast-moving Comanches. Castro was so disgusted with the white men's ineptitude that he and his warriors deserted.[28]

Within a few years the Rangers had become an effective fighting force with capable leaders, and the new Colt revolver made combat on horseback possible. But they did not scorn the help of Indian allies. When Captain Jack Hays, the most famous and successful Ranger leader of the 1840s, charged alone into a mass of Comanches, Flacco of the Lipans followed close behind. Historians of the Rangers have not emphasized the role of these Indian allies, but contemporary accounts reveal how frequently they were present. The Rangers made use of the services of these smaller tribes throughout the pre–Civil War era, gaining many of their most notable successes with Indian aid.[29]

In April 1858 Captain John S. "Old Rip" Ford, with a force of 102 Rangers and 113 Indians, crossed the Red River into Indian Territory, seeking to attack Comanche bands. The state government had lost patience with federal efforts at frontier defense and had determined to strike out on its own initiative. Ford's allies were members of the smaller tribes of the region, located by the federal government on the Brazos River Reserve. They included Caddos, Anadarkos, Tonkawas, Wacos, Shawnees and Delawares from the East, and Tahuacanos, and were led by their agent, former ranger Shapley P. Ross. It was thanks to them that Ford was able to locate a large Comanche village on the Canadian River; in the ensuing battle the allies, armed nearly as well as the Rangers themselves, played as important a part as the white men—as indeed their numerical proportions demanded. Ford gave them full credit for the part they played.[30]

Not all of these smaller tribes were invariably friends of the Texans. On occasion there were hostile acts between them, and their reward for serving the whites was small indeed. When Texas forced the federal government to cancel the Brazos Reservation in 1859, the tribes were forced north of the Red River. At that time men of many of these tribes were serving with U.S. troops against the Comanches. The frontier population, or a vocal part of it, demanded the removal of these Indians, and accused them of depredations. The leader of these Indian haters, John R. Baylor, was a representative "fighting Texan"; so, however, were Jack Hays, Old Rip Ford, and Shapley Ross, who led Indians against other Indians. None were humanitarians or "Indian lovers," but it is evident that the attitudes of Texas frontiersmen toward Indians in general are not easily classified. Certainly some persons made distinctions on the basis of tractability, willingness to serve white interests, and personal friendly acquaintance.[31]

Within a few months after Ford's campaign, several episodes

occurred that indicate a change in the U.S. Army's defense policy in Texas; possibly spurred by Ford's example, the army decided to launch a punitive campaign against the Comanches north of the Red River. Major Earl Van Dorn, with 225 men of the Second Cavalry Regiment, marched from Fort Belknap, Texas, in September 1858. Van Dorn complained to Agent Shapley Ross at the Brazos Reserve that Ross had shown favoritism toward the Rangers by encouraging his Indians to serve with them, but not with the federal troops. Ross replied that, on the contrary, he had offered the services of his warriors to the regulars several times and had been refused. Whatever inhibitions had affected Van Dorn's predecessors apparently did not trouble him; he gladly accepted the services of 135 members of the associated tribes, under the leadership of L. S. Ross, the agent's son. This young man was home from college, and apparently regarded the enterprise as an enjoyable way to spend his vacation. The Indian scouts located Comanches encamped in present southwest Oklahoma and the combined forces attacked, causing heavy casualties; several officers were wounded, including Van Dorn and Ross.[32]

Van Dorn made another expedition the following spring, following the Comanches into southern Kansas; an incident of this campaign suggests that military opinion was still divided on the proper role of Indian allies. With Van Dorn again were 58 Brazos Reserve Indians he had requested from Agent Ross. He surprised a village at Crooked Creek and gained another bloody victory. Van Dorn wanted his Indian allies to stay out of the fight, but their leaders insisted that to do so would disgrace them, a consideration that should have appealed to a professional soldier. Van Dorn may have feared that his troopers would shoot some of the friendly Indians by mistake; the scouts wrapped white cloths around their heads to distinguish themselves, a common type of answer to this perennial problem. The question of whether Indian allies should participate in combat as well as scouting would crop up repeatedly in later years, creating sharp differences among senior officers.[33]

Among the small tribes involved in campaigns against the Comanches, the Tonkawas stand out as frequent allies of the whites. This tribe was on bad terms not only with the Comanches, but with virtually all their neighbors. They were known to be cannibals, and so other tribes viewed them with abhorrence. Ford described them as the "black beasts" of the Brazos Reserve; all untoward events were blamed on their evil influence on the supernatural world. They were a people in decline, decimated by their enemies and by the diseases resulting from their association with whites. The attachment was based less on affection than on necessity; there was often mutual suspicion and dislike. Historian T. R. Fehrenbach comments that the Tonkawas and Lipans, even when they understood "what kind of gratitude they could expect from whites," continued to serve them out of their vindictive joy in destroying their traditional enemies. This seems a harsh judgment on people trapped in a truly desperate situation, between far more powerful peoples, and seeking some thin hope of survival. The Tonkawas continued their association with the Texans and the U.S. Army as long as the Indian wars on the Southern Plains lasted.[34]

The army's association with Indian allies in the trans-Mississippi West before the Civil War was a reflection of the seriousness of particular conflicts with the Indians. Where contact between white and Indian populations was great enough to incite serious trouble, the whites were likely to turn to Indians to augment their forces and to enable them to locate and strike the Indians they regarded as hostile. In New Mexico the U.S. Army inherited a pattern of Indian alliances dating back to Spanish times, perhaps without realizing it. In the Northwest and in Texas, frontiersmen and local authorities established alliances with Indians who were then called on by the federal military when they were needed. This phenomenon suggests two things: first, that not all frontiersmen were irrevocably dedicated to the extermination of all Indians, regardless of tribe; second, that the regulars were often reluctant to acknowledge a need for Indian allies, especially in a combat role. Colonel George Wright, in his expedition to chastise the Columbia Plateau tribes in 1858, took only 30 Nez Perces along with a force of about 600; obviously he intended them to serve chiefly as scouts, although their services actually extended beyond such duties.[35] When military policy in Texas became more aggressive, the army followed in the footsteps of the Rangers, although the officers were still dubious about the part Indians could play in battle.

Nevertheless, by the end of the 1850s a school of thought had developed within the army, of indeterminate numbers but including experienced frontier officers, favoring some sort of permanent, systematic organization of Indian auxiliaries and scouts. In 1852 Captain Randolph B. Marcy, explorer of the Southern Plains, recommended attaching Delaware scouts and guides permanently to each company of troops on the frontier. Captain George B. McClellan, First Cavalry, went a long step further. He had gone to Europe in 1855 to observe and report on the Crimean War and whatever lessons the U.S. Army could learn from the combatants. As a cavalry officer he was especially intrigued by the Cossacks, whom he regarded as ideal "irregular" cavalry and scouts. McClellan was convinced that "in many of the tribes of our frontier Indians, such as the Delawares, Kickapoos, &c., we possess the material for the formation of partisan troops fully equal to the Cossacks"; they would prove useful, he believed, in both Indian and "civilized" warfare.[36]

Lieutenant William Burnet, First Infantry, compared the Brazos Reserve Indians to the French army's native auxiliaries in North Africa. In giving these Indians an increasing role, first as guides and scouts, then as combat troops, the army was gradually developing an auxiliary force comparable to the French organizations. The Indians were far more effective in frontier defense than the Rangers, Burnet said; he believed they liked the work and were coming to look on the federal government as their friend. He feared, however, that the removal of the Indians from Texas had aborted these desirable trends. In 1860 the British traveler and ethnographer Captain Richard Burton, touring the West, concluded that the U.S. Army should imitate the British in India by raising native regiments. Officers he talked to agreed, but they judged that the public's fear of the atrocities that might be committed by the "savages" would block such a measure.[37]

The old pattern of Indian alliance with whites against other Indians repeated itself in the trans-Mississippi West, though in a haphazard fashion. The coming Civil War would be a period of far more serious and widespread Indian conflict, and would bring large numbers of volunteers and westerners into the field. One of the by-products would be a change in the intermittent and hesitant pattern of cooperation between Indians and the army.

Chapter Two

The Amateurs Take Over—
The Influence of the Civil War

The Civil War coincided with the intensification of Indian-white conflict in most parts of the West. Some writers have assumed that the Indians knowingly took advantage of the almost complete withdrawal of the regular army from the West. While it would be hard to prove that this was not the case, other causes can be identified. Quite simply, the basic causes of "Indian trouble" continued to operate: westward emigration continued, new gold rushes occurred, and the incidents that led to "war" multiplied accordingly. Six new territories (Colorado, Dakota, Nevada, Idaho, Arizona, and Montana) came into existence during the war years. The Indians may have seen the period in terms other than those of opportunities for savage rampages.[1]

The idea of a frontier stripped of troops and left to the mercy of the Indians is only partially true. In Texas, certainly, the Confederacy never really took up the responsibilities of the departing regulars. Elsewhere the military role fell to the Civil War volunteer units, recruited to fight for the Union and diverted to another task. Many of these units were from western states and territories, and their attitudes toward Indians tended to reflect frontier viewpoints. Except for a few senior officers, all were nonprofessionals who owed their military roles to the war itself. Frontiersmen or not, their attitude toward Indians and Indian warfare was often very different from that of the regulars. In many parts of the West there were more, not fewer, troops than before, and the attitudes of the new soldiers and commanders brought a new intensity and even a new level of brutality to Indian campaigning.

Since colonial times the American volunteer soldier has traditionally regarded war as an unpleasant, if necessary, interruption of his own life and the normal course of events. The unpleasantness is tolerable only if every effort is being made to bring it to an end quickly; a rich nation should exert every resource against the people responsible for the abnormal state of affairs—that is, the enemy. There are few objections to the use of excessive force or matériel, if they hasten victory, increase the soldier's chance of survival, and produce a final, decisive settlement of the problem. The citizen-soldiers of the Civil War certainly wanted the Union saved and normal conditions restored, beyond any chance of further disruption. They demonstrated their attitude by increasingly indiscriminate looting and destruction of Southern property as the war dragged on. A special ruthlessness was the natural response of volunteers who were unexpectedly thrust into the task of fighting an enemy whose ways of making war were particularly repugnant and whose skin color and culture made them seem far more alien than Southern rebels.[2]

To many volunteers and westerners it seemed that a short cut and a definitive answer to the problem was extermination, a word that was frequently used. The attitude behind it, already well developed in colonial times, was that Indians were scarcely human, incorrigibly vicious creatures motivated chiefly by delight in robbery, slaughter, and torture. To terminate the existence of such creatures was no wrong, but would ensure the safety of decent white people. If literal extermination was neither intended nor achieved, a bloody defeat might nevertheless serve as an object lesson, showing these cowardly murderers that they could not indulge their hellish desires with impunity. Thus one achieved a quick, final solution and made the West safe for women and children. These attitudes may well have made the volunteers more effective than the regulars, in the most immediate military sense, yet probably provoked even more hostility in many cases. Many regulars retained a suspicion that whites were as responsible for conflict as Indians, and regarded frontier civilians with some disdain; such notions seldom troubled the volunteers. Without the regulars' discipline, and with officers whose viewpoints were much like those of the enlisted men, they tried to solve the Indian problem once and for all.[3]

However ruthless fighters they might have been, the volunteers still needed the aid of at least some guides and scouts of skill and experience. The conditions of Indian campaigning required such aid if the troops were to be effective. In fact, the Civil War years saw a new emphasis on the use of Indian allies, and a degree of organization not seen since the War of 1812. This situation may seem paradoxical in view of what has been said about frontier and volunteer attitudes toward Indians. Surely dedicated Indian haters would neither value nor trust such people as comrades in battle. The example of the Texas Rangers and their frequent cooperation with Indian allies, however, has already suggested that such assumptions are at best too simple and sweeping. Governor Isaac Stevens of Washington Territory, dedicated to the dispossession of the Northwest Indians in the 1850s, recruited as many Indian allies as he could find; on one occasion his Nez Perce escort saved his life. The mountain men of the Rocky Mountain fur trade, often stigmatized as wholesale killers of Indians, lived, worked, and fought beside Indians, both displaced easterners like the Delawares and Shawnees and indigenous tribes like the Flatheads, Nez Perces, and Shoshones. It seems unwise to assume that frontier "Indian haters" invariably nourished implacable hatred for all Indians at all times; such unmitigated hatred may be more than most people can sustain. It was more common for frontiersmen to regard all Indians with some prejudice, yet to make distinctions between those considered really evil and dangerous and those relatively friendly and perhaps useful. Naturally they based these distinctions on the assumed hostility or friendliness of the Indians toward the whites, on their willingness to be useful to the whites, and the degree to which their customs and culture were repugnant to white standards. There were always some frontiersmen who knew Indians well enough to view them as individuals, and even to make allowances for cultural differences.[4]

Only a few illustrations of the complexities involved are possible here. John M. Chivington's name has gone down in infamy for the Sand Creek massacre of Southern Cheyennes in 1864. Yet Chivington, a Methodist minister, had earlier been a missionary to the Wyandot Indians in Kansas; he founded the first Masonic lodge in Kansas, the majority of whose members were

Wyandots. He probably regarded himself, and was regarded by others, as an authority on Indians because of these experiences. Albert Pfeiffer, allegedly a Dutch nobleman, was government agent for the Capote Utes in the late 1850s; he also led them in slave raids against the Navajos. Pfeiffer nourished a special hatred for the Apaches, who had killed his wife. The Utes, however, were said to have held him in the highest respect. We shall see other instances of whites who were closely associated with some Indian tribe and who to some degree absorbed the tribal viewpoint; probably for that reason, they often regarded some other tribe or tribes with the deepest antipathy. Nor were these men always free from more broadly racial biases, or always above exploiting their friends in some way. John J. Healy of Montana traded whiskey to the Canadian Blackfeet for several years, until the Northwest Mounted Police put him out of business; he then made the U.S. government an offer to defeat Sitting Bull with a force of 100 white volunteers and 200 Blood (Blackfeet) Indians.[5]

Aside from these mixed attitudes and the practical considerations of Indian campaigning, another factor compelled the volunteers to consider Indians as allies. They found the measure attractive because of their very desire to end the problem once and for all, by bloody examples or extermination if necessary. Here again we have Jefferson's "merciless Indian savages, whose known rule of warfare, is an undistinguished destruction of all ages, sexes and conditions." The common belief of whites on the frontier and elsewhere, nourished by tales of Revolutionary raids and massacres, was that Indians in their warfare with whites and other Indians invariably slaughtered, scalped, and tortured, with no regard for honor or mercy. If the enemy was like that, then one need have few compunctions about using allies who presumably followed the same rules. If one desired to wipe out the enemy, or at least to decimate him, such allies might be all the more desirable.[6]

Scouts were generally necessary in the Indian wars if one wished to come in contact with the enemy at all, except under conditions in which the Indians held the advantage. There is some reason to believe, all the same, that many of the western tribes were less wary during the Civil War than they were a few years later. Their experience of war with the whites was less at that period, and their contempt for white ineptitude in the wilderness may have led them to underrate the soldiers and fail to discern their strong points. "Wilderness" is, of course, a white concept, but it expresses how alien the Indians' accustomed environment was to whites. In any case, many of these Indians simply failed to understand that the whites considered themselves to be at war with "the Indians" as a whole, or with a particular tribe, and so would attack anyone designated as a "hostile." Many Indians, in their turn, retaliated against whites who considered themselves innocent of any offense.

The Navajo troubles in the Southwest were aggravated in the 1860s by increased hostilities with the Apaches of New Mexico and Arizona territories. Part of the military response was increased recruitment of Indians hostile to the offending tribes. Two men dominated the southwestern campaigns: Brigadier General James H. Carleton, an experienced, capable, and ruthless regular, and his field commander, the old scout and frontiersman Christopher "Kit" Carson, now commander of the First New Mexico Volunteer Regiment. Carson was virtually illiterate, but Carleton knew him from previous campaigns and trusted his abilities as an Indian fighter. After subduing the Mescalero Apaches, Carleton prepared to launch a final, decisive operation against the Navajos. The Utes served, as before, at first as scouts and trailers; soon large numbers were operating against the Navajos "on their own account." Carson praised their services and urged that they be allowed to keep captive Navajos, as well as livestock, as part of their reward; according to custom, the captives would probably be sold to New Mexicans as slaves. Carleton refused the request. Carson also recruited auxiliaries from Zuñi pueblo and from the Hopi towns. He apparently had some suspicion that the Hopis were covert allies of the Navajos and wished to alienate them from the enemy; eventually he praised the services of these allies from the sedentary tribes.[7]

With the Navajos confined to a reservation in eastern New Mexico, Carleton turned his attention to the increasing danger offered by the Comanches and Kiowas to the Santa Fe Trail, his principal line of communication with the East. Once more he selected Carson for command and sent him off to the Texas Panhandle with a force of 350 California and New Mexico volunteers and 75 Indians, including Jicarilla Apaches and Carson's old friends the Utes. Carleton's first intention had been to make the expedition primarily an Indian affair, with Carson leading a force of several hundred Jicarillas and Utes and another trusted officer leading a force of Navajos from their reservation to attack farther south. This would be an inexpensive campaign that would alienate the Rocky Mountain tribes from those of the Plains, precluding any possible coalition against the whites. The Navajos, however, declined to assist their conqueror. The Utes and Jicarillas were reluctant to provide large numbers of men unless the army could provide their families with protection and rations while they were gone, something Carleton lacked the supplies to do; since Carson wanted white troops to protect his supply train in any case, the expedition became a more conventional one. In late November 1864 they attacked the winter camps of the Kiowas, present in far greater numbers than expected, on the Canadian River near the abandoned trading post of Adobe Walls. The far superior strength of Kiowas and their Comanche allies turned the attack into a retreat; Carson handled the withdrawal ably, but acknowledged himself lucky to have extracted his forces with such light casualties. George Bent, a well-qualified judge of such encounters, himself half Cheyenne, concluded years later that Carson's Indian scouts were responsible for his escape.[8]

Relations with the Arizona Apaches had deteriorated to a disastrous extent as the Civil War began. For some years to come whites were safe only in a few towns, or traveling in large, armed bodies. The military operations in Arizona in this period were the responsibility of the volunteers from California, a state with a dismal record for its treatment of Indians. They received aid from contingents from various tribes of Arizona, notably the sedentary peoples of the Gila Valley and the southern part of the territory, long at enmity with the Apaches. These Papagos, Pimas, and Maricopas joined at various times with irregular collections of whites for murderous expeditions against the Apaches; indeed, these expeditions had contributed to the deterioration of relations with the Apaches. At General Carleton's orders, these Indians received obsolete muskets and ammunition, both for their own defense and for attacks on the Apaches. The new territory of Arizona, despite its lack of tax resources, organized a militia of five companies, as the Californians prepared for departure at the war's end. Company B consisted of Maricopas and Company C of Pimas, the latter commanded by Lieutenant John D. Walker; Walker was a part-Wyandot who had marrried into the tribe and led his warriors dressed in a breechcloth. The Arizona volunteers continued in service into 1866, when the regulars returned to Arizona. During this same period, Papagos and some friendly Apaches seem to have served semiofficially in various forays; a scalp bounty offered by the territory at this time probably furnished added incentive. The Pimas and Maricopas would continue to serve with the returning regulars in 1866–67.[9]

In the Pacific Northwest there were persistent troubles with small but widespread groups of Shoshones and Paiutes, loosely designated as "Snakes"; these troubles erupted sporadically in the broad area, part of the Great Basin, where Oregon, Idaho, and Nevada meet. Volunteer forces coping with the problem turned to Indian allies for all the usual services: reconnaissance, trailing, and combat with or without white assistance. Most prominent among these allies at this time were the so-called Warm Springs Indians, named after their reservation in Oregon, which housed a conglomeration of small groups, generally hostile to the Snakes. In 1864 they evidently received only subsistence and red headbands to avoid cases of mistaken identity; they were allowed to collect both material plunder and slaves. Captain John M. Drake was impressed with their services, and especially with their chief, Stock Whitley. These Indian troubles continued into the postwar period, and so did the services of the Warm Springs Indians, at least intermittently, until 1873.[10]

Indian troubles on the Plains intensified during the Civil War because of increased white intrusion, maladroit management of Indian relations, and misplaced aggressive action by the volunteer forces. The new troubles with the Comanches have been noted. A new level of hostility developed with the Sioux and Cheyennes from western Minnesota to Colorado Territory, endangering frontier settlers and threatening to cut off the major travel routes to the mountain gold fields and the Pacific coast. The immediate white reaction, civil and military, was furious outrage at the "bloodthirsty savages," who were conceived to have no excuse but their own homicidal tendencies. To serve their immediate military needs, most commanders turned for aid to those Indians they thought trustworthy. Most commonly they called on tribes known to be hostile to the powerful Sioux and their Cheyenne and Arapaho allies; commanders with frontier experience, however, on occasion enlisted trusted Sioux. Just before the infamous Sand Creek massacre, Major Edward Wynkoop of the Colorado Volunteers suggested to his superiors that these same Cheyennes and Arapahoes, soon to be victims, should be employed against the Kiowas and Comanches; their chiefs had expressed willingness to render such service.[11]

In 1862 the Santee Sioux of Minnesota, after years of accumulating grievances climaxed by inadequate food allowances, rose against the whites. Defeated after bloody fighting, the diehards fled to the Dakota prairies. Military operations extending out onto the Plains brought the army into conflict with the western, or Teton, Sioux. Although outrage against the Santees led to the largest public execution in American history, the military nonetheless turned for aid to Indians, among them Sioux. The mixed-blood Sioux leader Gabriel Renville approached Brigadier General Henry Sibley, a former Indian trader and now a volunteer officer, with an offer to recruit mixed-bloods as scouts to patrol the western approaches to the settlements. Renville also recruited some full-bloods, arousing suspicion in some quarters, but he insisted that the men he had chosen were reliable, and they were signed up.[12]

In 1863 and 1864, General Alfred Sully, a regular with extensive western experience, also campaigned in Dakota, making use of the services of a variety of Indians. The agent for the Yankton Sioux in southeastern Dakota recruited a contingent and offered them to Sully, who gave them outdated uniforms and some rations. They acted on their own in several forays and killed a number of hostiles. It took them twenty years to collect their pay, a delay that was the more unfortunate since their poverty was a significant factor in their readiness to enlist.[13]

Accompanying Sully on his expedition deep into western Dakota in 1864 were a motley lot of scouts. They included a contingent called the "Nebraska scouts," who seem to have included some whites and a number of Winnebagoes recently deported to Nebraska Territory from Minnesota. After the engagement at Killdeer Mountain (the largest but hardly the bloodiest or most decisive of the western Indian wars), Sully found himself lost and short of water in the Badlands. A young Indian showed the expedition the way to the Little Missouri River and their supply steamboat. These campaigns were less than decisive, but the commanders consistently recognized their need for the help of Indians.[14]

The difficulties with the Sioux, Cheyennes, and Arapahoes along the Platte River road—the most important route of emigration, mail and telegraph communications, and wagon freight to the mountain gold fields—called forth the services of more Indian allies. By 1864 hostilities with the Sioux—and the Cheyennes after Sand Creek—were a threat to the trail and to settlements in Nebraska and Kansas. Commanders fresh from the Civil War battlefields found that they could march and countermarch along the trail from post to post without deterring the far more mobile raiders, and that offensive sweeps with cavalry through the hunting grounds generally failed to discover hostiles. As an indication of the failure to secure results by conventional military means, Colonel R. R. Livingston started a great prairie fire from Fort Kearny west along the trail into Colorado, hoping to drive both Indians and buffalo out of the Republican River region and force them north of the Platte. The idea, an adaptation of an old Indian strategem, shows a certain ingenuity, as well as desperation, but results were minor.[15]

Even while the situation along the trail was worsening, Colonel William Collins recruited a small force of Sioux to act as "police" and keep order among friendly Sioux camped near Fort Laramie. Such duty was not unlike that performed by warrior societies within the tribe. On at least one occasion a group of Arapahoes accompanied Ohio cavalrymen on a scouting expedition into the mountains of Colorado and fought beside the soldiers. These episodes contrast with the usual sweeping statements that "the Sioux" or "the Arapahoes" were hostile or friendly at a given time.[16]

With Union victory in sight in the spring of 1865, the commanders on the Plains were able to plan large-scale offensive operations against the Indians north of the Platte. Plans provided for a three-pronged invasion of the Powder River country of Wyoming and Montana territories, the great hunting ground and central stronghold of the Teton Sioux and Northern Cheyennes. Three strong cavalry columns (all volunteer units) were to strike north from the Platte Valley: one from Columbus, Nebraska, under Colonel Nelson Cole; one from Fort Laramie, under Colonel Samuel Walker; and the strongest, under Brigadier General Patrick Connor, from Laramie via the new post of Fort Connor on the Powder River. They were to rendezvous somewhere on the Tongue River, near the Yellowstone, in Montana Territory. Very long marches would be necessary, especially for the eastern column under Cole, over country almost unmapped and known to few whites. The guides allotted to the two eastern columns proved to be ignorant—or their knowledge was not properly used —and these columns did little more than stumble about in an unknown wilderness, losing most of their horses to starvation, feeding on the dead animals, and harassed by Sioux and Cheyennes who were perfectly at home in what to the inexperienced troops and commanders was a virtual desert. It was an excellent example of how not to conduct an Indian campaign.[17]

Connor's western column enjoyed more success. Connor himself was a former regular enlisted man, an officer of Texas volunteers in the Mexican War, and colonel of a California regiment. He had campaigned against Bannocks and Paiutes earlier in the war and was the only column commander with experience in Indian campaigns. His men, California, Ohio, and Iowa cavalrymen, were also experienced in Indian fighting. His chief guide was the old mountain man Jim Bridger, perhaps the best-qualified man available. In addition, Connor had the services of two companies of Indian scouts: Captain Frank North's Pawnees and Captain E. W. Nash's "Omaha" scouts. Most of the latter were in fact Winnebagoes, recently settled with the Omahas on their Nebraska reservation. Although Nash officially commanded the Winnebagoes, their first sergeant was Chief Little Priest, a formidable warrior. Officially, both scout contingents were independent companies of Nebraska volunteer cavalry; this formal enlistment of Indians as soldiers set a precedent for the postwar period.[18]

In accordance with western thinking on such matters, Connor issued an order that all male Indians over the age of 12 were to be killed; General John Pope quickly canceled this instruction. Yet Connor's attitude toward the hostiles did not deter him from making full use of his Indian scouts, especially the Pawnees; he seems to have harbored a certain distrust of the Winnebagoes, although there is no record that they proved disloyal at any time. While Fort Connor was under construction in August, the scouts intercepted several small war parties of Sioux and Cheyennes moving north from raiding along the North Platte. On some occasions they managed to lure the hostiles into their very camps by pretending to be Sioux themselves. Apparently they took no prisoners; some of those killed and scalped were women. The Cheyenne mixed-blood George Bent believed that if Connor had sent his scouts out on long-range reconnaissance instead of merely sweeping up small parties, he could have surprised the Northern Cheyennes' main camp on the Powder.[19]

As the column rode north from Fort Connor, the Pawnees located a camp of Northern Arapahoes on Wolf Creek, a tributary of the Tongue. Connor personally led a surprise attack on the Arapaho village, scoring a great success by contemporary standards. He was displeased with the scouts, however, who fell out to loot the enemy camp, giving special attention to the horse herd. He estimated the number of enemy warriors killed at thirty-five; such estimates were notoriously unreliable. Women and children were commonly victims in such attacks on villages, whether this result was intended or not.[20]

Connor's further progress was less spectacular, but the scouts continued to play an important part. Frank North was sent out to locate the other two columns and found them together, virtually horseless, hungry, their wagons burned for lack of draft animals, and with hostiles hovering about. Connor concluded that both bodies should return south, since the hostiles were now alerted and hence only limited success could be expected. Indeed, the government had already sent an order recalling the expedition, which Connor did not see until his return.[21]

An incident of the latter part of the expedition shows both the scouts' combativeness and their attitude toward their enemies. A detached force, including the Winnebagoes, encountered a body of Arapahoes who waved white flags to show peaceful intentions. As soon as their dust was sighted, the Winnebagoes jumped on their horses and raced helter-skelter for the presumed enemy; one witness said the California troopers felt shamed by the scouts' bravery. The detachment commander, seeing the white flags, told Little Priest to halt his men. The chief asserted that this was an impossible task, but when the officer pointed a revolver at him, he managed to halt the eager warriors.[22]

When Connor decided to release the Arapaho women and children the expedition had taken prisoner on the Tongue River, he gave them a cavalry escort for some distance to protect them from his Pawnees and Winnebagoes. The scouts expressed their disapproval by saying that it would be better to kill them, since otherwise "they would produce more bad Indians." They would have been in agreement with Colonel Chivington, who reportedly told his men at Sand Creek to kill regardless of age or sex, because "nits make lice."[23]

The history of the Powder River expedition suggests some of the difficulties of campaigning against Plains Indians. Defects in planning and inherent problems of logistics and tactics kept it from being the decisive blow that was hoped for. For the eastern and center columns it was a near disaster. The Northern Arapahoes were the tribe that suffered most, and they were the smallest and least belligerent part of the Sioux-Cheyenne alliance. Some asserted that the expedition had at least drawn the hostile bands north, away from the Platte River road. The following year the government attempted to negotiate a peace, but this effort foundered from mutual incomprehension, lack of centralized Indian authority, and the whites' ultimate unwillingness to concede what to the Indians was a minimal necessity—undisputed possession of adequate hunting grounds on which to continue their familiar way of life indefinitely. There is no evidence that the expedition had given the Indians an overwhelming impression of the whites' power; they may even have concluded that they had driven the soldiers out of their country, and not without reason.[24]

However unsatisfactory the final results, the difference between the experience of Connor's column and that of the other two showed the advantages of experienced leadership and troops accustomed to Indian fighting. Connor's final report on the whole expedition is not available, so we do not have his final assessment of the services of the Pawnees and Winnebagoes. His extensive reliance on them for scouting, combat, and courier duty suggests both their value and Connor's confidence in them.

The scouts, along with Bridger, made possible what contact there was with the enemy. Moreover, this contact occurred on the soldiers' terms, not on the Indians', as it did for the other two columns. Moreover, the scouts did much more actual fighting, especially in proportion to their numbers, than the white cavalry. A member of the expedition wrote many years later of Connor's relations with his troops: "he loved these men—the Second Colorado, the Second California and the Eleventh Ohio. I have heard him say that with these three regiments and ninety Pawnee scouts under Major Frank North, he could whip all of the Indians on the plains, and I believe that he could have done it."[25] The failure to mention the Winnebago scouts may indicate that Connor's mistrust of them had persisted. Neither the Minnesota Winnebagoes nor the Nebraska Pawnees could have had an intimate familiarity with the Powder River country, nor was such familiarity needful with Bridger as chief guide. It was their skill in trailing and general reconnaissance, and their ability to fight "horse Indians" on their own terms, that was of first importance.

There is a continuity of practice in the use of Indian allies from the Civil War volunteers to the postwar regulars. Pimas and Maricopas in Arizona Territory and Warm Springs in Oregon continued in service as before, because the same conflicts continued. On the Northern Plains there was a more noticeable break in continuity. North's Pawnees were stationed at their reservation in Nebraska Territory in the winter of 1865–66, drawing pay and rations while protecting their own people from possible Sioux incursions. After accompanying one expedition in January, they were discharged in April. The Winnebagoes continued in service at Fort Connor, renamed Fort Reno, until June, frequently serving as couriers under dangerous conditions and skirmishing with the hostiles. First Sergeant Little Priest was severely wounded in November, in an encounter in which he held off a number of the enemy single-handedly with his Henry repeating rifle; his wounds eventually proved mortal.[26]

Colonel Henry Carrington's column encountered the Winnebagoes going home past Fort Laramie in June 1866; the Indians wanted to turn back and serve with Carrington, but the colonel had no legal authority to enlist or pay them. Jim Bridger told

Carrington that the Sioux, negotiating with federal commissioners at Fort Laramie, had demanded the withdrawal of the Winnebagoes. This demand, as reported by Bridger, probably reflects
the judgment of the Sioux on the scouts' effectiveness, and also
Bridger's own expert opinion. It may also indicate that the eastern warriors were overeager to collect Sioux scalps, under whatever circumstances, as in the incident with the surrendering
Arapahoes. Carrington thought the Winnebagoes should have
been retained in service until peace was ensured, in order to have
"a few soldiers who knew the Indian styles of warfare, and were
up to their tricks." The government provided no substitutes.[27]

In fact, the very presence of Carrington's command ruined
whatever chance existed for a peace treaty. His assignment was
to establish and garrison posts to protect the Bozeman Trail
through the Powder River country to Montana. Such leaders as
Red Cloud saw clearly the implications of such a move, undertaken without their consent. Carrington established two new
posts, Fort C. F. Smith and Fort Phil Kearny, on the trail. The
Sioux and Cheyennes continually harassed the garrisons, which
were hard put to defend themselves, let alone protect parties of
travelers.[28]

Carrington continued to hope for Indian allies, and in August
1866 his superiors authorized the enlistment of fifty. During the
summer the Crow tribe told Bridger that they could offer the services of 250 warriors, a proposition Bridger thought desirable.
The country through which the trail ran was disputed by the
Sioux and the Crows, the former having gradually pushed the
latter out over the previous thirty years by weight of numbers.
Moreover, the Crows had been traditional friends of the whites
since the earliest days of the fur trade. When they made their offer, Carrington had no authority to enlist them and no extra
arms to equip them. When he received authority to enlist Indians, he attempted to get the Winnebagoes, who were better
armed. The Crow offer remained in abeyance, while the Nebraska Indians were never assigned to the Bozeman Trail forts.
Hence Carrington was without Indian allies at the time of the
Fetterman massacre in December 1866, when over half of the
Fort Phil Kearny garrison perished. Indian scouts could certainly
have prevented the massive ambush that caused this defeat,

though there is no knowing if Captain Fetterman would have heeded their warnings.[29]

Although not officially enlisted, the Crows still acted as allies of the harassed troops along the Bozeman. Until the posts were abandoned in 1868, the Crows were frequent visitors, often providing useful information about the intentions and numbers of the Sioux, and fighting them in conjunction with troops or alone. Fort C. F. Smith, on the Bighorn River in Montana Territory, was even more isolated from support than Fort Phil Kearny, but it was also more centrally located in Crow hunting grounds. The fort was virtually cut off from the outside world through the winter of 1866–67. Only a few couriers, white and Indian, managed to carry messages in and out. The post commander reported in February, however, that hostile action had virtually ceased since October. He attributed this peacefulness in part to the weather (which had not prevented the Fetterman massacre at Phil Kearny in December), but primarily to the presence of the Crows in nearby encampments. The Crows continued their cooperation in the summer months. Troops and Crows together on occasion pursued horse-stealing parties of Sioux raiding at Fort Phil Kearny. Colonel Henry W. Wessels, the post commander, found the Crows "particularly active and enterprising" in fighting off a raid on June 18, 1867.[30]

Relations between the Crows and the army depended to a great extent on the local commanders, because of the informal nature of the alliance. Lieutenant Colonel Luther P. Bradley, commanding at Fort C. F. Smith in the summer of 1867, had little faith in the Crows; he kept expecting some hostile act from them, yet could report nothing except the trading of some powder to the Sioux. Before his arrival the previous commander, Captain N. C. Kinney, had given Chief Iron Bull and some warriors "permission" to drive off a party of Sioux. They did so with pleasure, but insisted on burning to death a captive Sioux, despite Kinney's protests. Although the Sioux had apparently made attempts to win the friendship and aid of the Crows, such an act seems to be a convincing demonstration of their lack of success. Nonetheless, Bradley placed no faith in information brought by the Crows of a concerted attack planned by the Sioux and Cheyennes on Forts Phil Kearny, C. F. Smith, and Reno.

The intelligence proved essentially accurate, since heavy attacks were made on outlying detachments of the first two posts a few days after Bradley expressed his distrust. The troops beat off the hostiles with new breech-loading weapons, which could inflict losses the Indians were not prepared to face.[31]

In the absence of Crow testimony from this period, one can view this informal but mutually advantageous military alliance only from the white side. We have official reports, and a few members of the Bozeman Trail garrisons left accounts of their experiences. Both Lieutenant George Palmer and Private James Lockwood give accounts of friendly visits back and forth, implying intercourse in more than one sense between Crows and soldiers. Crow hunters helped the C. F. Smith garrison to eke out its scanty rations during its winter of isolation; Lockwood, however, found boiled dog unpalatable when he was invited to Iron Bull's home for a feast. These accounts demonstrate a mixture of respect and gratitude toward effective allies with ethnocentric contempt for many of their customs and mores. This ambivalence was quite characteristic of the white soldiers' view of Indians when they were allowed to confront them in a broader context than that of combat. Since Palmer's notes were originally a series of newspaper articles, one can view the progressive modification of his ideas. Early in his service on the Bozeman he asserted, "There is not one redeeming trait about the character of any Indian, living or dead." A few months later he had concluded that Indian troubles were at least partly the fault of corrupt white agents. Although he found the Crows lazy and of lax morals, he ended by concluding that "no other Indians are braver or better fighters than the Crows," and remarked on their loyalty to their own people. Despite his disapproval of their morals, hygiene, and industry, he had to recognize their humanity.[32]

While the government was finally able to make a treaty with the hostile Sioux in 1868, it agreed to abandon the Bozeman Trail forts, and thus the trail itself. This meant giving up the Powder River country, at least temporarily, to the Sioux. The government had in effect betrayed the Crows, who had willingly helped the army to hold the posts for two years. In any case, the Sioux and Cheyennes had been in effective control of much of the region for some years. It is interesting that it was the hope of doing justice to "the Indians" that in part prompted the treaty. The Crows did not perceive their interests as being the same as those of the Sioux and Cheyennes.[33]

The intensification of Indian-white conflict during the Civil War years did not end with Appomattox. During the war years, however, the protection of settlers and travelers and the suppression of hostilities fell to wartime volunteer units, many of them from western states and territories. The nonprofessional soldiers took an especially brutal and punitive approach to hostile Indians, as indeed the Union forces took toward all of their enemies. At the same time, they turned readily to the use of friendly Indians. By this means they hoped to increase their military effectiveness and achieve a permanent solution to the problem of Indian resistance. Some of these arrangements with Indian allies were informal, with the Indians being offered loot and the other benefits of intertribal warfare, and perhaps military weapons. In several cases, however, the Indian scouts were regularly enlisted as volunteer troops in formally organized and officered militia units. A similar step was taken among the "civilized tribes" of Indian Territory, by both Union and Confederate authorities, for direct service in the civil conflict; this step may have eased the way for enlistment of "wild Indians" for service in the West. Since the Indian troubles did not end with the Civil War, the need for Indian allies remained also. As the western military problem returned to the hands of the regular army in 1866, the precedent of integrating Indians into the military establishment would continue.

Western Tribes

Chapter Three

Regularization

In the United States, and indeed in the Western world in the nineteenth century, an increasingly industrialized civilization was tending toward regularization. Much that had been haphazard, informal, and traditional was being reduced to written rules and regulations, organized and bureaucratized. The army had for many years employed Indians on an occasional, hit-or-miss basis, using anyone available as the occasion demanded, according to the good or bad judgment of commanders. In the post–Civil War era the practice was to be reduced to regulations; Indian scouts were to become, in theory, regular soldiers, and their employment was to be on a rational basis, proportional to need.

The regularization of Indian scouts was symbolic of the society's intention to bring all Indians under the regulation and control of the United States government. To many people the supposed lawlessness of the Indians seemed an anomaly in nineteenth-century America; the Indian scouts would be the instruments of white law, and they would also be among the first Indians whose activities were regulated. Such subjection was the long-term goal of the federal Indian policy, through all its turns and inconsistencies, and the symbolism of this military instrument was simply a by-product.[1]

The informal arrangements between Crows and soldiers on the Bozeman Trail marked the transition in at least two ways. In 1866 the regular army was in the process of reassuming military responsibility for the West from the Civil War volunteers. The Crow alliance was of the traditional type: the Indians were attached to the military force to the extent they wished to be, until they changed their minds; their reward was whatever glory, re-

venge, or material benefit they could secure through their efforts. Colonel Carrington had wanted a more formal arrangement, and after August 1866 he could have had one, if he had not
put off the Crows in the hope of obtaining the services of the
Winnebagoes. In that month the regulations governing the army
at last allowed the enlistment of an Indian scout force on a regular basis.

In theory the "Act to increase and fix the Military Peace Establishment of the United States" increased the army from a
prewar strength of 18,000 to 54,000. Cavalry regiments, especially needed in the West, increased from six to ten. Forty-five
regiments of infantry were provided for, but they were never
brought up to strength. The army never came close to this proposed establishment, because of Congressional economizing.
Indeed, the employment of Indians scouts may have seemed an
economical measure, since it would increase the effectiveness of
the small regular force, and Indian enlistments could be termi-
nated in case of need, unlike the fixed five-year enlistments of
white and black soldiers.[2]

The relevant portion of the act of 1866 was a clause authorizing the president to enlist a force of Indians, "not to exceed one
thousand." Their function was "to act as scouts," and they
would receive the pay and allowances of cavalry soldiers. They
could be discharged whenever the need for their services abated,
or at the discretion of the local department commander. A general order from the Office of the Adjutant General implemented
this provision of the act on August 1, 1866. Colonel Carrington's efforts to enlist Winnebagoes or Pawnees for service on the
Bozeman Trail was made under this authorization.[3]

Within three years Congress reduced the number of infantry
regiments to twenty-five, and by 1874 the lawmakers had cut
the enlisted strength of the entire army to 25,000, plus about
2,000 officers. The lack of any serious immediate threat to national security meant that the only people likely to express
much concern over the strength of the army were frontier people
who thought themselves threatened by Indians or bandits, and
occasionally urban citizens frightened by labor unrest. Military
historians have concluded that never had the organization and
efficiency of the army been of less concern to the general society.[4]

The most obvious direct influence on the Indian enlistment provision was the precedent established during the Civil War, when tribes from Indian Territory were enlisted in three "Indian Home Guard" regiments; this action came in response to the Confederacy's enlistment of units from many of the same tribes. As with the enlistment of blacks during the war, westerners and other "amateurs" established a policy that federal officials and the regular hierarchy finally had to accept. By no coincidence, Senator James H. Lane of Kansas took the initiative in enlisting both blacks and Indians under the Union banner, in the face of official disapproval; to him, as to many other westerners, the times seemed to demand extreme measures. In 1866 the Congress regularized the experiment with black troops by providing for four black regiments; the provision for Indian scouts, in a more modest way, made another emergency expedient permanent.[5]

The army gave the measure a mixed reception at first; a striking illustration is the enlistment of the Warm Springs scouts in Oregon for service in the continuing small wars with the Paiutes or "Snakes." This was a persistent, sputtering guerrilla war in the Oregon-Nevada-Idaho region, undoubtedly involving plenty of provocation on both sides. The white settlers naturally saw the matter from one side only, and they wanted a solution. After the act of 1866 was passed, the Adjutant General's Office allotted 100 scouts to the Department of the Columbia (Oregon, Washington, and Idaho). Oregon's governor, George Woods, asked the department commander, General Frederick Steele, to allow these Indians to be organized into two companies under commanders selected by the governor, to act independently of the regulars. Steele refused, probably as much because of the proposed freedom from regular control as from any objection to Indian scouts as such. Woods appealed to Steele's superior, General Henry W. "Old Brains" Halleck, then commanding the Military Division of the Pacific; he was again refused. Woods then telegraphed to Secretary of War Edwin Stanton in Washington, who ordered Halleck to accede to Woods's wishes. Two companies, not quite up to the authorized strength, were signed up under William McKay and John Darragh. The commanders were referred to as second lieutenants, later as captains, but their official federal status was that of "interpreters." They received officers' pay, faced the same dangers as army officers, and were definitely in command.[6]

As matters developed, the two companies operated mostly in conjunction with the regular forces. For much of the 1866–67 campaign they were under the command of Lieutenant Colonel George Crook, who had become familiar with the Northwest before the Civil War, and who in these operations began to gain a reputation as an Indian expert and troubleshooter. Crook had also raised a band of friendly "Snakes," led by his mixed-blood chief scout, Archie McIntosh; this was an early instance of Crook's preference for scouts closely related in language and culture to the people he was fighting. The government supplied at least some of the Indians' horses, although they were originally expected to provide their own. More or less complete cavalry uniforms were issued, including the elaborate dress hat with feather, tasseled cord, and crossed-saber insignia; this piece of finery certainly reduced the chances of mistaken identity. The Warm Springs companies received fairly up-to-date breech-loading carbines, but the Snake scouts had to make do with muskets labeled "Harpers Ferry, 1845." A newspaper correspondent judged that the Snakes were the better scouts and should have been furnished the more modern weapons.[7]

The military commanders judged that the Indian scouts contributed greatly to success in the campaigns of those years. Crook's assessment is evident in the fact that he became the army's most noted advocate of Indian allies, both as scouts and as combat troops. Generals Halleck and Steele, who had opposed the organization of the Indians on Governor Woods's terms— probably in fear of divided authority—both praised the scouts highly in their 1867 reports. Halleck alluded, in this connection, to his need for more troops, then wrote: "The officers are unanimous in favor of greatly increasing the number. As guides and scouts, they are almost indispensable." Steele's report was in even more significant terms, especially in regard to the scouts' role in combat.

Being armed, mounted, and supplied, and backed by troops, they cheerfully lead the way into the middle of their enemies. In the late expedition they have done most of the fighting and killing. They have also proved themselves very efficient when acting alone; they are very useful as guides and spies and in destroying the spies of the enemy. It is my opinion that one hundred, in addition to those now employed, would exterminate the hostile bands before the next spring, with troops enough in the settlements to prevent their getting supplies from that source.

Steele's conclusion that the Indians should serve as a major part of the army's striking force, even allowing white troops to be relegated to defending settlements, goes further than most regulars would have wanted to go. It was not so far from the opinions of his field commander, George Crook, and Steele may have been influenced by Crook's recommendations.[8]

Steele found it especially praiseworthy that the scouts had done most of the killing, and this comment is significant in another way. The general's expressed hope that the hostiles would be exterminated was to be taken literally. He apparently issued an order during this campaign to the effect that no prisoners of whatever age or sex were to be taken. This may be the only case in which a regular officer of such seniority issued an unequivocal and unqualified extermination order. Generals Sherman and Sheridan frequently used the word, but never issued specific orders; indeed, public opinion in the East would hardly have allowed them to do so. Other so-called extermination orders, such as Connor's, prove under examination to have applied to males above a certain age, and to have had other qualifications. Colonel Chivington, of course, was a volunteer. To some people, inside the army and out, success in the Indian conflicts could be measured by the number of dead Indians. There were others, like Crook, who measured success in the reestablishment and maintenance of peace at a minimum cost. This division of opinion would recur during the Indian wars. Steele may have imagined that his ''savage'' auxiliaries would be especially effective instruments of an extermination policy. Apparently they did kill some captured women and children on at least one occasion, but they objected strongly to the order, and seem to have evaded it at other times. The reasons they gave for objecting were that the Snakes would retaliate on their own families, and that they wanted the captives as slaves. These were not humanitarian sentiments, but they suggest that certain limits were recognized, if not thoroughly articulated, by the participants in intertribal warfare in the region. Steele's order somehow offended the local proprieties.[9]

Certain shortcomings of Indian scouts, from a military point of view, appeared during this campaign. The scouts preferred to go home after a few months in the field to visit their families and provide for their needs, and no doubt to recuperate from the rigors of campaigning. The sensible provision allowing short-term enlistment and discharge at the discretion of the department commander made it possible to accommodate them. Otherwise, the army would have lost their services in any case. One could properly call the men of many western tribes warriors because the average man was expected to participate in war fairly regularly during his active life. Warriors, however, were not a special class set aside exclusively for this task by their society, like the soldiers. They would not and could not devote all their time to war, for they had lives, duties, and responsibilities outside of fighting. From the army's point of view, this was a handicap.[10]

When Crook needed to enlist new scouts, he made a successful attempt to obtain them from the very hostiles who had just surrendered. Indeed, he made this proposal at the end of the peace talks, and found several young fellows ready and willing to put on the uniform. These same restless young men were quite likely the ones from whom renewed trouble might otherwise have arisen. Instead they were kept busy at an evidently congenial occupation and attached to the society that had defeated them. The pattern was an old one, and Crook and some other commanders would follow it increasingly in later years.[11]

The Indian disturbances of the late 1860s increased the enlistment of scouts under the act of 1866. Colonel Philip Régis de Trobriand, commanding a district along the upper Missouri in Dakota Territory, was eager to enlist Arikaras, Mandans, and Hidatsas against the Sioux. He had heard, through the army grapevine, of the exploits of the Pawnee scouts along the Platte in 1867; the example seemed to him to have great potential for his own situation. After the inconclusive Civil War campaigns, the river had become a sort of static military frontier between the whites and the Teton Sioux. The latter, Sitting Bull and Gall of the Hunkpapas prominent among them, harassed the military posts, the trading establishments, and the villages of the sedentary tribes. Trobriand saw a scout contingent as a counter to the perpetual forays. Near the old trading post of Fort Berthold lay Like-a-Fishhook village, where the Arikaras, Mandans, and Hidatsas had confederated for defense against the Sioux. Ravaged by smallpox and other diseases introduced by the whites, their numbers much reduced, the "Three Tribes" had fallen on hard times. At first the chiefs said they feared that enlistment of their young men would weaken their defenses; in fact, they may have feared losing their traditional authority and control over the young warriors. The colonel had to enlist some Yanktons from downriver. He was sure, however, that the Arikaras were, man for man, a match for the Sioux. In May 1868 the first ten Arikaras signed up for six months at Fort Stevenson. They were issued the full uniform, though they retained their mocassins, and insisted on the elaborate plumed hat. For furnishing their own horses they received 40 cents per day; they were first issued long infantry rifles, which were soon replaced with Spencer repeating carbines.[12]

The Arikaras fought with or in place of white troops for several years thereafter, their most famous service being with Custer in the campaign of 1876. One incident has a special poignance. On August 26, 1872, near Fort McKean, one white sergeant and six infantrymen, with two Arikara scouts, were attacked by a large party of Sioux. The two scouts were killed, while the white soldiers escaped. No details are furnished to tell whether the scouts either sacrificed themselves or were deserted as they covered the retreat of their white comrades.[13]

Major John Green of the First Cavalry initiated another form of Indian-military cooperation in Arizona Territory in 1869. Green, a tough German immigrant and former enlisted man, apologized to his department commander for accepting the surrender of Chief Miguel and his band of White Mountain Apaches, instead of attacking them. The Apaches, men, women, and children, had come out with white flags to meet Green's column; he and his officers agreed that to open fire in the circumstances would have been "cold-blooded murder." Professing himself ready to shoot on sight if extermination was the official policy, Green still thought that with proper handling and a military post to protect them, they would be quite susceptible of being "civilized." The major then noted that Miguel had offered the services of his warriors to the army, and suggested that the use of

Apaches against Apaches would bring a speedy end to the problem. The department commander, Brigadier General E. O. C. Ord, endorsed Green's opinions, making a special point that a military post and a reservation from which whites would be excluded would indeed be necessary for the protection of these Indians. Green was ordered to establish a post, later named Fort Apache, in the White Mountain homeland. The Apaches were immediately issued beef rations and encouraged to produce hay and wood for the post. This was the beginning of an Apache-military association that later caused much distress to the civil agents at San Carlos reservation.[14]

These incidents reveal that there was still a haphazard quality about Indian enlistments. The scout detachments did not prove to be the American equivalent of the "irregular" or "native" cavalry units employed by the British and French in their colonies, which were standing organizations with officers permanently assigned. The American scout units were temporary collections of Indians enlisted for a particular need, to be discharged in the interests of economy as soon as they were no longer needed. This lack of continuity was accentuated by the fact that scout officers were on temporary assignment from infantry and cavalry regiments. Nevertheless, some scout units maintained a degree of continuity and some officers remained on this duty for long periods.

The law of 1866 authorized 1,000 Indian scouts for the whole army: this was only a small proportion of the intended enlisted strength of 54,000, but just as an economizing Congress more than halved the overall strength of the army in the next eight years, so the actual strength of the scout force was to be cut drastically. This cut, however, was self-inflicted. By administrative decision, the Adjutant General's Office imposed limits on scout strength well below 1,000 during much of the post–Civil War period. In 1874, when the entire enlisted strength was reduced to 25,000, the number of scouts for the whole frontier force was fixed at 300. In 1876 Congress passed a military appropriation that fixed the 300-man limit legally, only to repeal it within three weeks to restore the 1,000-man limit. The legislators had learned that operations against the Sioux were not going well and that a new effort at pacification was needed.[15]

The total number of Indian scouts was reckoned as part of the total enlisted strength of the army. Legally, each Indian on the rolls meant one fewer white or black regular soldier. The drastic reduction of the army after 1866, with the consequent forced retirement of many officers—a source of much bitterness—had been painful in the extreme. Because regulars enlisted for five years, a 1,000-man scout force would mean 1,000 fewer regulars; that many spaces must be kept open for scout enlistments, even though these were short-term enlistments and all slots might not be filled. The administrative officers were not prepared to suffer any more losses of full-enlistment regulars for the sake of signing up savages who were in today and out tomorrow. To them the term "scout" probably suggested, as it still does, an Indian or two following a trail for a cavalry detachment, which if guided properly would catch and defeat the enemy. Civilian scouts were being hired for the same purpose, and would no doubt serve as well or better. In fact, the regular units were generally below strength during this period, since the army offered few inducements to enlist and desertion was easy. No doubt the Adjutant General's Office clung to a pious hope that the line units could at least be maintained at the strength allowed, when things settled down and Congress was finally satisfied. Unfortunately, the shifting demands of the actual western situation contrasted with the stable state of affairs that administrators naturally strove to maintain.[16]

Meanwhile the department commanders bombarded the commanding general and the Adjutant General's Office in Washington with requests for authority to enlist more scouts, pleading urgent necessity and the uniquely difficult problems within their commands. There were seven geographical departments in the West, and each commander claimed that no department had such hordes of actual and potential hostiles within it as his own; the number of scouts never seemed sufficient to carry on operations and protect the citizenry from wholesale slaughter. The department and field commanders undoubtedly thought that they, who were trying to carry out the army's mission, were being hamstrung by Washington paper shufflers concerned only with figures. The adjutant general no doubt thought that the commanders could see no further than their own commands, exaggerated their difficulties, and had no understanding of the problems of administering an army on a limited and uncertain budget. The commanding generals (Ulysses S. Grant, 1864–68; William Tecumseh Sherman, 1868–82; Philip Henry Sheridan, 1882–88; John McAllister Schofield, 1888–95) were generally sympathetic to the field commanders, but were also painfully aware of Washington realities and forced to balance needs and resources. In fact, the commanding general of the army had no direct control over the Adjutant General's Office, which reported directly to the secretary of war.[17]

Specific numerical allotments of Indian scouts were evidently made to the separate departments in 1866–67, judging from commanding officers' complaints about insufficient numbers of scouts allotted at that time. A memo from the Adjutant General's Office of 1876, however, states: "There does not appear to have been any distribution of this number to the several Departments or Divisions made from this office." This statement may mean only that no such allotments had been made, since the office limited the overall total to 300 in 1874. In fact, the memo writer suspected that commanders, especially General Sheridan, were simply ignoring the official limits "in view of recent hostile operations." The commanding general's report for that year more or less admits as much; in this report Sherman puts the official total of scouts at 214, adding in a discreet footnote, "No reliable data as to number of scouts, it probably exceeds this." At the beginning of the spring campaign of 1876, General Sheridan, claiming that most Indian hostilities occurred within his command, requested a clear directive as to how many scouts he could enlist, since his subordinates frequently requested permission to enlist them. By January 1877 nearly 700 scouts were on the rolls in Sheridan's division, 494 of them in Crook's Department of the Platte. Sheridan then declared that he had allowed this large number of enlistments in deference to the officers in the field, rather than in any personal belief in the need for them. Possibly Sheridan was covering himself here; denying the field commanders what they considered necessary for success would be less excusable by his and Sherman's standards than running over their budget. At the same time, the tone of the statement may have foreshadowed the future clash between Sheridan and Crook over the role of Indian scouts in the Apache campaigns.[18]

The commanders' correspondence and reports provide a good

picture of their problems and their efforts to evade the official limitations. In the post–Civil War period two geographical military divisions were concerned with Indian problems: the Division of the Missouri with headquarters at Chicago and five geographical departments; and the Division of the Pacific, with headquarters at San Francisco and most of the time with three departments. When department commanders begged for enlistment of more scouts, it was often the division commander's job to juggle quotas, telling one department commander that he must discharge so many scouts so that another department could enlist the same number—generally not so many as the latter believed necessary. Then he could listen to the complaints of both, or pass them on to Washington in the hope of relief. On occasion he simply told the department commander that the request could not be filled. In an emergency he could let restrictions go by the board for the time, knowing what his superiors and the public would say if difficulties with the Indians were not promptly settled.[19]

In early 1877 General Irvin McDowell, in San Francisco, received a request to allow enlistment of 100 scouts in the Department of the Columbia (General O. O. Howard) in case of difficulties in removing the "non-treaty" Nez Perces to a reservation. McDowell thought that half the number ought to be sufficient. In any case, Sherman informed him by telegraph that the only possibility was to discharge an equal number in the Department of Arizona. Yet Colonel (Brevet Major General) August Kautz, in Arizona Territory, was of the opinion that the only thing that was preventing massive outbreaks from the Apache reservation at San Carlos (where discontent reigned for various reasons) was the presence of scout companies at nearby forts. He believed one scout company to be more efficient than half a regiment (six companies) of cavalry in pursuit of Apaches. Kautz finally agreed to discharge twenty-five scouts in Arizona, thus contributing to Howard's relief. Indeed, McDowell had seriously underestimated Howard's needs; the Nez Perce war developed into one of the most spectacular of the Indian campaigns, and one of the most embarrassing for the army.[20]

On occasion commanders simply ignored limits and hoped to be covered. This is evident in complaints from Adjutant General Edward Townsend to Sherman and in various categorical orders to department commanders that any emergency authorizations must stay within prescribed numbers, and that these enlistments must terminate as soon as possible. Nonetheless, the office had to inform Sherman in March 1877, in reply to a request for information, that there were discrepancies between scouts authorized and the number actually in service, notably in Crook's Department of the Platte: "nothing definite can be stated as to the number in service at any given time." For an administrator this must have been a truly lamentable admission.[21]

There were various ways of evading the restrictions without actually violating the letter of the law. Such evasions inevitably confuse research into the subject, since the term "scout" was naturally used for anyone who performed a scout's duties. Many writers simply referred to "our Indians" in their reminiscences. As had been the practice for many years, the army still employed civilian scouts. The white scouts and guides who figure so prominently in fiction and art came under this heading; they were officially employees of the Quartermaster Department. This category included the civilian "chiefs of scouts" who sometimes led enlisted Indians with or in place of army officers; some of them were even referred to by military titles. It was possible to employ Indians in the same way, as had been done before the Civil War. The Arikara scout Bloody Knife, a personal favorite of Custer's, had been enlisted on several occasions; he went to the Little Bighorn in 1876, however, as a civilian scout—a status that did not prevent his death in battle. When Colonel Edward Hatch, commanding the District of New Mexico in 1880, was laboring to run down the elusive Apache leader Victorio, he addressed the usual pleas for scouts to higher headquarters. Pursuit was hopeless without them; Apaches from Arizona were the best, but Indians of some sort were indispensable. If the official limits would not allow enlistments, he wrote his adjutant in Santa Fe, then they must be signed up as civilian "guides, packers &c."—that is, to be paid by the Quartermaster.[22]

For more than two centuries Indians had accompanied white military expeditions for such inducements as loot, prisoners, glory, revenge, and the promotion of better relations with the whites. This had often been the procedure followed by the Texas Rangers and with the informal Indian-hunting expeditions conducted by civilians in Arizona; territorial and military authorities during and after the Civil War frequently adopted such expedients. The Crows cooperated with the Bozeman Trail garrisons in 1866–68 without formal enlistments. Pimas, Papagos, and Maricopas sallied out both as Arizona militiamen and as "volunteers." Tucson citizens staged a massacre of surrendered Apaches at Camp Grant, Arizona Territory, in 1871, but the majority of the participants were Papagos. Both whites and Papagos viewed Apaches in much the same way.[23]

Regular commanders accepted the services of these informal allies when they thought it expedient to do so. In October 1874 Lieutenant Richard Pratt led out from Fort Sill, Indian Territory, a motley collection of eighty-seven scouts, five of them white, the rest representing ten Indian tribes. Fifty of the Indians were enlisted scouts and thirty-two were described as "volunteers." When General George Crook marched north against the Sioux in June 1876, he was accompanied by some 250 Crows and Shoshones; this was at a time when the entire army was allowed 300 scouts. These allies were armed with government-issued carbines and ammunition, but were not officially enlisted. Their long-standing enmity with the Sioux and the influence of the Shoshone chief Washakie, steadfastly friendly to the whites, brought them to join the expedition.[24]

On occasion soldiers and Indians made arrangements even less formal. In 1877 Colonel Nelson Miles, commanding along the Yellowstone, was attempting to mop up remaining Sioux resistance in his area. Large numbers of Sioux had retired to Canada with Sitting Bull, and their return was momentarily feared. Scattered bands still moved about, defined as hostile because they had not surrendered, as so many of their tribesmen had done. Not only had Washington again reduced the army's scout quota to 300, but Congress had failed, for political reasons, to make any appropriation for the army for the fiscal year. For ten months, as one historian puts it, "the army's services were gratuitous." It was hardly the time to sign up large numbers of Indians, but Miles found a way to use the services of the friendly Crows; his method recalls the policy of the colonial powers of the previous century. In the spring and summer the Crows customarily hunted buffalo in the Powder and Yellowstone country of eastern Montana and Wyoming territories, skirmishing with the Sioux who hunted in the same region. Miles placed Lieutenant Gustavus Doane, a restless, enterprising officer with a liking for independence, in a supervisory position over the Crows, furnished the men with rations and ammunition, and trusted them to scour the country for Sioux in conjunction with their customary activities. Doane was to enlist some seventy scouts, but the rest were referred to as "allies." Their rewards were presumably the usual ones of intertribal warfare—glory, horses, and vengeance. Doane's position was akin to that of an Indian chief, particularly in lack of arbitrary authority and the need to persuade instead of order. He found this situation trying, although witnesses testify to his able handling of the assignment.[25]

By this means Miles used the services of Crow allies with a minimum of expense; he simply turned them loose with good weapons and provided some military direction of their efforts. While a portion of the men hunted and guarded camp, the rest scouted for Sioux well into the summer, until the Nez Perce war called for their services elsewhere. Naturally the Crows did things largely their own way. Lieutenant Hugh Scott, visiting their camp that summer, saw Crow warriors ride in with Sioux scalps.[26]

Such allies are naturally hard to follow in the records. Local commanders often made whatever arrangements they judged best. It is by chance that we have a detailed account by a Mohave Indian of Major William R. Price's arrangements with that tribe along the Colorado River in Arizona territory in 1867. These Indians served Price in obscure operations against Yavapais and Walapais; the narrator's account suggests that Price allowed or encouraged indiscriminate killing. If Price did indeed tell Mohave leaders that his troops could not catch the enemy in the mountains, his policy may really have been to follow the path of least resistance.[27]

The Army Act of 1866 regularized the practice of Indian-military cooperation by making it possible to integrate Indians into the regular army establishment as soldiers. Commanders in widely separated areas of the West found the Indians' services so useful that they begged for authority to enlist more. There could be no more eloquent testimony to the scouts' value than the repeated appeals for their services by hard-pressed department commanders. Yet the problems caused by congressional economizing were accentuated by limitations imposed by the army's own administrative staff. Much of the time only 300 Indian scouts were available to an army trying to maintain peace over about half the continental United States. Failing to obtain freedom of action from Washington, field commanders often either ignored or evaded official restrictions in order to secure the Indian allies they needed. Thus the old patterns of friendly alliance and officially authorized or condoned war parties continued, in conjunction with the newly regularized form of military service. In whatever way their services were secured, the ubiquitous presence of the Indian scouts and auxiliaries testifies to their indispensability, in the judgment of the frontier army.

Chapter Four

Military Attitudes
toward Indian Scouts

Reading the pleas of military commanders for increased enlistments of Indian scouts, one can see how the need for scouts appeared to the men responsible for field operations. The value of
the scouts seems to have been obvious to the whole frontier
army. From the passage of the act of 1866 on, the role of the
scouts clearly tended to expand in proportion to that of the rest
of the frontier army. Yet the ubiquity of the scouts and the apparent agreement on their usefulness concealed serious differences of opinion concerning the actual role Indian scouts should
play in campaigns and engagements. In addition to their vital
function as scouts per se, the Indians became an increasingly important part of the army's combat force, at times the only part
that could find and engage the hostiles at all. The implications
of this development were decidedly unpalatable for a portion of
the officer corps; a few officers, however, accepted the situation
with so much enthusiasm that they were severely criticized by
their colleagues.

Certain widely available official sources allow one to gain at
least a general picture of the changing role of the scouts. During
this period military posts were required to prepare every three
months a "Tabular Statement of Expeditions and Scouts."
These reports had separate columns for the numbers of officers,
soldiers, and Indians that took part in any force that left the
post. In 1882 the Military Division of the Missouri published a
list of engagements with Indians since 1868; the Office of the
Adjutant General compiled a similar list in 1891 covering the
entire West since 1866. Both of these reports were necessarily
based on the "Tabular Statements" and other reports. They give

place, date, troops engaged, and casualties, and sometimes list Indian scouts among the "troops engaged." Thus we know that Major A. J. Alexander had at least one encounter with Indians at Salt Creek and Cherry Creek, Arizona Territory, on October 9, 1868; troops engaged included "1st Cav., E; 8th Cav., I; 14th Inf., F; 32nd Inf., A; and Indian Scouts." Thirteen Indians were reported killed, while the army suffered no losses; tribal affiliation is given for neither the scouts (probably Pimas and Maricopas) nor the enemy. The mixed nature of the command—cavalry, infantry, and Indian scouts, the regulars representing four different regiments—is not unusual.[1]

Unfortunately, the published sources are inconsistent in their recognition of the presence of Indian scouts: a failure to mention them does not necessarily mean that none was involved. Only white troops are mentioned in connection with some engagements listed in these sources, yet researchers have learned from original reports and post records that Indians did indeed play a part in these affairs. Even one or two scouts may have played a decisive part by tracking and locating the enemy and making a surprise attack possible. While the scouts would be listed in the "Tabular Statement" for that quarter, the officer commanding may have considered their presence so routine as not to require mention in his report.[2]

Even in such admittedly imperfect sources, one can discern an increasing tendency to mention Indian scouts among the recorded "troops engaged," meaning that they were a significant portion of the whole force. In the late 1870s, especially in the Apache campaigns, Indian scouts were often the only troops engaged on the army's side; on many occasions only one white man, an officer or civilian scout, was present. In many other small affairs less than a dozen regulars and roughly the same number of scouts were involved. Sometimes Indian scouts engaged the enemy under one of their own leaders, with no direction from whites; many such episodes may have been reported inadequately, if at all.[3]

On the basis of published information, 1882 marked a statistical high point of scout service. Of ten engagements listed, seven involved Indian scouts; in one, scouts were the only troops engaged. In 1885 eleven engagements were recorded, seven of them listed as involving scouts, and in four only scouts participated.

The total number of engagements with Indians, however, declined fairly steadily from the late 1860s. In 1868 there were 140 engagements; Indian scouts are mentioned in connection with only 15, but we cannot therefore assume that Indians were not involved in any of the remaining 125 engagements. In Custer's famous attack on the Southern Cheyennes on the Washita River in Indian Territory (November 27, 1868), Osage scouts found the Cheyenne camp and made surprise possible; only one of the two official lists mentions their presence. During the late 1860s, moreover, hostiles often sought out and attacked small detachments and even ran off stock near posts; they were more likely to make such attempts in the absence of scouts. Such attacks are included, of course, among listed engagements. Since the scouts were necessary, and Indian campaigning declined in scale and frequency, it is not surprising that the scouts should become statistically more prominent. In 1888 there were two engagements, one in Arizona Territory and one in Montana; in both scouts were the only troops fighting. The 1885 figures, however, represent the Geronimo campaign, in which up to 5,000 troops tried to cope with an Apache band with a peak strength of 35 men and 8 boys "capable of bearing arms." Indian scouts played such a prominent part in the fighting that actually occurred because of the elusiveness of the hostiles and the policy of the department commander, General George Crook, who believed that only scouts could handle the problem.[4]

Statistics can give only the most general notion of the importance of the Indian scouts. Armed engagement was only one of the methods by which Indian resistance was broken, even if one considers only military operations. The scouts' significance was out of proportion to their numbers, and their influence was exercised in a variety of ways. If a growing industrial nation had to call on the services of "primitives," perhaps it was because they rendered services that no one else could perform.

Naturally army officers varied widely in their estimates of the value of Indian scouts and auxiliaries. Many who left a record of their opinions considered the matter within a much broader frame than that of the stereotyped "military mind." It is true that only a few got beyond the conception of the civilian assimilationists and reformers—the liberal, progressive orthodoxy of nineteenth-century America, confidently ethnocentric and regarding Western civilization, especially its American variant, as the culmination of human development. It would be unreasonable to expect them to see much deeper, except in the area of practical understanding based on experience.[5]

Both the positive and the negative judgments of these officers are revealing in regard not only to the actual value of Indian scouts, but to the patterns of thought to be found within the army itself. The positive judgments must be discussed at length below, but can be summarized here.

Approving judgments were based both on the deficiencies of the regular army and its western military difficulties and on certain positive benefits expected from the employment of scouts. In the first place, the regulars suffered from limitations imposed by lack of numbers, at least in the view of the senior officers. No general, of course, has ever had enough troops. When General Henry W. Halleck asked for more scouts for the Pacific Division in 1867, he specifically stated that they were necessary because he lacked sufficient numbers of regulars. In 1869 General Sherman complained that he had not a single regiment in reserve: "All are on duty, and I have constant calls for more troops, which cannot be granted." Beyond the simple limitations of numbers were the regulars' difficulties in coping with the situation, owing to their organization, training, equipment, and basic cultural inheritance. General August Kautz's estimate that a scout company was of more value than six cavalry companies suggests the problem.[6]

Aside from remedying the deficiencies of the regular army, as revealed by western conditions, the scouts were expected to produce positive benefits that could be gained in no other way. Scout service was expected to facilitate assimilation, and sometimes to draw off the energies of potential troublemakers. The activities of the scouts, it was believed, would have important psychological effects on the hostiles. The knowledge that the army could find and strike the hostiles because it had Indian help would induce a feeling of hopelessness. Particularly if scouts were drawn from the same or related tribal groups as the hostiles, solidarity would crumble and an obvious avenue to surrender and survival would open. In the same way, the scouts provided a means of conducting relations with an enemy of alien language and culture—the lack of such a link having contributed to many of the conflicts of the period. By these various means conflict could be minimized and actual wars shortened.

Military men often expressed opinions unfavorable to Indian scouts at the time of the wars and in later memoirs. These judgments generally fitted under three broad headings: disbelief in their capabilities as soldiers, distrust of their loyalty, and awareness that the use of Indians reflected unfavorably on the capacity of the regular army to carry out its mission. These judgments varied in degree and in consistency. The problem of atrocities— that is, violations of the white code of military conduct, the objection that would occur first to the humanitarians—was rarely mentioned by the military.

Doubt concerning Indian capabilities was particularly a matter of degree. Few men with any western experience could deny the need for the scout or trailer in the narrowest sense of the words. Without a man who could follow a trail, it was unlikely that the army could locate or attack the enemy. If the enemy knowingly allowed himself to be overtaken, it was because he had an advantage, as a number of officers learned to their sorrow. Opinions differed, however, on the honesty, reliability, and courage of the men who carried out these indispensable duties. Various officers recorded their suspicion that scouts were not performing the trailing function very assiduously, for fear of the enemy. To the officers, such conduct indicated lack of soldierly courage, if not downright disloyalty; the notion that the Indians were being sensible would have been unacceptable to these officers. In 1882 Lieutenant David McDonald insisted on closely pursuing Apaches despite the uneasiness of his all-Indian detachment; he barely got out of the resulting ambush alive, and his best scout, Yuma Bill, who had accompanied him as a matter of pride, was killed. Lieutenant Powhatan Clarke, describing a pursuit of a few "renegades" in 1890, could not quite rid himself of the notion that his Apache scouts were less brave and reckless of their lives than fighting men ought to be; neither could he down the suspicion that their methods really fitted the situation.[7]

The suggestion that information was liable to be distorted by fear of the enemy or sheer laziness was subject to a number of qualifications. In many cases whites expressed such opinions only about certain tribes, while rating others more highly. Some tribes were condemned wholesale as lacking martial qualities, while others were regarded as efficient, reliable, and loyal. Texas Ranger James Gillett had only contempt for the "cowardly" Tonkawas, but thought highly of the Pueblo scouts who fought with the Rangers against Apaches. It was generally agreed that when Navajos were employed as scouts against Apaches, they were not eager to come in contact with the enemy. Sensible or not, their wariness of the Apaches limited their usefulness. Pimas and Maricopas, though deeply hostile to the Apaches, had to undergo elaborate, lengthy religious purification ceremonies after killing an enemy, and this cultural requirement made their employment intermittent at best. It was impossible for some officers to accept such deviations from conventional white military practice.[8]

One gains the impression that the strongest adverse reflections on scouts' capabilities or reliability tend to come from the more conventional type of officer, who depicts himself in reminiscence as conforming closely to the stereotype of the "military mind." Such reflections come infrequently from men who had long and successful service as scout commanders. The man whose contempt for or aversion to Indians was deep and irreversible was not likely to volunteer for such duty, nor was he likely to stay with it long if he were assigned to it, or to enjoy great success in it. On the other hand, many of these men simply ignored Indian scouts as much as possible in reminiscent accounts. "The army" consisted of regular troops, and their adventures were the only subject that was interesting or important. Still, the most prejudiced might have a favorite Indian, and the most sympathetic often betrayed some condescension.[9]

Questions of honesty and general reliability are tied to those of loyalty. The opinion of George Crook, after more than twenty years' experience, was that "you cannot always be sure that an Indian is telling you the truth; he may lie to you; so will the white man. But if you make it to the Indian's interest to tell the truth, you get correct information; a white man will lie intentionally, and mislead you unintentionally."[10]

Military opinion on the Indians' effectiveness as fighting men ranged through the broadest possible spectrum. By European standards the courage and discipline of scouts and hostiles were deficient. Experienced frontier officers had seen individual Indians perform acts that required great, even suicidal courage; they were unlikely, however, to display the kind of obedient, unquestioning sacrifice of self exemplified by the charge of the Light Brigade or by innumerable Civil War episodes. Powhatan Clarke noted with good humor that an Apache "takes desperate chances in his way," but to these Indians standing up and letting oneself be shot at was a sign of insanity or at least a death wish. An officer of the Inspector General's Department inspected the scout companies in the Department of Arizona in 1877 and reported: "I think they make good and efficient soldiers when they act with white troops—alone they are not reliable, and without them the white troopers are almost helpless in the pursuit of Indians." It is not known how extensive this officer's frontier experience was, but in varying degrees his opinion was that of many army officers.[11]

Military doubts about Indian scouts approached most closely those of civilians in questioning their loyalty. Could one really trust them to serve faithfully against other Indians and not to betray the whites into the hands of the enemy, or turn on them on the field of battle? In only one instance, at the Cibicu in Arizona Territory in 1881, did scouts actually turn on the soldiers in the course of an engagement. Men going into action beside Apache scouts, however, could never forget even one such instance. Anton Mazzanovich, a former army enlisted man, was with the New Mexico Rangers when he and a comrade encountered seven Apaches with the red headbands of army scouts. Even though they knew the Apaches were scouts, the two whites were about to lead the other rangers in making "good Indians" of them when the scout officer came in view. Forty years later Mazzanovich was unrepentant: "They were treacherous and could not be depended on in an emergency."[12]

In less extreme form such views were probably held by many officers and enlisted men. Naturally these fears were most acute when the scouts were of the same tribe as the hostiles, or of some related group, which to most whites amounted to the same tribe. When Crook pursued Geronimo's Chiricahua Apaches with Chiricahua scouts, many civilians and soldiers, including the army's commanding general, could not bring themselves to believe that the scouts were not in some way betraying their trust. In no other Indian war did the scouts play so large a role as in Crook's Apache campaigns, and in no other did the dispute over loyalty become so acute.

The extensive use of scouts, especially in a combat role, inevitably presented implications about the capabilities of regular troops. These implications many army officers were not prepared to accept; they offended racial pride and *esprit de corps*, and injured the army's prestige. General Philip Sheridan, one of the chief Civil War heroes, commanded the army's largest geographic division for fourteen years, and the army for six. Recognizing that the services of scouts were of great value, he still held this opinion:

I doubt if any process whatever can, in one or two generations, develop the qualities necessary for the rank and file of our army. . . . Soldiers should possess the attributes of civilized men. . . . They [Indians] do not possess stability or tenacity of purpose. . . . They cannot appreciate responsibility or the sacredness of an oath . . . a race so distinctive from that governing this country that it would be neither wise nor expedient to recruit our army from their ranks. [13]

In a period when the army believed that it was being starved by Congress and ignored or scorned by the nation, the suggestion that it could not cope with the Indians without Indian aid was especially repugnant. Officers wanted to believe that they and their men did their best and were the best soldiers possible under the circumstances. They might dress like cowboys or mule skinners in the field (to judge from Remington's contemporary illustrations), but they took pride in the uniform and in their regiments. It was painful, therefore, to hear suggestions that they could not even cope with savages, and that they had better turn the fighting over to other savages. It was worse than painful, for if such ideas became widespread, they could affect the army's chances of ever securing larger appropriations or increasing its strength. Sheridan's reflections on Indian soldiers suggest that he had uneasy visions of an economizing Congress forcing the army to enlist large numbers of Indians as a panacea for both financial and military problems. [14]

Morale and effectiveness could suffer from the idea that Indians could do what white soldiers could not. In Dakota Territory in 1867, Colonel de Trobriand found that his recruits had been so filled with tall stories about the Sioux that they thought of the Indians as enemies to be avoided rather than attacked. At the same time, the morale of the Indians would rise if they conceived contempt for the white troops, and thus resistance would be prolonged and might spread.[15]

A significant exchange took place between Sherman and Irvin McDowell, commanding the Division of the Pacific, in 1881. In authorizing a doubling of scout strength in Arizona, Sherman insisted that the Indians should stick to scouting, while the fighting should be left to soldiers: "The moral effect will be bad if we have to get Indians to whip Indians." McDowell immediately asked for a clarification; did this mean that scouts could be used only for tracking, and that only white troops should engage in combat? He pointed out that scouts, from the nature of their duty, were always in advance of the troops; they would be the first to contact the enemy, and since the regulars were so much less mobile than the Indians, the scouts might be the only ones who had the chance to inflict any damage. Having been told, in effect, that his orders would make it impossible to operate successfully, Sherman let the people responsible decide how to use their resources. He insisted, however, that unless regular troops played a conspicuous role in defeating the Apaches, there would be bad effects.[16]

After General Nelson Miles took over the Geronimo campaign from Crook in 1886, his immediate superior, O. O. Howard, wrote to him about the newspapers' criticism of the army. The papers did not attack Miles personally, but "they still make flings at the uselessness of the soldiers, and the futility of attempting to do anything with such soldiers as we have." Howard encouraged Miles to get as many regulars into the field as possible and keep them on the move until the Indians were worn out; "as for the Apaches or other Indians out-shooting, out-marching, or outstripping our men in the long race, I do not believe it." Howard's advice demonstrates how some officers reacted to Crook's heavy reliance on his scout companies. Sheridan, like Howard, let Miles know that he wanted the regulars to be in at the death. What actually happened, as will be seen later, was quite different.[17]

In the post–Civil War period, the role of the Indian scouts and allies increased in importance as time went on. The recorded facts indicate that they could not be dispensed with; in every case of actual or potential conflict between Indians and whites, Indians were called on to help to defeat the hostiles or to prevent hostilities from breaking out. Yet this increasing role was played against a background of dissension and distrust on the part of those they served. Army opinion was divided between the belief that Indian allies were one of the best means of handling such conflicts, on the one hand, and an inability to recognize the Indians' military capacities and a refusal to accept the possibility that Indians might be better fighters than regulars on the other. There were, of course, many shades of opinion, reflecting racial bias, ethnocentrism, personal acquaintance and experience, and degrees of willingness to think about problems and adapt to them. The more closely an officer's mental world was confined to the army and the more obvious military values, the less likely he was to appreciate Indian allies.

Emotional reactions concerning the army's pride and public image, however, are not an answer to substantive questions; they indicate only the concerns and values of the people who expressed them. We must try to discover why a society with advantages in numbers and technology beyond all comparison had to turn to the "primitives" it regarded with such contempt to win undisputed control of the West.

Chapter Five

The Role of Scouts
in Indian Warfare

Even in the twentieth-century modern industrial nations have encountered great difficulties and have often met defeat in contention with guerrilla forces whose resources were laughably inferior to their own; hence it should not be surprising to find that the United States in the nineteenth century did not find it easy to subdue the Indians. "Indian fighting" was not unique to the United States; Britain, France, and Russia encountered somewhat similar problems during their imperial expansion in Africa and Asia, often on a much larger scale. Early in this century C. E. Callwell, a British officer, distilled the experiences of all four nations into a large volume on the theory and practice of "small wars."[1] The European nations often had to confront far larger numbers of the "uncivilized" than the United States, and to put far larger armies in the field; yet many of the solutions they adopted were similar to those of the United States Army. The most common of these practices was the use of "native" or "irregular" troops, for reasons very similar to those that moved the United States to enlist Indians. The French found their North African conquests facilitated by their Saharan Companies, made up of local tribesmen who furnished their own horses or camels. In the West African bush the British found native scouts indispensable to prevent surprise on jungle trails. General C. G. "Chinese" Gordon, the British hero of irregular warfare, was referring specifically to the Sudan when he advised: "Native Allies above all things, at whatever the cost. It is the country of the irregular, not of the regular."[2]

The parallel seemed evident to many American officers. Indeed, when such men as George McClellan, William Burnet, and later John G. Bourke advocated organization of Indian cavalry units, they preferred to cite French or British practice, or the Russian Cossacks, rather than American precedents. This preference may have stemmed from sheer ignorance, but it may also have been due to the fact that Indian allies in North America had historically been associated with massacre and torture. Such notorious "white Indians" as the Tories Simon Girty and Walter Butler had not been forgotten.[3]

The United States, however, enjoyed immense advantages in technology, and had to contend with far smaller numbers than opposed the colonial powers in Africa and Asia. Yet the United States had to turn to native allies also, reverting to practices followed by colonial powers in North America in earlier centuries. The advantages of the whites were bound to prove decisive in the long run, but their influence was not always obvious to the Indians and whites immediately involved in contact and conflict. The white population, after all, was thinnest just where it came in contact with the Indians. Indian chiefs who visited the East were often more awed by the sheer numbers of whites than by their technological achievements, but when they returned home their stories were not believed; such numbers were beyond the experience of any Indian who stayed at home. Besides, if the stories were true, the implications did not bear thinking about; therefore they must be false.[4]

Because of the way in which the United States had expanded during and after the 1840s, the army was not really covering a "frontier" or line of settlement; it was trying to police a "zone of contact" spotted and streaked with white settlements and communication lines, from the Missouri to the Sierra Nevada, and from the Rio Grande to the Canadian border. This immense area was the responsibility of an army of 25,000; the infantry and artillery were severely limited in mobility, and the cavalry, just under 11,000 in paper strength, had to carry a disproportionate share of the burden.[5] The popular image of a few troopers battling hordes of Indians, based on a few incidents such as "Custer's Last Stand," was a distortion; numbers on the actual battlefield were often not completely disproportionate. In the long run, obviously, the whites could afford to persist in hostilities and the Indians could not.

The technological disparity was immense. By the post–Civil

War period most western tribes had integrated into their way of life a number of items manufactured by whites which they could not possibly produce themselves. Chief Washakie, of the Wyoming Shoshones, ridiculed some of his tribesmen who suggested resistance by showing them a revolver and reminding them that while the whites could make such a weapon, all the Shoshones could make were bows and arrows.[6]

At the same time, it was not always easy to bring this superiority to bear in the field. Even after the Union Pacific was built, railroads penetrated the West slowly through the 1870s, in part because of the financial crash of 1873.[7] The rail lines did provide a supply base much closer to the campaigning areas than any that had been available before and during the Civil War. This was a major reason for the greater decisiveness of the postwar campaigns. All the same, in 1875 Fort Selden, New Mexico Territory, was 580 miles from the nearest railroad station and 263 miles from the nearest telegraph. Camp Robinson, Nebraska, soon to play an important part in the Sioux conflict, was 125 miles from a railroad and 82 from a telegraph line.[8] The great technological advantages symbolized by these inventions may not have been too apparent to the soldiers at these posts.

Those miles away from the railroad were still horseback miles. Out of sight of the rails and the telegraph wire, warfare, except for improved firearms, reverted to preindustrial conditions. Mules or wagons carried supplies; men walked or rode animals. On both sides, mounted men carried out reconnaissance and relayed their information in the same way. The power of striking the enemy was not much greater than that of a Roman legion, even though the firepower was far greater.[9]

Nor were the Indians hopelessly outclassed in firepower. The cavalry abandoned the Spencer repeating carbine in the early 1870s, reverting to a single-shot, breech-loading carbine; a board of officers declared that none of the repeaters then manufactured was rugged enough for military service, and that repeaters tempted men to waste ammunition. In any case, no other major power had yet adopted repeaters. The Indians were undaunted by such considerations and were glad to use repeaters when they could get them. They seem to have kept them functioning even when their condition would have horrified an ordnance officer, and with an ammunition supply even more precarious than that which prevented the army from engaging in target practice until the 1880s. In 1873 the army asked the Tonkawa scouts at Fort Griffin, Texas, to turn in their Spencer repeaters for the single-shot Sharps; they protested, through their commander, that they would rather obtain Winchesters at their own expense, if the army would provide ammunition. They were allowed to retain the Spencers. Some officers, of course, were prepared to swear that the Indian Bureau had supplied every hostile Indian with a Winchester and a carload of ammunition. Concerning the armament of hostile Indians, the only safe statement is that there was great variation over time and place.[10]

In the 1840s the revolver gave the Texas Rangers a great advantage over Comanches armed with bows and lances; according to the experienced Colonel Richard Dodge, this superiority persisted more or less through the Civil War, and often justified reckless charges by cavalry against great odds. In later years, however, the Indians acquired enough breechloaders to make headlong charges against them a risky proposition, unless one had the advantage of surprise. The breechloader not only had a higher rate of fire than muzzle-loading weapons, but could be fired from a prone position behind cover; possession of such a weapon put the Indian on a roughly equal basis with the soldier. The fact that Plains Indians developed the art of reloading metallic cartridges before the whites is a tribute to the ingenuity of these "backward" people, and a demonstration of both their supply problem and their familiarity with this type of ammunition.[11]

In fact, breechloaders and metallic cartridges had much the same effect on Indian warfare as on conventional war; they strengthened the tactical defense and increased the importance of cover and dispersion. The massed charge became suicidal. Testimony indicates that by the 1860s, the tomahawk, like the cavalry saber, had become more decorative than useful, and was reserved for dress occasions; the same was happening to the lance. Such testimony indicates the decline of hand-to-hand combat, despite some old warriors' knightly contempt for battles that were "just shooting." In fact, the traditional tactics of most Indians emphasized mobility, individual flexibility, use of terrain, and economy of lives; they seem to have found it easier to adapt to the new weaponry than the white military did. In the

1870s the army increasingly fought against enemies who could not be seen; only the smoke and flash of the concealed Indian's gun indicated his presence. This was a major reason for the surprise attacks on Indian camps; it was the only way the soldiers could make a decisive attack at all. The Apaches' tactics were especially well adapted to such conditions; they understood the use of camouflage long before the army.[12]

America led the world in machine-gun development, and the Gatling gun has received much attention in fiction. The weapon saw extensive use in the wars of the colonial powers; military historian John Ellis gives the machine gun primary credit for the European conquest of Africa in the late nineteenth century. Yet the Gatling, another striking symbol of the whites' technological superiority, saw only limited use in the Indian wars. Custer, for example, refused to take Gatlings with him to the Little Bighorn because he feared they would slow his march.[13]

There were several reasons for the limited use of this advanced weapon. As Custer's rejection of the weapon suggests, the Gatling was somewhat more cumbersome than later machine guns. Moreover, the Indians' tactics minimized the weapon's effectiveness; they did not charge headlong into automatic fire, as did Zulus and Sudanese. Finally, army officers just did not understand how to use this new weapon to the best advantage.[14]

The army was not unaware of the problems and special conditions of frontier warfare, yet its organization and training did not reflect any attempt to adapt to them. Its organization and tactics were always directed toward possible wars with conventional, European-style military powers, and tactical manuals and West Point teaching described this kind of warfare. Indian fighting, it was assumed, would soon be a thing of the past; conventional warfare would become the army's principal responsibility in the future. There were officers who, like George Crook, found western campaigning a worthwhile professional challenge; some found in the Indians themselves both objects of sympathy and of absorbing intellectual interest. Nevertheless, the principal direction of study for the officer interested in professional growth was supposed to be the practice of the European armies, especially the German. The country's most influential military thinker of the period, Colonel Emory Upton, saw little frontier service; his writings were devoted to conventional tactics and to ways in which the United States could adapt European military organization to its own situation.[15]

Consequently there was no official military doctrine, reduced to a set of principles, on how to conduct war or relations with Indians. Captain Randolph B. Marcy's *Prairie Traveler*, published "by authority of the War Department" in 1859, devoted some pages to Indian fighting and trailing, but as the title indicated, it was primarily a handbook and survival manual for travelers on the Great Plains, both civilian and military. Marcy was rare in his generation in his attempt to study and explain frontier problems in such a professional manner. The closest thing to a manual on the subject of Indian fighting was Edward S. Farrow's *Mountain Scouting: A Handbook for Officers and Soldiers on the Frontiers.* Farrow, a former scout commander in the Northwest, devoted much of his book to techniques of marching and survival, but he also including chapters on trailing, "Indian character," and skirmishing. Obviously Farrow thought that there was an unfilled need for such a work. He had the book privately published in 1881, rather late in the period of the Indian wars; it does not seem to have had much influence. William P. Clark's study of Plains Indian sign language, which General Sheridan encouraged, presumably for the army's practical use, would have been much more useful if it had been undertaken fifteen or twenty years earlier. In default of official doctrine, army officers depended on the accumulated experience and judgment of such men as Farrow and Clark. Some possessed the ability to learn and to step outside the conventional frame of reference; others did not.[16]

Of course the problem was not simply one of army deficiencies, avoidable or otherwise. The Indians possessed certain abilities, conditioned by their way of life, that gave them at least an immediate, short-term advantage. Most western conflicts involved the nomadic tribes rather than the sedentary farmers. For the nomads mobility was a way of life, and they operated for the most part in their home country; hence the army found that even cavalry could not keep up if the Indians wanted to run away. The scrubby-looking Indian ponies might not be a match for cavalry horses in a short race, but on a long pursuit they showed far more endurance. Indian ponies lived on grass all their lives, but the army horses were used to grain and lost strength rapidly without it. In any case, the Plains warrior usually had more than one horse. An Apache would ride a horse to death, then cut off a steak from the animal and proceed on foot. None of these practices was possible in the army, whose horses were government property. The nomads adapted their whole society to movement, and women and children hindered the fighting men far less than whites would have supposed. Indian women with children of various ages readily forded streams that the army deemed impassable.[17]

The Indians were accustomed to living off the country. Buffalo provided the Plains Indians with most of the necessities of life, and until the herds were destroyed they constituted a free commissary. The virtual extermination of the buffalo by white hunters destroyed the mobility and independence of the Plains tribes, and this was one of the greatest factors in the defeat of these Indians. General Sheridan showed his appreciation of this point by his statement that buffalo hunters should be encouraged and perhaps even supplied with military arms and ammunition.[18] The end of the buffalo, obviously, had no effect on the Apaches of the desert Southwest.

The Indians knew where water could be found throughout the year. The Apaches in particular knew which plants would provide food and drink in a country the whites perceived as a barren waste. The natives of plains, mountains, and deserts knew how best to adapt to extremes of weather. All this knowledge, which the whites found so hard to acquire, was part of everyday life to the Indians; it was so commonplace that they could hardly believe the whites could be so inept.[19] The experience of Cole's and Walker's columns in Connor's expedition of 1865 (see Chapter 2, above) was an extreme example of inability to cope with the country and the people who were so well adapted to it. Most of the animals died, the troops were starving, and the Sioux and Cheyennes harassed them without suffering any casualties.

An episode that illustrates the difficulties, and the army's understanding of them, is the experience of Major A. P. Morrow of the Ninth Cavalry in the campaign against the Apache Victorio in 1879–80. Morrow's fellow officer Thomas Cruse tells us that Morrow was "specially noted" for his pursuit of Victorio, and "had brought that wily Indian leader to bay at three different times and had finally driven him into Mexico." The real meaning of these words is that Morrow had fought Victorio three times and the Apache had escaped each time; Victorio finally got away entirely, and the best that could be said was that Morrow had managed to chase him out of the United States for a time, into the territory of a neighboring country. From the point of view of his colleagues, Morrow's accomplishment was highly creditable. They knew how much effort had been required to accomplish that much.[20]

Historians have often noted that the American Indians in general relied very heavily on scouting, movement, concealment, and surprise; indeed, writers have criticized them as having no other, more sophisticated plans or tactics. But the critics have seldom noted the extent to which the Indians forced the military forces of the United States to adopt the same methods. Writing in 1866, Randolph Marcy told his fellow officers that to fight Indians successfully they "must receive instructions from them, study their tactics, and, where they suit our purposes, copy from them." The army must strive to combine "discipline with the individuality, self-reliance, and rapidity of locomotion of the savage." In view of all that has been said about the army's deficiencies, it is only fair to say that it did respond to the Indians' challenge, first of all by its own increasing emphasis on mobility and surprise, and even more by its use of Indian scouts. Although no one said so specifically, an increasing use of Indian allies actually reduced the need to reform training and organization to enable regular soldiers to cope with the Indians. In truth, however, all intelligent professionals, whatever their opinions about Indian scouts, wanted improved training, better marksmanship, and hardier, more self-reliant soldiers—none more so than George Crook, the most devoted champion of the scouts.[21]

Commanders assessed the need for Indian scouts on the basis of what their own experience had taught them, or relied on the advice of the more experienced, as Colonel Carrington relied on Jim Bridger. Inevitably the experience of officers varied considerably, as did their ability to learn from their own and others' experience. Sometimes knowledge appears not to have been communicated too well. Of those senior officers who figured prominently in Indian campaigns after 1865, few besides George

Crook had extensive experience with such service before the Civil War.[22]

Many officers, some with years of frontier experience, asserted that Crook was the originator of the Indian scouts; they knew that he was the most effective employer and most earnest advocate of the scouts, and they were apparently ignorant of the historical precedents. Lieutenant John Bigelow, later noted as a writer on strategy, was not sure whether Crook thought up the idea on his own or adopted it from the British native auxiliaries. Probably these men were far better acquainted with Napoleon's campaigns than with the history of their own Indian wars. If there was any continuous tradition on the use of Indian scouts or Indian warfare, these professionals were not aware of it.[23]

"Finding them, not fighting them, is the difficult problem to solve," wrote Colonel Wesley Merritt.[24] Officers with more experience than Merritt in fighting Indians might have disagreed, but no one denied the importance of finding them. In a vast country one had to locate relatively small numbers of fast-moving people. Reconnaissance is always a military necessity, but under frontier conditions it assumed special importance and required particular skills. Location, numbers, intentions, and identity were all vital intelligence.

The Plains tribes referred to a scout as a "wolf"; in the sign language the same sign stood for both. Among some tribes scouts wore wolf-skins with the wolf's head over the man's; the pelt served both for camouflage and to invoke the supernatural gift of the wolf's skill. Red Wing, of the Crows, said, "A scout is like a lone wolf, that must be looking, looking, looking, all the time."[25]

Scouting acquired such importance that the frontier army also used the noun "scout" or the phrase "going on a scout" for any kind of patrol, reconnaissance, or search-and-destroy mission. Scouting, however, covered the gathering of military intelligence, and this activity had several facets. Tracking or trailing—the latter was the more common term—was literally the following of a trail left by the enemy. This was a skill that Indian boys learned early, for both hunting and war. With such training, they naturally learned to see "sign" where most whites saw nothing.[26]

On one occasion white scouts Luther North and Buffalo Bill Cody accompanied a Pawnee who was following a trail that neither white man could see. Cody was skeptical until the trail crossed a sandy stretch where the tracks showed more clearly; he then acknowledged the Pawnee to be the best trailer he had seen.[27] Trailing skills included the ability to estimate numbers, to estimate how long ago a party had passed by examining horse dung to see how far toward the center it had dried, and whether a party of Indians included women by the position of urine in relation to the horse's hoofs; women rode mares, while an all-male party on stallions was more likely to be a war party. As Lieutenant James Shannon remarked after observing Apache scouts in action: "to the Indians, trailing is a science and not a matter of guess work."[28]

The Indian "wolves" were acquainted with the various uses of terrain and camouflage for concealment. Plains Indians are even known to have disguised themselves as buffalo in order to survey their enemies from a distance.[29] The value of such skills in reconnaissance is obvious. The old saw about the need to be most wary when there was no indication of Indians about is not merely a cliché of fiction; it occurs in instructions from General C. C. Augur to Colonel Ranald Mackenzie in 1874.[30]

Guides who knew the country were vital. Still, scout units were sometimes transferred to areas they did not know intimately, if their other skills were deemed sufficient to offset this disadvantage. The Pawnees served in present Wyoming in 1865 and 1876, and Arizona Apaches pursued Victorio in New Mexico Territory in 1879–80.[31]

A task of some importance was the identification of Indians encountered by the military. To the majority of whites, one Indian looked much like another; in a situation where mistakes could be fatal for one side or the other, and where surprise was judged to be essential to secure results, such ignorance could be disastrous. But the various tribes had their variations in clothing, hairstyles, methods of pitching tipis, and other readily visible traits well known to all tribes of their own region. A good, clear footprint was often enough to identify the tribe of the maker by the distinctive moccasin pattern. Plains Indian art of the period clearly demonstrates the general knowledge of the subject, of obvious value to the scout or warrior.[32]

Many whites regarded these scouting skills of Indians as inherent and hereditary; this notion fitted with the assumption that Indians were closer to being wild animals than the whites. They assumed that Indians had especially acute sight and hearing and "instinctive" cunning and wariness; one was not required to credit such people with intelligence or reasoning ability. An authoritative study of the Comanches finds them to have a decided tendency toward poor vision. The picture of a nearsighted Comanche goes far toward canceling the stereotype of the superhumanly keen senses of the child of the wilderness. Obviously these skills were part of the necessary training of hunters and warriors, learned in childhood and adolescence. It was a matter of knowing what to look for, not of animal instincts. At the same time, the animal stereotype had a different meaning to Indians who invoked the wolf than to those whites who were offended by the Darwinian theory. There must have been considerable individual variation. There is no reason to imagine that the lazy, the careless, and the congenitally inept were unknown among Indians, any more than among any other people.[33]

It follows that it was not impossible for whites who wished to apply themselves to acquire some of the skills characteristic of Indian scouts, although most started at an age when learning and overcoming ingrained habits came harder. A few men, such as Jim Bridger and Kit Carson, after many years' experience were probably as good as virtually any Indian, and better than the younger warriors. Such men, with their accumulated knowledge and the additional asset of ready communication with white officers, were invaluable; their very survival was their certificate of proficiency. Few whites, however, could equal the experience of a Bridger or a Carson, survivors of an era when white men in the West were indeed far outnumbered by Indians. White scouts and those of mixed ancestry were common enough on the frontier, but their quality varied widely. General Sheridan found Hays City, Kansas, in the late 1860s thick with "Indian scouts" full of tales of the Indians they had slain, "but the real scout—that is, a guide and trailer knowing the habits of the Indians—was very scarce." In Arizona nearly twenty years later reporter Charles Lummis observed that same "class of border toughs whose highest dream is to pose as scouts."[34]

The "half-breed" scout was a familiar figure on the frontier. Since he had probably spent most of his life in the Indians' environment, he was likely to have knowledge given to few whites. General George Crook, devout believer in Indians as scouts, was very fond of certain scouts of mixed blood, such as Archie McIntosh and Baptiste "Little Bat" Garnier.[35] But the closer such a man was to his Indian heritage, the greater the difficulty he had in communicating his knowledge to the whites. Colonel John Gibbon took note of the half-Sioux guide Mitch Bouyer as the only mixed-blood he knew who could give distances in terms of miles instead of travel time.[36] The difficulty was that the Indians' travel time for a given distance was generally much less than for a column of troops. Undoubtedly a certain bias was operating against the marginal man, a "half-breed" not quite at home in either world, creating distrust whether justified or not. Indeed, the white man who was closely identified with a group of Indians was also distrusted in some quarters.[37]

The language problem was especially pertinent in regard to Indian scouts. The white or mixed-blood scout with real experience was of use if he could breach the language barrier. If Indian scouts could communicate with whites, they could be of use in communication with Indians. Even if they had no common language, the sign language was known to the Plains tribes and to many tribes of the Intermountain region in regular communication with the Plains. Two people versed in this means of communication could carry on lengthy conversations without either knowing a word of the other's spoken language. It was another part of the equipment of the really proficient scout, and easier than learning the varied and complex tribal languages.[38]

Former scout James Cook listed the traits of the ideal scout in his memoirs. They included superb physique and vision, absolute honesty, resourcefulness, knowledge of Indian culture and language, good sense of direction, knowledge of country, keen observation, common sense, and marksmanship. Such a paragon must have been hard to find among any race or nation. Captain Arthur L. Wagner, preparing a textbook on "security and information" for the army in the 1890s, reflected the frontier experience in recommending the American Indian and his methods as a model for scouting and reconnaissance for any army in the world.[39]

Some military men persisted in regarding Indians as cowards because they fought only when they had the advantage or when escape was cut off. When their camps were attacked, they would fight with great stubbornness to cover the retreat of their women and children, as Custer found out. Few observers grasped the point that no tribe or band had the numbers to engage in frequent pitched battles or wars of attrition. Plains warriors on occasion displayed literally suicidal bravery, but virtually all would have regarded the bloodshed of Gettysburg or Cold Harbor as mass insanity—men cooperating, incomprehensibly, in their own destruction. To the frontier officer, Gettysburg represented "normal" warfare; today we find the Indians' viewpoint the more reasonable.

It was this preference for living to fight another day and the Indians' superlative mobility that made surprise attacks on Indian camps the only method by which decisive results could be obtained. Ideally the attack had to be made at dawn, in order to catch the Indians asleep, but with daylight soon appearing to show the troops what they were doing. In such attacks the troops inevitably shot women and children, knowingly or otherwise; officers insisted that such deaths were unavoidable, but their insistence itself suggests an uneasy conscience. There was no "rear area" in an Indian war. If Indian warriors tried to leave their families in a safe place, such as a reservation, the army would not allow them to do so; the warriors would be far harder to catch than the already elusive villages. Of greater importance than casualties, however, was the destruction of property— tipis, food, clothing and blankets, ammunition, and horses—and the crushing effect on morale. The effect was the greater in winter, the best time to campaign against Indians if horses and men could stand the hardship. The only purely military alternative was continual pursuit and harassment, which was hard on troops and mounts, and frustrating besides.[40]

In such a mode of warfare, the need for scouts is obvious. The enemy had to be located and his strength determined, then the troops must be guided, often over difficult terrain, to the village, trying to make a silent approach in darkness. The services of Indian scouts greatly increased the chances of accomplishing all this. If the hostiles became alerted or the troops failed to reach the village before daylight, the results could be disastrous; Custer attacked the camp on the Little Bighorn in mid-afternoon. Indians did not usually post sentinels at night, but there were usually hunting parties out from any camp who might serve the same purpose. Commanders had to assume that any warning would allow the hostiles to decamp or to prepare a warm reception for the attackers, although in fact camps that had received warning were sometimes surprised because of the misjudgments of hostile leaders.[41]

A classic illustration of many of these points is the battle of the Red Fork, or the Dull Knife Fight, in November 1876. This was part of the winter campaign against the Sioux and Northern Cheyennes undertaken after the highly unsatisfactory results of the previous summer's operations. Crook marched into the Powder River country with some 1,500 cavalry and infantry and about 360 Indians: 105 Shoshones, 100 Pawnees under Frank North, one Ute, one Nez Perce, and 151 Sioux, Cheyennes, and Arapahoes from the agencies. After trying to locate the village of the elusive Crazy Horse, the scouts brought in information of a large Cheyenne village in a secluded canyon in the Big Horn Mountains, on the Red Fork of the Powder River. Crook sent Colonel Ranald Mackenzie with the Indian scouts and the cavalry, about 1,100 men in all, to strike the enemy camp. Scouts moved out from Crook's camp to scare off possible hostile watchers, then Mackenzie's column moved by night, in bitterly cold weather, lying over the next day in a canyon in the face of the mountain range and moving again in the dark. Scouts kept Mackenzie informed of the Cheyennes' continued presence at the campsite. The leader of the Arapaho contingent, Sharp Nose, knew the country well and guided the column along narrow canyons, impatiently urging the troops on. Observers acknowledged Sharp Nose to be as good a guide as they had seen, besides being notable as a leader and warrior.[42]

Nearing the Cheyenne camp, the column heard drums; instead of being fast asleep, the Cheyennes were celebrating a victory over a party of Shoshones. In subzero darkness, trying to be silent, Mackenzie and his men waited for the Cheyennes to go to sleep. Lieutenant John Bourke judged that if surprise failed, in that terrain the army's casualties would be limited only by the amount of ammunition the Cheyennes had to expend. In fact, the Cheyennes had received warning from their scouts, but the chief of the Fox warrior society had refused to allow a retreat, even in the face of dire warnings from the tribe's most respected medicine man and prophet. The Fox warriors taunted and horse-whipped those who tried to strike their tipis. Luther North later concluded that the Cheyennes simply did not believe that the troops would attempt a forced march through the mountains at night. They did not realize how far the presence of Indian allies had extended the capabilities of the troops.[43]

Near dawn the Cheyennes finally went to sleep. Mackenzie led his column into the broader but still rugged valley of the Red Fork. A Sioux scout called Scraper, disgruntled at not having been made a sergeant, charged the village on his own in his war bonnet; three men who tried to stop him found themselves par-ticipating in this rash venture. Mackenzie had ordered that the hostiles be allowed to fire the first shot; if they did not open fire, they could be taken prisoner without bloodshed. When an early-rising Cheyenne fired on this impromptu advance party, the bat-tle was on. The column fanned out to a broad front as the valley widened, with the cavalry on the right and the Indian allies on the left. The Sioux, Arapahoes, and Cheyennes were sandwiched between the Shoshones and Pawnees, possibly because of linger-ing distrust of these erstwhile friends and tribesmen of the en-emy. The attackers quickly captured the village and part of the horse herd. Lieutenant Walter S. Schuyler, who had earlier worked with Apache scouts in Arizona Territory, led the Sho-shones onto a ridge to the left of the village, and the scouts' fire helped to drive the Cheyennes out of the village.[44]

The Cheyennes withdrew, however, into the especially rough ground north and west of the village, and as the light increased, the battle became a long-range gun fight, in which anyone who left cover on either side took an extreme risk. An attempted mounted charge by a cavalry company cost the life of Lieutenant John McKinney and wounded several men. Interpreter Billy Gar-nett recalled that the Sioux first sergeant Three Bears told Mac-kenzie in the bluntest fashion that the colonel must let his men take cover and fight individually, like the Indians, or the scouts would quit in disgust and he would suffer Custer's fate.[45]

Whether or not Mackenzie was influenced by Three Bears's brusque advice, the battle became a day-long stalemate. Prob-ably the Cheyennes were principally interested in covering the retreat of their women and children. At one point the army hospital area came under Cheyenne fire, and Mackenzie asked Frank North to detail some Pawnees to root the snipers out of the rocks. North called his men together with an Indian reed whistle; half a dozen men stripped down (they were in full uniform) and tied handkerchiefs around their heads to identify them to the soldiers, and then moved into the rocks. They killed one or two of the hostiles and ended the danger to the wounded.[46]

Mackenzie sent for Crook to bring up the infantry, whose long rifles would perhaps provide the firepower to end the fight in his favor. When darkness came, however, the Cheyennes withdrew. They had lost their tipis, most of their household goods and clothing, their winter supply of dried meat, and many of their horses. They did follow the departing troops and recover a portion of their horses. The rest Crook distributed among the Indian scouts. In subzero weather, without proper shelter, clothing, and food, the Cheyennes suffered severely, and several babies and old people died. This was all part of the desired result, but it seems to have troubled the consciences of some of their attackers, both white and Indian.[47]

This episode is related at length because it illustrates many important points. Indian scouts first located the hostile camp, then made the night march through the mountains possible, and finally played a prominent part in the fighting. In the opinion of most participants, Crook's policy of using large numbers of Indian allies, including tribesmen and former allies of the hostiles, paid off well. It was the following spring, after further harassment by Nelson Miles, that the Cheyennes, led by Dull Knife and Little Wolf, surrendered, but the severest blow they suffered came at the battle of Red Fork. Colonel Richard Dodge was probably right in asserting that Crook's decision to "fight fire with fire" was what made this result possible.[48]

In accordance with Crook's policy, the Indian auxiliaries played a large part in the battle itself, constituting about one-third of Mackenzie's force. Yet many army officers were unwilling to accept Indians as combat troops. Evaluation of the actual fighting ability of Indians as compared with regular troops is complicated by the great tribal and individual variation; moreover, many whites had favorite tribes and slighted others. Captain Anson Mills, an experienced cavalryman, observed Crook's Crow and Shoshone allies at the Battle of the Rosebud (June 17, 1876) and concluded that they were worthless. Yet he was virtually the only participant who left an account that expressed such an opinion. Disregarding Lieutenant John Bourke as prejudiced in favor of Crook's ideas, one finds that Lieutenant H. R. Lemly concluded that the Plains warriors were the best skirmishers to be found. Crook himself noted, in his report on this 1876 campaign, that his Indian allies could hit a running wolf from the back of a galloping horse, while his soldiers could hardly hit a galloping Indian while standing still on the ground. Crook was trying to explain the unsatisfactory results of the summer's campaign, but he was a professional soldier and a noted hunter and marksman, and was entitled to have an opinion on shooting ability.[49]

From the other side, White Bull of the Minneconjou Sioux, also a participant at the Rosebud, later drew some conclusions from his wide experience in fighting Indians and whites. He thought that the Crows and the white soldiers were about equal in a shooting fight, while the Crows were better in hand-to-hand combat; of all the enemies he had met, however, the Shoshones were the best and the bravest. The unspoken chauvinistic implication of White Bull's statement is obvious. Researcher Walter S. Campbell, however, noted that other old Sioux warriors he knew sometimes referred to the Rosebud fight as "the battle with our Indian enemies."[50]

White officers who expressed distrust or contempt for Indian allies would have rejected these assessments. They often reflected on the way in which Indian allies, especially those not formally enlisted, would quit and go home when the fancy took them. It may never have occurred to these critics that the Indians in turn often distrusted the courage and general competence of their white allies, and that they sometimes left because they were disgusted with what they saw as military incompetence or because they feared they would be left to suffer the consequences of defeat.[51]

Few witnesses would have questioned that the average Plains warrior was superior in horsemanship to the average cavalryman. Crook noted that a Sioux boy was in training as a cavalryman from the time he could first sit on a horse. The white

trooper was too often a city boy who began to learn horsemanship after enlistment, and received very sketchy training at that.
The frequently noted ability of Plains warriors to pick up
wounded comrades on the run, or to hang out of sight on the side
of a running horse away from the enemy, firing under the animal's neck, was far beyond the trooper's skill.[52]

There was less agreement concerning Indian marksmanship.
Others echoed Crook's praise of his allies' shooting, yet some
sources insist that Indians did not shoot well with firearms, perhaps because they lacked sufficient ammunition for practice.
There is general agreement that for the same reason the soldiers,
especially in the 1870s, were also poor shots. Some modern anthropologists argue that nonliterate people cannot be marksmen
because they lack the ability to close just one eye in order to
sight. One could quote many Indian war veterans on both sides
of this question, yet there must have been individual and tribal
variations.[53]

John S. Gray, a careful student of the Plains wars, concludes
that the Indians relied on the highly developed individual skills
of the warrior, fostered by a whole way of life, while the army relied on the disciplined obedience of men acting in concert as
their officers directed. This idea agrees with Crook's assessment
of the Apaches; he concluded that military discipline aimed at
making a man into a machine, while the Apache was a superb individual fighter, needing no one to do his thinking for him. Indeed, Crook makes the Apache warriors into such supermen that
it is a relief to turn to their own recollections and find their
human emotions and foibles revealed.[54]

An incident that reveals the relative combat value of scouts
and white cavalry occurred in the summer of 1867 along the
Platte in Nebraska. A company of Pawnee scouts under Captain
James Murie was rushed by rail to Plum Creek Station (now Lex-
ington) on the Union Pacific, where a number of Cheyennes
were hovering about; Colonel Richard Dodge also hurried to the
station with four companies of infantry. Dodge arrived to find
that, in compliance with his telegraphed order, the Pawnees had
already crossed the river to reconnoiter. From the roof of the station, Dodge relates, he watched the subsequent action with a
telescope. Murie with 50 Pawnees advanced against perhaps 100
to 150 Cheyennes. He had to cross Plum Creek over a narrow
bridge with the enemy waiting mounted on the other side and

riflemen stationed at an old stage station on their right flank. The Pawnees were in uniform but habitually stripped to go into action. According to Dodge's reminiscent account, the Pawnees, out of sight in a low spot, stripped down but retained their hats and their overcoats, secured over their shoulders by one button. Riding over the bridge in a column of twos, they looked much like regular cavalry. The Cheyennes expected, Dodge thought, that they could frighten the poorly trained cavalry horses with yells and flapping buffalo robes and, catching them in the worst possible position crossing the bridge, inflict a disaster on them. When the company was halfway across the bridge, the Cheyennes charged. The Pawnees threw off their hats and overcoats, gave the Pawnee war cry, and charged. The Cheyennes, with cries of "Pawnee! Pawnee!" fled with the scouts in pursuit. The Pawnees killed between fifteen and twenty, taking scalps. They took prisoner a woman and a boy.[55]

There is some confusion about the details of this episode, since none of the official reports, including Dodge's, mentions the overcoat ruse. Yet Dodge, a West Pointer and regular soldier of much western experience, implies that the Cheyennes were confident of beating fifty white troopers, but not fifty Pawnees. Even if his assessment of the Cheyennes' intentions is wrong, his readiness to believe this is significant. The Pawnees could beat the Cheyennes at their own game, as evidenced by the results.

The assessment of Major J. M. Walsh, Northwest Mounted Police, is valuable as an outsider's opinion. Having become well acquainted with Sitting Bull's Sioux during their sojourn in Canada (1877–81), Walsh told Colonel Nelson Miles that the Sioux holdouts could probably outfight the United States troops who had advanced to the border: "he had seen the best [cavalry] regiments of England, and did not think them equal to the Sioux as horsemen or shots." Reporter John Finerty tacitly agreed, expressing relief that Miles's command did not have to engage the Sioux on this occasion.[56]

Beyond the value of Indian scouts in finding and fighting the enemy, a further benefit was urged by their advocates; this was the psychological effect their presence had on the hostiles. If the scouts could help the army find the enemy in their safest retreats, then the hostiles would realize that they might run, but they could not hide. The consequent insecurity would make reservation life seem increasingly attractive. When the Apache chief Cha-ut-lipun surrendered to Crook in 1873, he explained that his people were surrendering because, thanks to Apache scouts, they could no longer sleep at night or light fires for fear of bringing the troops down on them; "We are not afraid of the Americans alone, but we cannot fight you and our own people together." The Cheyennes at the Red Fork also called out to the Cheyenne scouts to go home: "We can whip the white soldiers alone, but can't fight you too."[57]

A demonstration of these points in microcosm is offered by the "Sheepeater War" in Idaho Territory in 1879, a minor affair that would be farcical except that people suffered and died in it. The Sheepeaters were a Shoshonean-language group living in the rugged mountains of central Idaho; little known to whites, they were called "sheepeaters" because the mountain sheep was a mainstay of their food supply. Rumored depredations by these people led the army to send a few companies into the mountains in the summer of 1879. The regulars had very little success with these Indians, who moved effortlessly along the ridges of their familiar habitat, while the soldiers toiled through snowdrifts (in June) and deep canyons, under fire from the heights. Captain Reuben Bernard withdrew his exhausted command for fear of approaching winter, except for his Indian scout company. Twenty Umatilla and Cayuse Indians, with seven mounted infantrymen as sharpshooters, had formed at the Umatilla reservation in Oregon, under two quite junior lieutenants, Edward S. Farrow and William C. Brown. They had already led the troops to what limited success they had enjoyed in seizing a Sheepeater camp; now they saved the affair from ending as a fiasco. They kept up the pursuit until the harassed Sheepeaters, denied the chance to lay in their winter food supply, decided to open negotiations. A scout who spoke Shoshone served as interpreter. The terms were surrender and removal to a reservation. Fifty-one people came in, fifteen of them classifiable as warriors; they surrendered eight firearms, five of which were fairly up to date. Yet they had defied the efforts of over a hundred regular soldiers, led by an officer (Bernard) of exceptional experience. General Oliver O. Howard, commanding the Department of the Columbia, acknowledged that it was Farrow's scouts that turned the affair from failure to success, such as it was.[58]

If the scouts shook the morale of the hostiles, they could also offer an encouragement to surrender, as the Sheepeater episode demonstrated. Their value in this regard was especially great if the scouts and hostiles were closely affiliated. Their presence as fighting men suggested that surrender might not mean utter degradation or execution. To men with families to consider, they demonstrated the availability of an alternative to complete humiliation or resistance unto death. One could save one's family and one's band and still hope to retain the dignity of horses, arms, and the manly occupation of violence.

"It is not merely a question of catching them better with Indians," said Crook, "but a broader and more enduring proposition—their disintegration."[59] Crook had every reason to hope that the use of scouts from the same tribe would break tribal cohesion and the authority of hostile leaders. "Divide and conquer" had been white policy since colonial times. Little effort was required to turn some tribes against each other, as they were often already on hostile terms. In addition, tribal factionalism and individualism often offered cracks into which a splitting wedge could be inserted. The morality of playing on such animosities probably bothered the military leaders no more than it did their diplomatic contemporaries in Europe. In the short run they could end hostilities with less bloodshed by inspiring in the hostilities an "If you can't lick 'em, join 'em" attitude. In the long run they assumed that the weakening of tribal ties and chiefly authority would promote assimilation.

Indian scouts and allies could serve as the intermediaries in peace negotiations. In the spring of 1877 Crook sent the Sioux reservation leaders Spotted Tail and Red Cloud separately to Crazy Horse to convince the chief that surrender was the only alternative to destruction. Some whites would have been horrified to learn that these chiefs were allowed to leave the reservation without white supervision, and with large numbers of well-armed followers; yet Crazy Horse did come in to surrender.[60] In the fall of the same year, the Cheyenne scout Brave Wolf, on his own initiative, apparently entered the camp of the fleeing Nez Perces and tried to persuade them to surrender to his commander, Nelson Miles. The Nez Perces were not receptive, and Miles was apparently displeased by Brave Wolf's action. Yet Brave Wolf's stated motive, that after all, they were all Indians, and he hoped to end the war without further bloodshed, is impressive.[61]

In 1915, long after the supposed end of the Indian wars, there occurred an episode that illustrates the diplomatic approach, and how readily some army officers turned to it. A pointless encounter between a U.S. marshal's posse and a band of Utes in southeastern Utah resulted in the death of three white men, hysterical publicity about an "Indian uprising," and cries for military aid. The chief of staff of the army was General Hugh Scott, a former scout commander and an expert in the sign language; he had retained a deep interest in the Indians' culture and in their welfare. Setting out with one aide to attend to the problem, Scott also telegraphed for the aid of an old Navajo medicine man, Bi-joshii; this man had surrendered to him two years earlier after another, bloodless disturbance. Bi-joshii grumbled that it was a long, hard trip for an old man, "but my brother wants me to go and I will go." Together they were able to persuade the Ute leaders that it was possible to surrender to the whites and live. The whole affair was a minor and quite avoidable civil disturbance, inflated by minds steeped in "wild West" myths. What is significant is that Scott, the "old Indian fighter," knew exactly how to terminate the matter without further bloodshed, and that the mutual respect between the general and the Navajo medicine man made this outcome possible. The episode demonstrated that some whites and some Indians could, if they made the effort, establish relationships outside the conventional framework of racial hostility.[62]

The Indian scouts were not merely minor adjuncts of the army, engaged in finding someone for the soldiers to fight. Their reconnaissance and trailing function was indeed a prerequisite to any effective military action against hostile Indians. In addition they extended the army's capabilities by making it possible for the soldiers to operate, to an extent, like Indians themselves. They could and often did serve as an especially effective part of the fighting forces, and sometimes were the only ones who did any fighting at all. On occasion they also made it possible to end hostilities without further bloodshed by serving as intermediaries and as symbols of the possibility of an honorable accommodation with the whites. While some military commanders could think only in terms of the number of Indians killed, others were aware of these less violent possibilities and eager to take advantage of them. Thus both Indians and whites found that it was possible to cooperate for the end that both desired.

Chapter Six

"Indian Thinking":
White Leadership and Indian Scouts

Interaction between Indians and whites in the West led to relationships that ranged from bitter hatred and cynical exploitation to warm mutual respect and affection. A particularly close and demanding relationship was that between Indian scouts and the whites assigned to lead them. Persons of radically differing cultures, values, and views of the world found themselves in a situation that demanded close cooperation, understanding, and mutual respect. Even in the area of most immediate mutual interest, the conduct of war, they represented widely differing traditions. A mutual understanding of objectives and methods could be literally a matter of life and death.

No one could be less capable of the necessary adjustments than the "military mind" of popular stereotype, unless it was the stereotyped unchanging Indian. Real people, however, have at least the potential for genuine flexibility. Late in the period of the Indian wars, Frederic Remington made the acquaintance of an officer with experience in leading Apache scouts who denied that he and his fellows should be called "Indian-fighters": "It would often be better and more truthful to call us 'Indian-thinkers' rather than 'fighters.' "[1]

Effective leadership of Indian scouts depended far more on the personal qualities of the leader than on his formal, legally based authority. Undoubtedly this is true of all leadership, but in the regular forces the insecure or obtuse officer could fall back on the authority of his commission and the harsh disciplinary measures that regulations and custom made available. With Indian scouts these sanctions could easily produce the opposite of the desired result—not because Indians had no concept of law or constituted authority, as whites often imagined, but because their concepts of authority, law, and punishment differed substantially from those of whites.

The Cheyennes said that a chief should take no notice if a dog urinated on his tipi; that is, he should be above any personal considerations or biases. Obviously this proverb reflected the Cheyennes' awareness of the perennial problem of abuse of power for personal ends. To fall seriously below this standard was likely to cost the chief his position. For example, Little Wolf was one of the four "old man chiefs" of the Northern Cheyennes, and one of their greatest fighting leaders, hero of the famous fighting retreat from Indian Territory to Montana Territory. In 1880 he shot Starving Elk at Fort Keogh, Montana, for making apparently improper advances to Little Wolf's daughter. In consequence Little Wolf lost his position and became a virtual outcast, a punishment he regarded as just. On the other hand, the chiefs of Cheyenne warrior societies, and those of some other Plains tribes, enjoyed considerable power of arbitrary command. It is not easy to generalize about authority and obedience among western Indians; their societies were too diverse. Yet authority among them tended to be based at least as firmly on the character of the leader as on a formal commission or investiture. This was particularly the case among the nomadic peoples, whose freedom of movement limited the opportunities for arbitrary, unpopular exercise of authority.[2]

The officer in command of Indian scouts, whether or not in conjunction with white troops, had to make a special effort to cross barriers of culture and language in order to establish personal authority over his men. He was given no course of instruction in how to go about the task; the only book that tried to give advice on the subject, Edward Farrow's *Mountain Scouting*, was published late in the period. Most literature available to him generalized very broadly about Indians, was often denigratory, and had little information related to his specific needs. The officer assigned to such duty had to learn on the job, relying on his own good sense and ability to adapt. It is certain that some succeeded and were regarded with respect and affection by the men they commanded. It seems that the scouts sometimes felt protective toward such leaders, who had many traits they admired, yet had so much to learn about the most ordinary things.[3]

An officer in command of scouts first of all had to possess physical courage. Indians generally did not admire foolish waste of life, but any suspicion that the commander was less brave than his men was ruinous.[4] Under frontier conditions, physical stamina and endurance were also necessary; service with Indian scouts could strain a man to the physical limit. Several who persisted in such service, such as Frank North, W. P. Clark, and Charles Gatewood, died in their forties, their health broken or their resistance lowered by the hardships they had undergone.

Beyond these minimum requirements was the need for considerable flexibility and adaptability. It was necessary to adapt to very different ways of doing things than one was used to, either as a civilian or as a soldier. Rigidity and intolerant ethnocentrism could disqualify a man otherwise well suited for the assignment. An officer could not expect his men to throw their lives away at his command, after the fashion of Pickett's Charge. Those officers for whom such Civil War sacrifices represented the height of military virtue could easily become disgusted with Indian soldiers. Some could see virtue in the Indians' economizing with human life: "None of us were injured which was due to the fact that we used the hostiles' own tactics against them," wrote Apache scout commander James Watson of an action in Arizona.[5]

Scout commanders had to accept the importance of the supernatural in the lives of Indians—to them a matter of the most practical, down-to-earth concern. To many whites these "superstitions" were at best laughable, at worst a hindrance to military efficiency. Some officers, however, recognized the importance of religious ceremonial and protective "medicine" to the Indian warrior's morale. George Custer would remind his Arikara scouts to perform the proper ceremonies before going into action; "Custer had a heart like an Indian," scout Red Star later commented.[6] Before plunging into the mountains of Mexico on a hazardous expedition, George Crook asked his Apache scouts, the majority of his command, to hold a war dance. Thus the scouts were assured of spiritual protection, and also of Crook's respect for their beliefs.[7]

On the other hand, the formalities dear to the hearts of some officers meant little to most Indians; many of them they judged mere foolishness, or a definite nuisance. At the beginning of their service the Pawnee scouts were stationed at Fort Kearny, Nebraska; the post commander informed Frank North that, as a volunteer officer, he must drill his command in the manual of arms. North pointed out that, aside from his own ignorance of such matters, the Pawnee language had no words that could be adapted to the purpose. The order stood, though the drills must have been farcical. Before too long duty in the field rescued the Pawnees.[8] During the Little Bighorn campaign Lieutenant James Bradley strove to understand the viewpoint of his Crow scouts, yet he expected them to line up for a formal roll call each morning. An appeal to Colonel John Gibbon by the interpreters ended this irksome formality.[9] The Apache scouts could never understand why the cavalry had to line up and stand in ranks on the parade ground before an expedition, instead of just starting out.[10]

The essence of leadership of scouts, in the opinion of the most experienced of such leaders, was to let them use their own methods to the extent compatible with the ultimate purpose. George Crook, through an aide, distilled this concept into an order to a junior officer assigned to Apache scouts.

> The first principle is to show them that we trust them . . . they are quick to note any lack of confidence. . . . They appreciate the situation, and understand thoroughly what is expected of them, and know how best to do their work. They understand this business better than we do, and to direct them in details will merely disgust them and make them "time-servers." They will work in your presence, and when away from you loaf. The only directions that can be given them, with any probability of good results, is to explain to them what you expect of them, and let them do their work in their own way, holding them responsible that it is done. . . . They know better how to obtain the information which is needed—namely the presence of the renegades—than we do, and should be allowed to use their own methods in getting it. . . . We cannot expect them to act automatically as drilled soldiers do. Their best quality is their individuality, and as soon as this is destroyed their efficiency goes with it. . . . The question is how to get the most valuable service, and hence the caution sought to be conveyed in this letter, which is based on long experience in the use of Indian scouts and auxiliaries.[11]

The order accords with Crook's expressed philosophy and known practice. As John Bigelow shrewdly observed, "General Crook makes of his Indian auxiliaries, not soldiers, but more formidable Indians."[12] Furthermore, he regularly took their advice, or at least consulted with them, on matters of strategy and tactics. Interpreter Billy Garnett claimed that in the campaign that led to the Red Fork battle, Crook based some of his major decisions on the counsel of his Sioux and Arapaho scouts. Earlier the same year he consulted frequently with the aged chief Washakie of the Shoshones, who had been a warrior before Crook was born and whose leadership had enabled his people to hold their own against much stronger enemies. Lieutenant Charles Gatewood did not need Crook to tell him these principles; he habitually discussed the next day's march with his Apache scouts each evening, always inviting the Indians to give their opinions.[13]

Colonel Ranald Mackenzie of the Fourth Cavalry learned this lesson the hard way. In 1871 his Tonkawa scouts trapped two Comanches in rough terrain on the edge of Texas's Staked Plain. Never a patient man, Mackenzie stood behind his scout commander, trying to hasten the Tonkawas' moves against the enemy. His reward was an arrow in the thigh. In their own good time the scouts, moving acrobatically over the rocks, disposed of the two Comanches. Mackenzie's correspondence nonetheless indicates his full appreciation of the necessity for scouts, and frequently records his confidence in them, particularly the Tonkawas and Seminole Negroes.[14]

Crook once explained in some detail the qualities he looked for in a scout commander. Efficiency, he noted, was the all-important quality Indians expected from a war leader; virtually all studies agree that a war chief who wasted lives and otherwise performed ineptly was not likely to be able to recruit followers again. His medicine was not strong enough. Scout commanders had to have good health, stamina, courage, patience, good judgment, and discretion. Crook preferred younger officers who were in good health "and whose ambition is a guiding motive, rather than . . . officers of more experience, upon whose vigor and energy the effects of long service have began [*sic*] to tell."[15] No doubt the ideal leader described was something of a self-portrait, intentional or not.

Scout commanders were generally lieutenants, although when Crook formed battalions of Apache scouts he put captains in command. These lieutenants were not necessarily the callow youths of latter-day fiction. Promotion was very slow, and almost entirely by seniority. Lieutenants might be in their thirties or older. Charles Gatewood, one of the most experienced scout commanders, was a forty-three-year-old first lieutenant when he died in 1896. Such appointments made for an experienced but aging officer corps, from whose members ambition, energy, and independence of thought had often dribbled away over the years.[16]

Paradoxically, this situation ensured that officers of high quality often commanded scout detachments. The restless and adventurous, and those whose intelligence demanded something more challenging than post routine, sought the assignment. As Hugh Scott noted, one would be ahead of the main column, and would be sure not to miss any excitement. A junior officer with many years to wait for promotion could enjoy independence and responsibility beyond his rank. After a few years of reservation and Apache scout duty, Lieutenant Britton Davis concluded that he could not bear to return to ordinary routine; he resigned from the service at the age of twenty-six.[17]

Frank North's most recent biographer describes him as "a restless, intelligent person who had a great distaste for the humdrum of ordinary activity." He was also an asthmatic who may have been driven to overcompensate for his condition, somewhat in the manner of Theodore Roosevelt.[18] Another example of congenital restlessness was Lieutenant Gustavus Doane, Second Cavalry, leader of Crow scouts against Sioux and Nez Perces in 1877. He was an early explorer of Yellowstone Park and led a hazardous boat expedition down the canyon of the upper Snake River. He regularly submitted requests to be sent on expeditions to central Africa or the Arctic; the latter request was granted but produced no results because the government provided a wholly inadequate ship. He also designed a new type of tent, which the army adopted, and unsuccessfully sought appointment as superintendent of Yellowstone Park. Clearly Doane was the sort of man whose physical and intellectual restlessness could find release in duty with Indian scouts.[19]

Deep ambivalence characterized military attitudes toward Indians, with sympathy and admiration on one hand, distaste, condescension, and racial stereotyping on the other. One person could entertain all of these attitudes at once. The ambivalence, of course, simply mirrored the attitudes of the general society; for the soldier the emotions were likely to be stronger because he confronted the object of the attitudes at firsthand.[20]

Some officers felt only revulsion for "Mr. Lo" ("Lo, the poor Indian . . ."). For others the native Americans became an absorbing and sometimes lifelong interest. Army officers were prominent among the pioneers of anthropology in the United States. Crook's aide, John G. Bourke, assiduously collected information from the various tribes as he accompanied the general about the West; the Bureau of Ethnology published a series of his fearfully erudite papers. Army surgeon Washington Matthews was the first white American to study seriously the culture of the Navajos, and he also worked among the Hidatsas. The first book on the Plains sign language was by Signal Corps officer Garrick Mallery, who became one of the chief experts of the Bureau of Ethnology.[21]

The sign language, and other facets of Plains culture, also became an absorbing interest to William Philo Clark, one of the scout commanders most admired by both whites and Indians, whom the Indians called White Hat. Clark commanded the entire body of scouts at the Red Fork battle, supervised the Sioux at the Red Cloud agency, and commanded Crow and Cheyenne scouts in Montana Territory in the late 1870s. He was highly regarded by the Indians, with whom his expertise in the sign language enabled him to communicate without an interpreter. Little Wolf's band of Northern Cheyennes surrendered to Clark in the spring of 1879, after their epic flight north from Indian Territory; this bloodless achievement was possible in part because Clark's Cheyenne scouts made it plain that they would fight even their own kin if the officer ordered them to do so. Little Wolf became Clark's first sergeant on Miles's expedition to the Canadian border. The two became fast friends, and planned an illustrated work on the sign language. This project proved abortive, but Clark's posthumously published *The Indian Sign Language*, though unillustrated, contained a wealth of historical and cultural information. Clark's intelligent and respectful interest in Indian culture undoubtedly contributed substantially to his successful relations with the Indian scouts and others under his charge. His early death in 1884 undoubtedly was a loss not only to the army, but to the study of history and anthropology.[22]

An officer whose interest in Indians was equally deep, but of a different order, was Richard Pratt, and his evident success as a scout commander requires a somewhat different explanation. As an officer in the black Tenth Cavalry as well as a scout leader, he believed absolutely in racial equality and equal rights. Yet he thought also that Indian culture should and must perish, so that the Indians themselves might survive. For much of his eight years on the Southern Plains he commanded scout detachments that included members of a majority of the tribes of the region. His greatest fame, however, was as superintendent of the Carlisle Indian Industrial School, which he ran very much as a military institution. An uncompromising proponent of assimilation, he disliked the Bureau of Ethnology, and by implication the science of anthropology, because he feared that they would glorify and perpetuate ways of life that he wished to see eradicated. Clearly Pratt was in the tradition of the pietistic reformers and assimilationists of his era, people whose capacity for empathy with Indians was usually severely limited by their ethnocentrism.[23]

Pratt's success as a scout commander was probably due to his ability to see individual Indians as people, and to respect and admire their virtues despite his ethnocentrism. His first acquaintance with Indians came when he commanded a group of Cherokee scouts in Indian Territory, well-assimilated Indians who broke down his preconceptions about "atrocious aborigines." Conversations with his Cherokee sergeant convinced him that the man was "both a manly and perfectly normal member of the human family." He was even more impressed with the Pawnee scout Big Spotted Horse, "a tall fine specimen of a man who relished perilous service," and who would carry out assignments that no white scout cared to undertake. From personal experience Pratt came to believe that many tales of thrilling experiences among the bloodthirsty savages were based on exaggeration and misapprehension. His ability to see past his own ethnocentric and authoritarian attitudes and to meet an Indian as a rational, quite possibly admirable person enabled Pratt to achieve success with his scouts; he was remembered with strong affection by many Indians.[24]

Officers who liked the scouts they commanded often developed paternalistic attitudes toward them. These attitudes were not necessarily incompatible with respect for the Indians' rationality and maturity; they sprang from realization that the Indians were confronted with a culture that their training had not prepared them to understand and a society and political system in which they had no power. Lieutenant Edward Casey, highly respected in his profession as a tactician, took command of a company of Indians in the Eighth Cavalry in 1888, part of an experiment in integrating Indians into the regular establishment. This Cheyenne company, stationed at Fort Keogh, Montana, became known as "Casey's Scouts." The Northern Cheyennes were in distress at this time because of short rations, the failure of their attempts to farm, and troubles with neighboring white ranchers. Whites blamed them for all shootings of ranchers' cattle and for all unsolved murders, with or without evidence; there was much agitation for removing the Indians and opening the reservation to settlement. Enlistment as soldiers provided some Cheyennes with a means to support their families, and the company was able to act to some extent as a police force. Casey repeatedly wrote reports in which he defended the Cheyennes against hysterical charges, insisting that the troubles were largely the fault of white greed and mistreatment of Indians, and that the whole tribe could not be held responsible for the acts of a violent few. He urged his superiors to use their influence to prevent the proposed termination of the reservation; ultimately the reservation was not opened to white settlement, and the army's influence may have helped.[25]

Casey's ultimate fate was heavily ironic, for he was killed by a Sioux during the Ghost Dance troubles of 1890 while his company was maintaining surveillance of a large camp in South Dakota. The killer, Plenty Horses, was acquitted by a jury after army officers testified that the killing should be considered an act of war. The verdict infuriated Casey's friend and admirer Frederic Remington, but Casey's fellow officers believed he would have approved the decision.[26]

An officer whose feelings remained strikingly ambivalent after several years with Indian scouts was Lieutenant Charles B. Gatewood. He was with Apache scouts or on reservation duty for some seven years, as long as any officer in the army. Some historians have written that Gatewood did not really like or trust Indians, in spite of his remarkable record; if the tale were true, it would indeed be noteworthy, considering how much of his career was devoted to such service. In fact, like so many whites on the frontier, Gatewood liked some Indians and disliked others, both individually and as groups. His writings about his reservation duties, in which he acted as de facto agent, judge, and police chief, show a considerable sense of humor. At a period in his life when his health had failed badly and frustration about his career and lack of promotion had accumulated, Gatewood reflected adversely on the trustworthiness of the Chiricahua Apache scouts in the Geronimo campaign. Apparently at that time (1886–87) he believed that the Apaches had lost any affection for him; this belief probably reflects his own physical and emotional state as much as any attitudes of the Indians. Gatewood was the man who persuaded Geronimo to surrender for the last time in 1886. If it were true, as some historians assert, that he was the only officer the Apache leader trusted enough to negotiate with, then he cannot have displayed much overt aversion to Indians.[27]

Not all white leaders of scouts were army officers. Civilian scouts and "chiefs of scouts" are prominent in the accounts of Indian campaigns. Lieutenant Augustus Tassin defined a chief of scouts as "some white dare-devil of a frontiersman of the Wild Bill genus" and described him as "guide, interpreter, and general medium of communication between the Indians and the officer in command." Such men were officially employees of the Quartermaster Department. Their value was in specialized knowledge not usually available to officers. To be really useful they had to know the country, have some expertise in trailing, and be able to communicate with the Indians in their own language or, on the Plains, in the sign language. The best of these men sometimes remained in service for years and became famous frontier characters. Officers often took their advice, though the army did not always acknowledge this fact, and they sometimes commanded without any officer's supervision. The ones most esteemed by the military generally eschewed the fancy bucksins, long hair, and other trappings of the "scouts" of the Wild West shows.[28]

Frank North of the Pawnee Scouts was the most famous of these civilian leaders. During the Civil War, when he first commanded the Pawnees, he held a commission as a captain of Nebraska volunteers; in later years he and the other white officers with the Pawnees were in fact civilian scouts. North nonetheless retained the title of captain, later wore the uniform and insignia of a major, and apparently drew a major's pay. North's peculiar status persisted because the army recognized that he was the only white man the Pawnees would follow.[29]

In Arizona the chief of scouts above all others was Al Sieber; most officers were glad to take his advice. Sieber may or may not have known how to trail as well as the average Apache, but he knew enough to oversee their work. Sieber claimed his success was due to his always keeping his word to the Indians: when he said he was going to kill one of them, he did. Perhaps the Apaches found this characteristic not unworthy of respect, but he probably employed a bit more psychology than this statement implies. At any rate, Sieber was employed by the army for nearly two decades.[30]

An obscure civilian scout and an Apache scout unit struck the decisive blow in the 1879–80 campaign against the Apache band led by Victorio. For over a year, white, black, and Indian troops had pursued and skirmished with Victorio through New Mexico, west Texas, and northern Mexico, but it was a relatively inexperienced Texan, H. K. Parker, who caught the chief in the Black Range of New Mexico. Parker and his scout company slipped up on three sides of the hostiles and sprang an ambush that Victorio himself could not have bettered. Parker reported killing thirty "men, women, and children" without suffering any loss, and running off a large portion of the band's horses. This was a great deal more than the army had accomplished till then, and historians of the campaign have assessed it as the beginning of the end for Victorio. The army did not emphasize the importance of this engagement; it was bad enough that no regulars were present, but in addition there was not even a commissioned officer in command.[31]

An officer who did not care for Indians himself thought that men like Charles Gatewood, who spent long periods alone with scouts, often became "almost Indian-like in habit and thought." Such a statement reflects mostly the writer's prejudices, excited perhaps by the lack of formality and "spit and polish" of men like Gatewood. The question arises, all the same, whether such men did consciously or unconsciously absorb Indian modes of behavior or even thought. To adopt certain Indian methods of warfare or of living in the field was only good sense. There is little evidence, however, that even those who took a serious interest in Indian culture became seriously alienated from their own culture or significantly assimilated to that of any Indian tribe. Such a shift, as many Indians found, is exceedingly difficult for an adult.[32]

Fur trappers and traders probably attempted this type of acculturation more than any other white group. Edwin Denig, an experienced and intelligent trader on the upper Missouri, concluded that Indians would never respect a white man who imitated them, or who was accomplished in those areas in which they themselves were proficient, such as hunting, trailing, and war. They respected, rather, the white man who was rich in trade goods and could do things of which they were ignorant. Probably this statement reflects Denig's own unwillingness or inability to excel in the Indians' accomplishments; moreover, Denig's experience was confined largely to Indians of the upper Missouri. Still, many people do often regard with contempt or resentment the outsider who tries to push his way into their group, particularly if they regard themselves and their culture as basically superior to that outsider's group. Edward Farrow, drawing on his experience among Indians of the interior Northwest, observed that nothing so pleased them as to have whites follow their customs. It is likely that Farrow had in mind an observation of the proprieties much less thorough than the "going native" that Denig scorned.[33]

The white men who most thoroughly attempted to assimilate themselves into Indian life were those the frontier called "squaw men"—those who married Indian women, remained with them over long periods of time, and adopted the tribal style of living. Generally speaking, such men were not among the most celebrated leaders of Indian scouts in the post–Civil War period. Regular officers were unlikely to adopt such a mode of life, which would decidedly inhibit their careers. The first leader of the Pawnee Scouts, in 1864, was Joseph McFadden, who was married to a Pawnee woman and lived with her people. From all accounts McFadden was unable to exercise any control over the Pawnees; rather than tell them to do something, he asked them if they wanted to do it. Alfred Sorenson, supposedly basing his account on Frank North's recollections, says that the Indians would not respect a white man who lowered himself to their level from his superior position.[34] There is no reason to believe that the Pawnees regarded whites as their superiors, even if they were in some ways more powerful. There is no doubt that they greatly respected North, who knew their language and culture well, but who followed the life-style of his own people and married a white woman. If North had openly displayed such attitudes of racial superiority as those expressed by his biographer, his relationship with the Indians could hardly have continued. The difference between him and McFadden may simply have been one of personality, or it may have arisen from the more basic attitude described by Denig. It may also have been that McFadden's marriage identified him with his wife's band, one of four divisions constituting the Pawnee tribe, and thus lowered his influence with others. The leader in the Plum Creek fight of 1867, James Murie, was a Scot married to a Pawnee woman.[35]

In fact, there were some other "squaw men," often men of mixed ancestry themselves, and of varying degrees of cultural adaptation, who led Indian scouts or auxiliaries with some success. The McKay brothers, William and Donald, three-quarters Indian in ancestry, distinguished themselves as leaders of the Warm Springs scouts. John D. Walker married into the Pima tribe and led the Pima company of Arizona volunteers in the 1860s. Walter G. Marmon married a woman of Laguna pueblo and was the commander of a Laguna battalion in the New Mexico militia in the 1880s. There are enough examples from widely separate regions to suggest that "squaw men" were not automatically disqualified among all tribes from respect or leadership. They may have owed their official position, in the first place, to white authorities, but they could not have lasted long if they were despised by the Indians. Most certainly, however, the "squaw man" was despised by much of white society, and this was probably a major factor in his relative lack of prominence. In any case, the army's preference for putting a commissioned officer in charge reduced the role of this type of "marginal man."[36]

Various Indians, generally well-assimilated men, received commissions on both sides during the Civil War, and Lieutenant Donald McIntosh, largely Iroquois in ancestry, was killed at the Little Bighorn, but no traditional Indians served as officers, even in the inferior capacity allowed to native officers by the British in India. The highest rank available to an Indian was that of first sergeant. This was the rank given to Little Wolf, who had outwitted and outfought many an army officer, and to Washakie, who had led several hundred warriors in battle for two generations. The language and cultural problems that would have resulted from the commissioning of Indians chiefs as officers, however, even if racial bias were overcome, would probably have required more flexibility than the army was capable of. Obviously the respect and obedience such leaders received from their own men had little to do with their nominal military rank.

The relationship between Indian scouts and their white leaders tended to be short-lived. Such officers were on temporary assignment from their regiments and eventually had to return. Some left sooner than others, since the duty was not to their taste. Since the scout companies themselves were temporary organizations, it was hard to form an esprit de corps based on a leader's personality or shared experiences. Company C, Apache Scouts, based at San Carlos Agency, Arizona, was a unit that enjoyed more continuity than many others; still, in some nineteen months in 1877–78 the company had to be mustered in four times, each time by a different commanding officer than on the previous occasion.[37]

Among the exceptions was Frank North's long relationship with the Pawnee Scouts. It was acknowledged that they would follow no other leader.[38] Charles Gatewood was particularly fond of the men of his first scout company, with whom he served in the Victorio campaign; he made a point of having his picture taken with them when their six-month enlistment ran out. Commanding many of the same men soon after, he persuaded Lieutenant Thomas Cruse to join him as second in command of "a good bunch of *real* soldiers." Later, when he commanded a unit of Yuma and Mohave scouts, the White

Mountain Apaches of his old company kidded him about how he had come down in the world, and suggested that he leave the army and marry into their tribe. Gatewood agreed with them about the Yumas and Mohaves, but did not take up the offer.[39]

The outstanding example of a long association between a white army officer and a scout unit was that of Lieutenant John L. Bullis and the Seminole Negro Scouts. In many ways the relationship was more like that between a chief and his band than that between a commanding officer and his men. The Seminole Negroes were descendants of Southern slaves who ran away to the Seminoles in Florida, allying and to some extent intermarrying with the Indians. Fearful of reenslavement after the Seminoles' removal to Indian Territory, they fled to Mexico with some Seminoles under Chief Wildcat. For some years they served the state of Coahuila as a defense against raids by Comanches and Apaches, but their relations with their Mexican and Indian neighbors gradually deteriorated. In the early 1870s they made an agreement with the U.S. Army to cross the Rio Grande and take up service as scouts. Possessing the skills appropriate to Indian scouts, they enlisted under the same provisions. The scouts believed they had been promised grants of land, but no record of such an agreement was ever found.[40]

John L. Bullis commanded this unit from 1873 to 1881. From their village on the military reservation at Fort Duncan, and later at Fort Clark, Texas, Bullis led his men on many expeditions in the no-man's-land along the border, in conjunction with regular troops or without them. On a number of occasions they crossed the border to attack Indian camps, without the consent of Mexico. Of sixteen Indian scouts awarded the Medal of Honor, four were Bullis's men. The patriarchal nature of their relationship is exemplified by the fact that Bullis was expected to examine each newborn child in the camp and express his approval; on at least one occasion he performed a marriage ceremony. He worked to prevent the removal of his scouts to Indian Territory—perhaps to their ultimate disadvantage, since they never received the Texas land grant they expected. Bullis himself was less successful in later relations with Apaches in Arizona; methods that worked well with one group may well have failed with another.[41]

The story of the Seminole Negroes is one example of a tendency to institutionalize scout units at certain posts. The Ton-kawas resided for some seventeen years near Fort Griffin, Texas, the men serving as scouts; Richard Pratt was their commander in 1873–74. The Northern Cheyennes, with some Sioux, at Fort Keogh, Montana; the White Mountain Apaches at Fort Apache, Arizona; and a dissident band of Hidatsas at Fort Buford, Dakota Territory, provided scouts over a number of years. The men lived with their families, with their tribal or band structure more or less intact. Such villages represented a modest approx-imation of the "military colonies" that army officers like H. C. Cushing, in the 1880s and 1890s, would advocate as the solution to the Indian problem. The Seminole Negroes were not dis-banded until 1914, and Apache scouts served at Fort Apache un-til the post was turned over to the Department of the Interior in 1922. These situations were objectionable to the Bureau of In-dian Affairs, although they were probably more satisfactory to the Indians than reservation life. The Indian Bureau eventually secured control of most of these people. The army seldom showed much interest in placating the bureau, but as Indian troubles diminished, so did the need for scouts. The Indians, of course, had no voice in the matter; the option of being free from any government agency's control was never open to them.[42]

Yet these fragile symbiotic relationships, dedicated to violent purposes, represented an attempt by certain groups of Indians to adjust to the problems posed by the increasing white presence in the regions in which they lived. For a people such as the Tonka-was, the army post also represented an alliance against the over-whelming power of a far more obvious enemy. These relation-ships also represent, though they are largely ignored, some of the most striking examples of Indian-white military cooperation.

In order to cooperate militarily, Indians and white leaders had to make adjustments to each other. Professional officers had to modify or abandon certain preconceptions about the conduct of war and about the relationship between officer and enlisted men. Some displayed sufficient intelligence, empathy, and flex-ibility to succeed, while others did not and soon abandoned the assignment. For a man able to make the adjustment, the job of-fered the chance for independence, responsibility, and a more varied experience than fell to the lot of the regimental officer. It also offered great hardship and increased personal danger. Some of the men involved developed an abiding personal interest in the welfare and the culture of the people with whom they served. What was really necessary, however, was a respect for that culture and for the Indian's individuality and way of doing things. Beyond that consideration, what was necessary was the qualities required for leadership among any people.

The Indians, too, had to make adjustments to customs and procedures alien to them, whose immediate value was not always apparent. Their reasons for making the effort, and for choosing military cooperation with the whites, were not always apparent to the whites, even to the leaders who knew them best.

Military Organization of the West, ca. 1875

Chapter Seven

Renegades, Patriots,
and Pragmatists

Bad Soup, one of Sitting Bull's diehards in Canada, denounced Nelson Miles's Indian allies in these words: "They arm the Crows and Cheyennes, the Bannocks and Assiniboines, to murder our young men. Are the Americans afraid to fight themselves, that they hide in a cloud of Indian renegades?"[1] We do not know if the word "renegades" accurately translates what Bad Soup meant, but the word raises important questions about the motives of Indians who served the whites. To what extent were these Indian scouts consciously and deliberately betraying their own people to serve their own selfish interests? To what extent, in other words, were they mercenaries for the whites and renegades to their own people?

The phrase "their own people," which so readily occurs to whites, is in fact profoundly misleading. We cannot understand the scouts without understanding what that phrase meant to them. Some scouts fought against people of an entirely different tribe, while others fought people of their own tribe—that is, people to whom they had a clear sense of kinship through language and culture. A group of people might be Indians first of all to whites, and then distinguished as Sioux, Arapaho, Crow, or Apache; to the people themselves they were first of all Lakota, Inuñaina, Absaroka, or Nde. Tribal names generally conveyed a sense of "The People" or "Our People." This did not automatically meant that no other group had any human value, for a group might have warm feelings for allies of long standing,[2] but people were conscious of the difference between themselves and those who were not "Our People." As the white presence became increasingly obvious and important, a consciousness un-

doubtedly developed that there were "Indians," including one's
own people, and there were "whites." The Plains sign language
had generally recognized signs for each tribe, but as late as the
early 1880s William P. Clark found no general sign for
"Indian." The tribe, he found, was always specified, for this was
the distinction of greatest importance.[3]

Everywhere in North America, and certainly in the trans-Mississippi West, a sense of identity as Indians was slow to develop.
In the East, Tecumseh the Shawnee tried to develop a sense of
Indian solidarity and common ownership of land in the face of
white encroachment; although his message made an impression,
the pace of events overcame him. He had no equivalent in the
trans-Mississippi West. Certain tribes made alliances or "non-
aggression pacts" of greater or lesser duration. Such was the
long-standing alliance between the Sioux, Cheyennes, and Arapahoes, or the Kiowa-Comanche alliance. A peace agreement between Kiowas and Comanches, on one hand, and Southern
Cheyennes and Arapahoes on the other, made in 1840, later developed into a loose alliance against the whites. As mentioned
earlier, there are indications that the Sioux sent out feelers to
the Crows in the late 1860s about possible alliance against the
whites, but the Crows were not interested. In the 1870s, Sitting
Bull apparently made attempts to win over the Blackfeet even
before he fled north of the border. Later, in Canada, his people
took in the Nez Perce refugees in 1877, and he continued his efforts to etablish good relations with formerly hostile tribes such
as the Blackfeet and Assiniboins. As a sign of his personally
friendly relations with the principal Blackfoot leader, Crowfoot,
Sitting Bull gave his son the name Crowfoot. The Blackfoot
chief nonetheless preferred to remain at peace with whites on
both sides of the border.[4]

Intertribal warfare was exploited by the whites, but it had
been endemic on the Great Plains for centuries. Alliances were
made and unmade by Indian tribes, as by "civilized" nations,
for reasons that seemed good and sufficient at the time. Today's
friend might be tomorrow's enemy—a state of affairs by no
means confined to the Great Plains. Competent scholars have
concluded that far more Indians perished in intertribal warfare in
the nineteenth century than in wars with the whites.[5]

Students of the Plains tribes have emphasized the importance of warfare in tribal society. Coups counted against the enemy and the number of horses captured gave a man prestige and position, not to mention wealth. While this aspect of intertribal war has received primary emphasis from many writers, one school has pointed out the broader tribal objectives served by such warfare. Individual warriors may have gone to war with the thought of proving their valor and acquiring horses, but the society was served by its assertion of control over the buffalo range.[6]

In this condition of affairs, it is not so surprising to find that some tribal chiefs might seek an alliance with the whites if they saw an advantage in this course for their people. In fact, such alliances were founded in the early days of the fur trade, long before the United States government became involved. Flatheads, Nez Perces, Pend d'Oreilles, and Shoshones found the mountain men, with their formidable rifles, helpful allies against the powerful and aggressive Blackfeet; the trappers, greatly outnumbered by the western tribes, were equally glad to have friends to travel with and, if necessary, fight beside.[7]

In later years, when the United States Army became a significant force on the Plains, certain tribes naturally began to consider if this new power would make a valuable ally against powerful enemies. The question had an additional significance, of course, because the wiser chiefs increasingly realized that the white presence in itself meant drastic changes in the lives of their peoples. The question of accommodation or resistance to this power acquired ever greater importance in tribal councils. In many cases, however, the chiefs found their Indian enemies such an immediate menace that any problems created by the whites seemed entirely secondary.

In the nineteenth century the Teton Sioux represented such a menace to many tribes on the northern Plains, and ultimately the Sioux found many of these tribes leagued with the whites against them, while others remained neutral in the face of Sioux attempts to win them over. This difficulty in acquiring allies was in no small part due to their past history.

In the latter eighteenth century, the Teton Sioux crossed the Missouri and began their triumphant expansion to the west and south. They established an alliance with the Cheyennes and

Arapahoes, but other nomadic and sedentary tribes found themselves under increasing pressure from this far more numerous people. The Arikaras, Mandans, and Hidatsas eventually found consolidation in one village necessary for self-defense. The Pawnees found their buffalo hunts in the Republican Valley increasingly dangerous, and their home villages on the Loup and Platte were subject to frequent raids. Beginning in the 1830s, the Sioux gradually pressured the Crows out of first the Powder River country and then the Bighorn region to the west. After 1840 the eastern Shoshones experienced increasing danger from the Sioux and their allies as they hunted buffalo east of the Continental Divide, besides being raided by these same tribes west of the divide. None of these peoples could make a lasting peace with the Sioux, for the seven divisions of the Teton Sioux had no central political authority capable of binding them all to a peace agreement. Thus there was no Sioux grand strategy, but the same basic goals and needs prompted the expansion of all seven divisions. With an expanding population, they took advantage of circumstances to enrich themselves in the ways that were significant for the time and place.[8]

For tribes subject to Sioux pressure for decades, the combination of revenge and self-defense would constitute a powerful motivation, even without the other possible motives of individual warriors. The suggestion that they were betraying "the Indians" would have been meaningless to them. They knew too well who their enemy was.

Among the tribes that would aid the white soldiers against the Sioux, the Arikaras appeared to whites in a particularly unfavorable light. Edwin Denig, a thorough student of the upper Missouri tribes, reflected harshly on the morals and habits of the Arikaras in the 1850s. Yet he attributed no small part of these problems to the lack of opportunity for young Arikara men to distinguish themselves in war: "Instead of being considered a great warrior he desires to be known as a great rake." He thought them poor warriors, but their awkward position under Sioux domination must have proved inhibiting. The hereditary chiefs apparently restrained the young men, not only to conserve manpower but from fear of losing control of the rank and file. When scout enlistment began in the 1860s, there was initial opposition from some chiefs, but at least one chief, White Shield, seems to have approved. Each Arikara chief had his own police force, and it was the head of White Shield's police, Son of the Star, that encouraged members of this body to enlist as scouts.[9]

The Crows had established a friendly relationship with whites in the early days of the fur trade. They frequently claimed that they had never killed a white man, though they cheerfully robbed them often enough. A relatively small tribe, they were caught between the Sioux to the east and the Blackfeet to the northwest, both far more numerous than they. White observers from the 1830s on predicted their early extinction through war casualties and a low birth rate. In the twentieth century elderly Blackfeet declared that this would indeed have been the Crows' fate if the United States had not intervened.[10]

White judgments on the Crows varied widely, in the usual fashion, but many observers commended them for their intelligence, of which their friendliness toward whites was taken as a sign. Scout Baptiste Pourier observed that while Sioux on the march preserved no order, the Crows kept their columns closed up and allowed no one to ride ahead of the leader—except, presumably, their scouts. This characteristic was probably related to their numerical disadvantage, which necessitated greater discipline and more precautions than were deemed necessary by their more numerous enemies.[11] Some whites, not appreciating the Crows' need to conserve their fighting strength, judged them to be cowards. Others thought them at least as good fighters as the Sioux, though forced to stand on the defensive. Indeed, the young warriors, eager for glory, were often restive under the restraint the chiefs tried to impose on them.[12]

When asked to furnish scouts for Colonel John Gibbon's column in the 1876 war against the Sioux, the Crows had mixed feelings. As Chief Blackfoot had observed earlier, previous military expeditions had marched into Sioux country, proclaiming that they would sweep through it like a whirlwind, then had returned without positive results. The Crow reservation had remained subject to raids. The Battle of the Little Bighorn, where the Sioux and Cheyennes had one of their largest gatherings ever, took place on the Crow reservation. "We are not the whirlwind," declared Blackfoot with sardonic pride, "but we go to the Sioux . . . we meet them and fight, but we do not turn back." When the Crows with Gibbon heard of Custer's defeat, their worst fears were confirmed, and they fled from the wrath to come. Remembering the abandonment of the Bozeman Trail forts in 1868, they must indeed have been pleasantly surprised by the army's continued operations against the Sioux in 1876–77.[13]

In 1877 the Crow chiefs told Lieutenant Gustavus Doane that they wished to adopt some surrendered Sioux and Cheyennes. Indeed, they said that the desire to recruit in this fashion was one of the principal reasons the Crows had joined the army's effort against the Sioux. At first this seems an unlikely motive for war. Yet earlier observers noted a special Crow propensity to adopt captive women and children to make up their losses in population. The treatment they gave the adopted captives was so good that they usually won them over. Such reports may not convince us that the Crows were fighting principally for recruiting purposes, but they can serve as a reminder that the purposes for which Indians fought were not always simple or obvious.[14]

Those Crows who explained their reasons for joining the whites in war, however, usually gave the more obvious reasons. Aside from the individual warrior's desire for prestige and wealth, higher policy aimed at both defeating their powerful enemies, the Sioux, and establishing better relations with the whites. The need of the Crows for powerful allies against the Sioux was evident, despite the chiefs' doubts about white military prowess. The hope of gaining the gratitude of "Washington" was equally pragmatic, as Chief Blackfoot explained to Colonel Gibbon in 1876: "All other Indian tribes do evil to the whites, but I and my people hold fast to them with love. We want our reservation to be large, we want to go on eating buffalo, and so we hold fast to the whites."[15] Half a century later Plenty Coups, who as a young notable had consistently advocated the white alliance and had fought with Crook at the Rosebud, assessed the situation in the same terms as Blackfoot. The people who fought the whites, however bravely, ended with very little; the Crows had a large reservation in their homeland. "When I think back my heart sings because we acted as we did," declared Plenty Coups. "It was the only way open to us."[16]

The motives of the Eastern Shoshones were similar. Various Shoshonean groups had been driven from the Plains late in the eighteenth century by such people as the Crows and the Arapahoes. The Comanches had split off from the Shoshones and had gone south. Their separated brethren found themselves a home in southwest Wyoming, in the valley of the Green River. They continued to hunt buffalo east of the Divide, and guns obtained from traders gave them the means of holding their own. By the 1840s, Washakie had established himself as the preeminent chief; he seems to have acquired an almost dictatorial authority that was most unusual among the nomads. Shoshone society was highly individualistic, yet it was evidently possible for an able man to assert unusual authority in a time of need. Washakie first met whites in the early days of the fur trade; he was well acquainted with Jim Bridger, who helped him to obtain guns for his people. Born around 1800, he dominated his people from about 1840 until his death in 1900. His policy was consistently one of peace and cooperation with the whites, even in the face of great provocation. In times of tension he lost followers by this policy, but many of them would return later. Since the Oregon-California route ran through the Green River country, opportunities for friction were many, and the hunting environment inevitably deteriorated; yet knowledgeable whites knew they were safe among Washakie's people.[17]

Washakie's clear understanding of the situation led him to ask for a reservation in the Wind River Valley, on the eastern side of the divide; this location was away from the Oregon Trail and the Union Pacific route, and offered his people hope for a permanent home. "The Sioux may trouble us," Washakie remarked, "but when the Sioux are taken care of, we can do well." Established there in the early 1870s, with a military post for protection, the Shoshones cooperated with the army in defense against frequent raids by Arapahoes, Cheyennes, and Sioux. Mining settlements in the region believed that the Shoshones also shielded them from raids. Washakie, though well past the age for a warrior, still led his people in battle. In 1878, at General Crook's request, the army renamed the post at Wind River Fort Washakie.[18]

Although the federal government continually sought to put an end to intertribal warfare, it also exploited and exacerbated such conflicts by employing one tribe in its conflicts with another. The ultimate purpose of both the army and the Indian Bureau was the same—total white control of the Indians—but the means employed were often contradictory.[19]

This contradiction was clearly exemplified when the federal government, going to war with the Sioux in 1876, took advantage of intertribal animosities. Arikaras served with Terry and Custer, and Crows with Gibbon. Crook recruited a large body of Crows and Shoshones to accompany his command in their advance from the south in June. In accordance with his philosophy, Crook took a much larger number of Crows than did Gibbon, without formally enlisting them. Including about 80 Shoshones led by Washakie himself, Crook had about 250 allies —clearly evidence of his faith in them.[20]

The allies, armed with up-to-date Springfield carbines, joined Crook near present Sheridan, Wyoming. The expedition entered the region south of the Yellowstone, the Indians scouting ahead. On June 17, 1876, they encountered Sioux and Cheyennes in force on Rosebud Creek, Montana Territory. The resulting encounter was unusual in that it was a pitched battle in which neither side was surprised, and both sides fought in the open for some hours. It consisted of a series of disconnected skirmishes, charges and retreats, and attempts to cut off detached parties. On more than one occasion Crows and Shoshones, according to their custom, came to the rescue of troopers wounded or dismounted. They were somewhat handicapped by the soldiers' inability to tell them from the hostiles. Some writers thought a charge by the Shoshones saved the day by preventing the hostiles from splitting the command in two. John Bourke, who accompanied one such charge, thought the allies' manner of fighting exactly suited to the circumstances. Eventually the Sioux and Cheyennes withdrew, leaving Crook with the battlefield but no decisive victory. White observers were disgusted to note that their allies mutilated the hostile dead and killed some wounded, yet the emotions that prompted these acts were largely responsible for their presence in the first place. The Oglala He Dog later declared that the hostiles would have pursued Crook during his subsequent retreat, but they feared the Crows and Shoshones would strike at the dispersed Sioux and Cheyenne camps. Some Sioux remembered the Rosebud battle as "the battle with our Indian enemies," and White Bull regarded the Crows and Shoshones as equal to the white soldiers as fighters, perhaps better. Some soldiers were inclined to agree.[21]

1. White Horse, Pawnee Scout, about 1868 or 1869. He wears the traditional Pawnee scalp lock, which was being replaced at about that time by the longer hair style associated with the nomadic Plains tribes. He appears to be wearing a uniform coat; the revolver and tomahawk may be studio props rather than his own. (Photo by W. H. Jackson. Smithsonian Institution, National Anthropological Archives.)

2. Frank North, leader of the Pawnee Scouts, 1867. He wears the insignia of a major, his nominal rank as scout commander, though he was officially a civilian scout. (Photo by Clifford of Omaha. Courtesy of the Nebraska State Historical Society.)

3

3. Pawnee Scouts, about 1870. Standing, Baptiste Bayhylle, mixed-blood interpreter and sergeant of scouts. Seated, left to right, Man Who Left His Enemy Lying in Water, Night Chief, One Who Strikes the Chiefs, and Sky Chief. The last, who was killed by the Sioux in 1873, was probably not a scout. (Photo by W. H. Jackson. Courtesy of the Nebraska State Historical Society.)

4. Loakum Ar-nuk, a Warm Springs scout, in the northern California lava beds during the Modoc War in 1873. Obviously a posed picture. He has a military hat and cartridge box, civilian clothing, and a Spencer carbine. (Photo by Eadweard Muybridge. Smithsonian Institution, National Anthropological Archives.)

5. Warm Springs scouts photographed by Eadweard Muybridge during the Modoc War in northern California, 1873. They wear a mixture of white civilian clothing and military hats and overcoats. The right rear man and the front row have Spencer carbines. The left rear man has a Sharps and the other two unidentified weapons. (Smithsonian Institution, National Anthropological Archives.)

4

5

6. Washakie, chief of the Wyoming Shoshones and consistent ally of the whites. He led Crook's Indians in the battle of the Rosebud, June 17, 1876, and he and his warriors assisted the army on many other occasions. (Photo by W. H. Jackson, 1870. Smithsonian Institution, National Anthropological Archives.)

7. Plenty Coups, young Crow
leader and advocate of cooperation with the whites. Plenty
Coups served with the Crow
scouts at the battle of the
Rosebud. (Photo by Charles M.
Bell, Washington, D.C., 1880.
Smithsonian Institution, National Anthropological Archives.)

8. *Medicine Crow, one of the leaders of the Crow scouts at the battle of the Rosebud. His hair style is characteristic of his tribe. (Photo by Charles M. Bell, Washington, D.C., 1880. Smithsonian Institution, National Anthropological Archives.)*

9. *General Crook in council with Crow allies, Wyoming, 1876. An eyewitness sketch by artist-correspondent Charles St. G. Stanley published in* Frank Leslie's Illustrated Newspaper, *September 2, 1876. Stanley's depiction of the dress of the Crows matches contemporary descriptions. The white men in the center, left to right, are interpreter Louis Richaud, scout Frank Grouard, and General Crook. (Library of Congress.)*

10. *Charles St. G. Stanley's drawing, in* Frank Leslie's Illustrated Newspaper, *October 14, 1876, of Crook's troops and scouts crossing Goose Creek in Montana the day before the battle of the Rosebud. The poles are coup-sticks, not lances. The presence of the woman shown in the picture is confirmed by Crow testimony. (Library of Congress.)*

13

11. Three Bears, Oglala Sioux, first sergeant of the Sioux scout contingent with Crook in the fall and winter campaign of 1876–77. (Courtesy of the Nebraska State Historical Society.)

12. Standing: Lieutenant (later Captain) William Philo Clark, leader of scouts on the Northern Plains and author of The Indian Sign Language. His companion has been variously identified as the famous Cheyenne chief Little Wolf and as Little Hawk, a Minneconjou Sioux. (Smithsonian Institution, National Anthropological Archives.)

13. Sharp Nose, Northern Arapaho, 1st sergeant of the Arapaho scouts with Crook in the fall and winter of 1876–77. His services as a guide were vital to the expedition. (Smithsonian Institution, National Anthropological Archives.)

14. *Chato, Chiricahua Apache leader and 1st sergeant of scouts. After surrendering in 1883, he served against the hostile Chiricahuas in 1885 and 1886. In 1886 he was arrested and sent into exile and imprisonment with the people he had been fighting. Photo by John K. Hillers, probably taken during Chato's 1886 visit to Washington, just before his arrest. (Smithsonian Institution, National Anthropological Archives.)*

15. *General George Crook, in campaign outfit and on his mule, Apache, in Arizona, 1885. Left, Chiricahua Apache scout Dutchy, a hostile a year earlier; right, Alchesay, White Mountain Apache scout and Medal of Honor winner. (Courtesy of the Arizona Historical Society.)*

16. *Casey's Scouts at Fort Keogh, Montana, about 1890. Many of the men, Northern Cheyennes, were former hostiles and had also been scouts for Nelson Miles in the 1870s. Lt. Edward Casey, center; Lt. Robert N. Getty, left, wearing cap. (Photo by Christian Barthelmess. Smithsonian Institution, National Anthropological Archives.)*

15

16

17. Desar, Apache scout with the
10th U.S. Cavalry, New Mexico.
(Photo by Henry A. Schmidt,
1892. Courtesy of the Museum
of New Mexico.)

Crook retreated into Wyoming Territory, and Custer's defeat on June 25 turned the whole campaign into a humiliation for the army. In the subsequent months of campaigning, however, Indians continued to serve with the army's columns. Moreover, their own war parties were active, with army encouragement.[22]

On the southern Plains the Comanches held a position somewhat similar to that of the Sioux in the north, and they too ultimately found that they had created a host of allies for their conquerors. They had dominated the region by their numbers and forced some weaker peoples, such as the eastern Apaches, virtually off the Plains. By the post–Civil War period they were much reduced by disease, but the bands farther removed from white settlement still intended to continue their traditional way of life as long as they could. Their enemies included many of the smaller tribes of the area, both indigenous peoples and those removed from the East by the federal government. Various small groups had associated themselves for self-defense without much regard for language or other cultural considerations. In 1874 Richard Pratt recruited scouts from the "affiliated bands" at the Wichita Agency, near Fort Sill in the Indian Territory. In October he had a detachment including men of no fewer than ten tribes: Wichitas, Pawnees, Tehuacanas, Wacos, Keechis, Caddos, Delawares, and one each from the Araphaoes, Shawnees, and Comanches.[23]

The Tonkawas in the post–Civil War period had continued their special relationship with the whites, while remaining pariahs among the other tribes because of their cannibalism. Whether they ate human flesh as an article of diet or for religious reasons only, they were at intervals the victims of attack by other tribes that believed some of their members had been killed and eaten by the hated Tonkawas. They lived near the Wichita agency in Indian Territory after removal from Texas in 1859, but in 1862 most of them died in a massacre staged by several tribes, which may have resulted from their Confederate sympathies. Most of the survivors returned to Texas and offered their services to the Confederates in return for being allowed to live in their old homeland. While some of the men scouted for the Southern frontier forces, the rest remained about the settlements, regarded by the whites as beggars and thieves.[24]

In 1867 the Texas state government, which had been looking after the Tonkawas, persuaded the army to take responsibility for them. The army established them at the new Fort Griffin, Texas, on the Clear Fork of the Brazos River. The men willingly served as scouts, and the army in return provided rations for them and their families. Their very existence depended on the post, for they did not dare venture far from it for fear of their enemies; they were too weak to face any further losses. They wanted to live in Texas, but there was no land available to the federal government in that state to provide a reservation for them. The Bureau of Indian Affairs was unwilling to assume responsibility for the Tonkawas unless they could be moved to a permanent reservation, yet the tribe's leaders were unwilling to move to Indian Territory, for they were sure that such a move would mean extermination at the hands of their enemies.[25]

Despite accusations of cowardice, the services of the Tonkawa men as scouts were acknowledged to be invaluable. Indeed, no expedition out of Fort Griffin was complete without them, and some who were not enlisted scouts volunteered to accompany the soldiers. Some officers acknowledged that much of whatever success the Fort Griffin troops enjoyed was due to their skill, and the demanding Colonel Ranald Mackenzie was glad to have them with him. Lieutenant Robert Carter of Mackenzie's Fourth Cavalry could not free himself from condescension toward the Tonkawas, even in describing how they saved his life, but his detailed accounts of Mackenzie's campaigns make it clear how indispensable they were.[26]

Nonetheless, white attitudes toward them remained ambivalent. Observers described them as drunken, dirty, and debauched; the establishments on "the Flat" below the fort, which catered to soldiers and buffalo hunters, helped the Tonkawas to acquire this reputation. By 1872 the officer in command of the scout detachment declared that only ten out of a detachment of twenty-four were not so "demoralized" as to be unfit for duty as scouts. Many of the local civilians regarded them with contempt and distrust, yet some thought of them as friends and appreciated their role in defending the settlers. In 1868 Tonkawas returning from a successful expedition held a scalp dance, and both soldiers and local residents attended, thus tacitly joining in celebrating the victory over the common enemy. Most of them were known to the whites only by their English nicknames, such as McCord, Old Henry, Johnson, Job, and Canteen.[27]

Richard Pratt, who commanded the Tonkawas in 1873–74, made considerable efforts to control drunkenness and establish some order among them. Whether his efforts were the cause or not, the Tonkawas rendered useful service in the 1874–75 Red River war. Afterward, however, their occupation was virtually gone. In 1872 a general order from the Adjutant General's Office had prohibited the further issuing of army rations to Indians at any post, with the exception of enlisted scouts or occasional visiting chiefs. Since the majority of the Tonkawas were old men, women, and children with no other means of subsistence, the current post commander evaded the order. In 1874 unequivocal general orders forced the post commander, Lieutenant Colonel George P. Buell, to stop issuing rations to any of the 119 Tonkawas and 26 associated Lipans living near the post, except scouts. At Buell's urging, the Interior Department had purchased some cows and goats for these Indians, in the hope that they would become self-supporting, but they were still desperately short of food.[28]

Buell, with whom the scouts had served on many occasions, was distressed at seeing loyal allies starving on his doorstep. He wrote to higher authority that "while disclaiming any intention to reflect on any branch of the government," he thought "that these Indians should be cared for by someone." General Sheridan endorsed Buell's recommendation, calling the Tonkawas "a very deserving people." All the same, they remained at Fort Griffin, with an army officer as their de facto agent, until 1884, when the remaining 92 consented to move to Indian Territory. In the early 1930s there were 6 persons, all past middle age, who spoke the Tonkawa language, out of some 40 people claiming the tribal name; forty years later there were 57 who called themselves Tonkawas. It may be hard to see any benefit that accrued to them from their association with the whites, but it is equally hard to imagine what alternatives they had. As far as they could tell, any other course would have meant that there would be no Tonkawas at all.[29]

Indian allies played their part in conflicts in the Northwest, but here patterns of intertribal hostility are less clear. The Salishan and Shahaptin language peoples of the Columbia Plateau engaged in intermittent hostility with the Shoshonean people located to the south. Both of these groups probably considered their real enemies to be the Blackfeet and the Sioux, Cheyennes, and Arapahoes they encountered on their buffalo-hunting trips east of the Rockies. These trips had engendered alliances among various of the Plateau tribes, and also with tribes to the east, especially the Crows. The coalition of the Plateau tribes against the whites in the 1850s marked a high point of unified resistance, broken most conspicuously by that portion of the Nez Perces who furnished scouts for Governor Isaac Stevens and Colonel George Wright. By the 1870s, these patterns of alliance cracked under the pressures of choice imposed by whites. In the Nez Perce and Bannock wars of 1877 and 1878, tribes turned against each other less from deep-seated hostilities than from expediency and potential profit.[30]

An animosity of long standing between Bannocks and Nez Perces no doubt contributed to the Bannocks' readiness to furnish scouts to General O. O. Howard in his operations against the Nez Perces in 1877. Howard, the "Christian general," was distressed by the Bannocks' general insubordination and their tendency to kill and scalp without discrimination. They were the only troops under his command, however, who could maintain contact with the retreating Nez Perces in their flight over the Rockies. The Bannocks also displayed a great interest in acquiring Nez Perce horses.[31]

The Nez Perces had been on strong terms of friendship and alliance with the Flatheads and the Crows, but these tribes knew too well the probable consequences of antagonizing the whites. When the Nez Perces passed through the Flathead country in western Montana Territory, the Flatheads informed them that they retained their old friendship but were also friends of the white settlers in the region. The Flatheads would help the Nez Perces on their way, but would not tolerate any violence toward local whites. Relations between local Flatheads and whites must have been friendly for the Indians to take such a stand, but a common-sense appraisal of the situation must also have influenced them.[32]

The Crows are said to have answered requests for scouts against the Nez Perces by saying, "The Crow heart is Nez Perce, and the Nez Perce heart is Crow." Yet a number of Crows went off with Lieutenant Gustavus Doane and other officers to serve against their old allies. They confined their operations largely to stealing Nez Perce horses, and their depredations were indeed a blow to the fugitives' mobility. The Nez Perces were noted for the quality of their horses, and the temptation must have been strong.[33]

That the Bannocks had not joined the army from any special love of the whites was demonstrated the following year, when they in turn went to war. Mismanagement and settlers' encroachments had deprived them of virtually all subsistence; General Crook judged that they had decided to fight while strength remained. Their leader, Buffalo Horn, had scouted for the army in various campaigns; he may not have gained much impression of the army's efficiency, but in any case he and his people were desperate. The Bannocks found, in their turn, that most of the other tribes would not support them. General Howard found, early in the campaign, that his efforts to recruit scouts from among various Northwest tribes met with little response. This "unusual reluctance" he attributed to efforts made by the Bannocks to inspire a general uprising in the interior Northwest. After the army, with some help from a few Paiute and Christian Nez Perce scouts, had headed off the Bannocks' drive into Oregon, some other tribes turned against the hostiles. The Umatillas watched from a neutral hilltop while an infantry force stood off the hostiles outside the Umatilla agency; they then offered to take up the pursuit of the defeated Indians, for which, being mounted, they were much better equipped than the infantry. Inevitably a suspicion lingers that if the hostiles had prospered, the Umatillas would have been equally ready to join them.[34]

The Crows again played a part in the Bannock war, in a manner that suggested both their ambivalence and their self-interest. When Colonel Nelson Miles sought Crow allies to bolster his little force of mounted infantry in heading off some fleeing Bannocks near Yellowstone Park, the Crow chiefs were unreceptive, on the ostensible grounds that the command was too small. A number of warriors, however, declaring that they were not afraid of anything, followed Miles after he left their camp. The excursion began to resemble more an Indian war party than a military expedition. With a force of 35 soldiers and 75 Crows, Miles surprised the Bannocks and captured the lot. The Crows made off with the Bannocks' horses.[35]

The episode suggests the divided opinions of the Crows on these questions of war or neutrality. They were not on hostile terms with the Bannocks, and the chiefs were trying to exercise their usual restraint. "The young and the restless," however, slipped away in hopes of glory and horses. Something very similar had happened during the Nez Perce war.[36]

Were these scouts, serving against people toward whom they felt no long-standing animosity and some of whom were former allies, simply mercenaries for the whites? This question involves a study of individual motivation more than tribal politics. Individual scouts went to war, as some of the episodes just cited indicate, for reasons that were by no means wholly disinterested. On the Plains and in the Northwest there were constant references to the acquisition of horses from defeated hostiles as a reward for scout service. Crook held a grand distribution of captured Cheyenne horses after the Red Fork battle. Mackenzie apologized to his superiors for distributing horses to his Tonkawas and Seminole Negroes, explaining that they had to be given some reward for dangerous reconnaissances far from the main command. The matter was of concern to some civil officials because these animals might be the original property of white citizens, stolen by the hostiles.[37]

This sort of thing was not uniquely characteristic of scouts, however. Horse stealing had been one of the principal forms of intertribal war since the introduction of the animal. The possession of large numbers of horses was of both practical importance and status value. Although many tribes conducted horse-stealing raids on foot, war on a more serious scale required more than one horse for each man—one reason why the cavalry could not run down Indians who had any sort of start. Buffalo-hunting Indians required horses for obvious reasons. Horse stealing from any tribe not on the closest terms of friendship and alliance was not only acceptable, but one of the most proper activities for young men. The Crows gloried in their reputation as accomplished takers of horses. Military historian John Keegan has observed:

Soldiers have always looted; indeed, the robbing of the enemy, particularly an enemy killed in single combat, and for preference, of an object of display for its intrinsic or symbolic value— the finery or weapons of the vanquished—has always provided an important motive for fighting. But an economic motive operates too.[38]

For many Indian cultures the horse served all these purposes.

Pay also attracted many scouts. Reservation Indians in particular learned to appreciate the value of pay and soldier's rations to supplement the meager rations provided on the reservation. The value was accentuated for such groups as the Seminole Negroes and Tonkawas, who had no reservation and were entirely dependent on the army. These people were mercenaries in the sense that they were selling their marketable skills to the only purchaser available.

Indian scouts, then, might serve for reasons that were decidedly mercenary and self-interested. But this in itself did not distinguish scouts from other Indian fighting men. To gain in material wealth and status was for most of these men a perfectly legitimate aspiration, and one recognized by their culture. To acquire these things at the expense of bitter enemies was a virtue; to do so at the expense of people to whom one owed little or no loyalty was easily rationalized.

Less tangible reasons could be found for the readiness of scouts to join up, however. Reservation life, as Indians perceived it, was itself a factor. Official theory and policy on the reservations were dedicated to turning Indians into yeoman farmers. Except for people already accustomed to agriculture, the process of reeducation was both unattractive and painful. Indians without the necessary skills, living on land allotted them because it was unattractive to whites, commonly found farming unprofitable besides. For men accustomed to hunting and to war, the chance to escape for a time must have been powerfully attractive. "To Apaches a reservation is a prison," observed the Apache James Kaywaykla. Historian William B. White illuminates this point with his conclusion that the regimented existence of the reservation made it difficult to discharge normal human aggression—of which the frustration of such a life must have been a fruitful source.[39]

Such considerations would not apply, of course, to those with little or no experience of reservation life, or those who, like the Crows in the 1870s had been able to keep up a more or less traditional way of life while ostensibly under an agent. In 1868 Crook was able to enlist some young Paiute men immediately after their chiefs had surrendered; he specifically told them that they were going to fight the Pit River Indians in California. Lieutenant W. R. Parnell described them as "wild by nature," and he thought they were eager to ease the pain of defeat by beating someone else; he concluded that stories of warrior ancestors and the sheer excitement of war were powerful influences on these young men. Parnell's reflections may seem odd coming from a professional soldier, especially an Irishman who had served in the British as well as the United States Army. In any case, the eagerness of these young men to enlist indicates that they found the offer attractive.[40]

The role of glory, as such, in the Plains culture has received a thorough examination from the students of those tribes. The reminiscences of old warriors point out how the aspirations of the young men were directed toward war. There are any number of stories of youngsters who ran off to join war parties before their parents considered them old enough. A little more maturity might bring enough judgment to create fear, but few were willing to bear the odium that went with a conspicuous reluctance to go to war. Discretion was allowed and even required of older men, but not for the young. All this, to be sure, was perfectly compatible with tactics designed to minimize loss of life. Otherwise such a state of affairs could not have endured.[41]

Obviously such generalizations do not apply to all western Indians. The Pueblo peoples, notably, seem to have regarded war as an unpleasant occasional necessity. The Warm Springs scouts could see no good in exterminating the Paiutes. Many other people, even on the Plains, are said to have limited the casualties inflicted on the enemy—an attitude not incompatible with a glorification of warlike exploits. Authorities claim that some Plains tribes avoided killing all their enemies—assuming they were capable of doing so—because then there would be no one left to fight. The Papagos required the slayer of an enemy to undergo days of ritual purification. This custom was apparently a matter of contamination rather than absolution for sin, but it suggests that killing was not approached in a casual or gleeful spirit. It also limited the military value of such tribes from the army's viewpoint.[42]

Kit Carson required Zuñis and Hopis to furnish scouts against the Navajos because he suspected them of aiding the enemy to some degree. They proved useful, but a major reason for recruiting them was to make them prove their "loyalty" and to alienate them from the Navajos. Afterward they would supposedly have no choice but adherence to the whites. In 1879 Nelson Miles insisted that the Assiniboins furnish scouts for his expedition against Sitting Bull and the Sioux holdouts in Canada. The Assiniboins complained that they were caught between the Sioux and the whites. Miles also recruited the Bannocks he had captured the previous year, who were still prisoners of war at Fort Keogh. According to reporter John Finerty, the Assiniboins and Bannocks ran out on W. P. Clark's scout detachment when they fought the Sioux on Milk River, Montana Territory, while the Cheyennes and Crows stayed and fought. Presumably the purpose of alienating them from the Sioux was served to some extent. Otherwise "conscription" in this fashion was of limited and chancy value.[43]

It is evident that Indians who fought for the army against other tribes did not consider themselves renegades or traitors to a hypothetical "Indian" people. Historical emphasis on Indian–white conflict tends to obscure the fact that Indians interacted long before white contact became significant. Intertribal conflicts and alliances had an importance often more immediate than any problems or pressures created by whites. For many Indians an alliance with the army offered hope of turning the tables on a powerful enemy who represented an immediate and obvious menace. In some cases the army represented survival itself. Even chiefs who saw clearly enough that the whites would bring about drastic change in their own lives often decided pragmatically that resistance would only mean catastrophe, and that rendering assistance might work to their advantage.

Aside from such considerations of high policy, individual warriors found various gratifications through scout service. Material wealth, especially horses, could be obtained, and with it status. Men trained as warriors could acquire the military prestige their society admired. For warriors confined to reservations, scouting eased the painful processes of enforced acculturation, offering both temporary release and a means of assimilation that was suited to their inclinations and ministered to their pride. For some the shame of defeat was eased by the assurance that their courage and skill were valued by the victors. All this could be achieved at the expense of people to whom one felt no overruling obligation, and who might be hated enemies.

Chapter Eight

The Other Good Indians:
The Intratribal Conflict

In 1868 the Comanche chief Mow-way, with other army prisoners, was transferred from Fort Bascom, New Mexico, to Fort Leavenworth. Along the way one of the prisoners became ill. To Mow-way's surprise, the whites cared for the sick man and made every effort to save him. When the man died, Mow-way expected that the whites would throw his body on the prairie for the wolves; instead, they put him in a box with all his possessions and buried him in a carefully dug hole, which was neatly mounded over. "I could not understand why such mean people, as I thought the white people were, should be so kind to an Indian in sickness and after death."[1]

Probably the white man who recorded this story was amused by the ignorance of the poor benighted savage. For Mow-way, however, the actions of these whites were indeed incomprehensible and inconsistent with his previous knowledge of them. There was no reason for him to be versed in the Judeo-Christian tradition, nineteenth-century humanitarianism, or the military code regarding the treatment of prisoners. His previous experience, largely limited to conflict, suggested that the whites would be glad to have the prisoner die; they had given many indications that they wanted his people to die.

Mow-way's story should remind us of just how incomprehensible and inconsistent the actions of people can seem if one is not aware of their view of the world or the circumstances under which they have to make decisions. It would be a mistake to assume that American Indians did things for motives that seemed obvious to whites, yet it would also be a mistake to assume that any Indian was simply a collection of culturally conditioned reflexes. Mow-way had imagined that all whites, for whatever mysterious, evil reasons, wanted death for all Comanches. Similarly, many whites assumed a monolithic, unchanging "Indian."

Nothing about the Indian-scout phenomenon aroused such puzzlement, disbelief, and distrust among whites, military and civilian, as the willingness of some Indians to serve against people of their own tribe. Intertribal hatreds were relatively easy to understand, if one could get past the idea that all Indians were simply "Indians." But for Brave Wolf the Cheyenne to express willingness to fight his own kinsmen if he were ordered to do so, or for Chato the Chiricahua Apache to track down the Chiricahuas led by Geronimo, was something that common preconceptions about Indians could hardly adjust to. Some whites simply refused to believe it and could never bring themselves to trust the reliability of these scouts—or the judgment of the officers who employed them.[2]

While some whites could only despise Indians, regardless of their relationship to whites, others preferred to think in terms of "good" and "bad" Indians. Bad Indians, of course, were those who offered resistance or refused to accept what the whites had in mind for them. Good Indians were those who were cooperative, willing to try at least some aspects of "civilization," or even to support white military operations. Chiefs such as Washakie of the Shoshones and Spotted Tail of the Sioux were Noble Red Men because they had ruled out armed resistance and sought the best terms they could get. Dogged resistants such as Sitting Bull were at best "sullen," if not demonic. The tendency of recent years among whites has been to reverse the categories; Spotted Tail is transformed into the betrayer of the "patriot chief" Crazy Horse, and the Indian scouts become mercenaries and traitors. The problem with both perceptions is that they are value-laden, shaped by the emotions of the moment, and hence do not allow for dispassionate examination of the facts. The fact that active hostiles frequently became scouts—and vice versa—confounds both the older and newer perceptions, and introduces us to the complexities of human behavior.[3]

Whites exploited intertribal hostilities and intratribal divisions from early colonial days on. Uncas and his Pequot followers supported the Puritans against their fellow Pequots in 1637;

Uncas became a dominant figure among New England Indians for decades. This is not to say that whites always exploited these divisions with full understanding or Machiavellian cleverness. Uncas probably thought he was exploiting the whites.[4]

Recent students of the Indian past have focused on factionalism and internal politics in an effort to understand tribal history. They have concluded that such divisions existed among tribal societies without outside intervention. Like humans everywhere, Indians were contentious. They disagreed and fought among themselves both before and after contact with whites. Whites sought to exploit Indian divisions, intertribal and intratribal, and Indians often sought white aid in these same conflicts.[5]

Indians responded in various ways to the pressures created by the white presence, even as they responded to pressures from other Indians. As the power and intentions of the whites became increasingly evident, with all the attendant deterioration of the conditions that made the accustomed life possible, chiefs and others had to determine appropriate courses of action. Policy determination was naturally a fruitful source of disagreement between leaders and groups that might or might not have differed over other matters.

Historians of African reaction to European colonialism have discovered great diversity of response among groups in any one region, particularly among peoples not subject to the rule of a centralized state, even a "backward" one. Regarding the reaction of people in southeast Morocco to the French, historian Ross E. Dunn finds that "trade, negotiation, and collaboration went on simultaneously with resistance" and that the overall response over three decades was "multifarious, fluctuating, and inconsistent." John Iliffe finds "rational calculation of interest and probable consequence" to be characteristic of Tanganyikan confrontation with the Germans, and emphasizes that the policies of governors and colonial officers were only one factor among many variables.[6]

George Crook likewise found Indian actions to be based on more than "savagery" and "wildness." The Bannocks went to war in 1878, he asserted, because their food supply was disappearing, the government was providing no adequate substitute, and if they waited too long they would be too weak to resist. If they were desperate, it was because they fully appreciated the situation.[7] Reporting to his superiors in 1883, Crook declared: "The reasoning power of the Indian from his own standpoint is unequaled." Indians were generally handicapped by ignorance of the whites' "manner of life," but once aware of the power of the federal government, they would accept the new order if they were treated with "common justice," a quality Crook found to be sadly lacking in U.S. Indian policy and administration.[8]

The point is worth emphasizing because much anthropological literature leaves an impression, on the layman at least, that Indians and other "primitive" people were so bound by culture and tribal ties that they were capable of only a stereotyped response to any situation. Although written with quite different intentions, such literature tends toward the same conclusion as that of nineteenth-century writers who assumed that the monolithic "Indian" was "hewn out of a rock," incapable of changing or learning from experience. Certainly culture conditions the actions of all of us, but if only one course of action were conceivable within a particular group, how does one explain the varied actions of the actual Indians, or the responses noted by the African historians? As Francis Jennings points out, the one choice never open to the Indians was to stay exactly the same.[9]

Indians often lacked information about the whites' intentions, values, and motives, and therefore developed defective policies and strategies. Certainly southwestern tribes accustomed to raiding in northern Mexico could not understand why the United States, having fought the Mexicans, should insist after 1848 that raiding in Mexico should cease. Still less could they understand how the whites, because they had beaten the Mexicans, should now claim to rule territory and people that the Mexican government had never been able to conquer or control. During the Civil War a well-informed Indian could have noted that the whites, with the same basic language, religion, and cultural heritage, were fighting a bloody war (killing more whites than there were Indians in the West) over the status of a people both sides regarded as alien and inferior. What rational explanation could there be for such actions?

The word "tribe" is used here as it is used in most writing about American Indians. The term does not imply, however, that there was some sort of centralized government that decided policy to be accepted by all members of the tribe. When we say that some Indians served as scouts "against their own tribe," we may be expressing a perception of the situation not at all similar to that of the persons involved. In an explanation of anthropologists' findings in this area, Robert Berkhofer emphasizes that the social organization of the groups involved might not be coextensive with the tribe as it was recognized by whites. In their own minds, people might owe overriding loyalty to a smaller group within the tribe. A chief's first responsibility might be to ensure the welfare of his particular band or division, whatever was happening to the rest of the tribe. Berkhofer questions whether Indian activities in a given situation should be evaluated as simply the result of white actions, or as "self-originated and creative responses to white-posed problems."[10] The history of the Indian scouts makes it clear that the tribe did not automatically command the loyalties of all its members.

Texans, for example, generally thought of the Comanches as a single menacing horde, yet the Penateka Comanches, whose range was located closest to white settlement in Texas, made an effort to achieve peace with the whites immediately before the Civil War, even to the extent of cooperating with the Texans in attacking other Comanches and Kiowas. The Comanches' particularly loose governmental system facilitated such a move. The Penatekas had always had a sense of separateness from the other bands, and most of their war leaders had died at the hands of the Texans in the 1840s. They accepted a reservation in Texas in the 1850s, but were driven from the state with the smaller tribes in 1859.[11]

The smaller Kiowa tribe had a more elaborate and cohesive governmental structure, including a single head chief. After 1865, however, the strains of factionalism and white pressures destroyed tribal cohesion. Most reports suggest that the head chief, Lone Wolf, lacked the personality or prestige to dominate other strong-willed chiefs. Kicking Bird (Striking Eagle), a rising young chief, had apparently decided by about 1870 that accommodation with the whites was the only sensible policy. On at least one occasion, however, he led a raid into Texas to silence talk that his stand was a sign of cowardice. Whites perceived Kicking Bird as a good Indian, while regarding more belligerent leaders as bad men and congenital criminals. Hence civil agents and military authorities sought to enhance Kicking Bird's position. At the end of the Red River war in 1875, the army asked Kicking Bird to designate those of his people who were most responsible for the troubles, in order that they could be removed to prison in Florida. This was Kicking Bird's opportunity to eliminate his opposition, but he is said to have undertaken the task with great reluctance. In any case he died soon after, allegedly from a curse placed on him by a powerful medicine man who was one of those imprisoned. Many of the Kiowas regarded Kicking Bird with respect in later years, and hindsight makes it clear that resistance could hardly have produced any good.[12]

Another Kiowa who chose the path of collaboration was Big Bow, and his case raises the question of the part religious attitudes played in such choices. Big Bow was a formidable warrior and raider, hence a very bad man in the eyes of soldiers and Indian agents. Many Kiowas were leery of him because he was a complete skeptic in religious matters; he refused to try any means of invoking supernatural aid, preferring to rely on his own abilities. At the end of the Red River war he accepted the mission of persuading many of his people to come in off the Staked Plain to the reservation to surrender. He rendered this service in return for a promise from the military that he would receive no punishment for past deeds. Obviously this was a quite pragmatic accommodation with the new order, but one may ask if his religious doubts rendered him less ready to die for the old values and way of life.[13]

Big Bow's skepticism does not invalidate the usual assertions about the importance of the supernatural in the life of the Plains tribes, and of most Indians under their traditional culture. It was evidently possible, however, for some Indians to entertain doubts. The traditional faith of many Indians was shaken or destroyed by the various effects of the white presence: diseases, disappearance of game, evident technological superiority, and sheer power. For most Indians, religion was a part of the everyday, practical world. Our concept of the "supernatural" removes such matters from the everyday world in a way that most Indian cultures did not; these forces were among the most real and important parts of the "natural" order. Many Indians testified that at some point after the coming of the whites, the old religion ceased to work; in the old days it had worked, but now the same calls failed to produce a response. The fact that many Kiowas became Christian converts within a few years after the wars ceased seems significant in this connection. Not all Indians responded in this way, however; some only clung the more stubbornly to the old beliefs, while others attempted some amalgamation of Christian and traditional elements, as in the Ghost Dance.[14]

No one seems to have asked at the time whether the crumbling of former faith, or the desire to be associated with the manifestly greater medicine of the whites, had anything to do with enlistment as a scout. These factors could have had particular importance in the many cases of men who enlisted soon after surrender. The obvious power of the whites in war indicated that they must have a greater command than the Indians over supernatural powers. Such responses must obviously have been a matter of both the particular culture and individual personality. Many scouts seem to have clung to traditional beliefs, performing proper ceremonies to ensure safety and success, with or without the approval of their military superiors. Yet continued belief in certain powers might not be inconsistent with a conviction that the whites had command over other, very strong ones. For most Indians, what the Crows called the "other side camp" housed a multitude of powers that might intervene in the affairs of this world. Those scouts of various tribes who were especially anxious to obtain the full army uniform may have been seeking a device that would convey to them some of the white men's power.[15]

In his study of Protestant missions among the Indians, Robert Berkhofer concludes that acceptance of Christianity usually accompanied a considerable degree of acculturation in other respects. The degree of acculturation varied widely among groups of scouts, but those scouts who had tribesmen still actively hostile were less likely to be among the more acculturated. However, one may recall the Christian Nez Perces, who prayed, read the Bible in their own tongue, and kept the Sabbath, and who provided useful service against other tribes and against their non-Christian fellow tribesmen.[16]

Recruiting Indians of groups closely allied to the current enemy was a favorite tactic of George Crook. Then and since, such a move surprised and worried observers for whom enemies were enemies—unified fighting forces representing a cohesive entity. Yet there were certain obvious benefits to be gained by this tactic. Such scouts were more likely to be familiar with the country in which campaigning was done; they would know, for instance, where favorite camping grounds were located, or travel routes not immediately obvious to the outsider. They would have a better chance of knowing what reactions or procedures the enemy might follow in a particular case. John Bourke noted the Sioux and Cheyenne scouts' "complete familiarity with the plans and designs of the hostile Sioux and Cheyennes." In 1880 Luther S. "Yellowstone" Kelly watched some Cheyennes, with one Sioux, track down three Sioux raiders, their one-time allies.

Only a short time before these same Cheyenne scouts had been hostile Indians and had doubtless been in much the same predicament as the Sioux ahead . . . every detail of the chase was clear to Yellow Bull; every artifice used approved itself to his understanding, and he probably knew the very spot from which the Sioux would watch the pursuit.

The Sioux were cornered and surrendered after a conversation with the Cheyenne leader White Bull.[17]

Another possibility was opened up by such tribal divisions. The words "scout" and "spy" were used almost interchangeably in the nineteenth century, but only a little information is available about espionage in the Indian wars. In late 1876, Crook had Sioux and Cheyenne agents working under cover in the hostile camps. Before the Red Fork battle, a Cheyenne spy named Sitting Bear reported information on the location of the enemy camps. On the San Carlos reservation in Arizona Territory in the 1880s, certain "confidential Indians" reported at times to Lieutenant Britton Davis, in charge of the recently hostile Chiricahua Apaches. The Chiricahuas later claimed to have known all along who these agents were. Espionage during the Indian wars may not have had all the sophistication of the twentieth century, but apparently it was, as always, an accompaniment of war.[18]

Crook expected that scouts would play a role in breaking tribal unity; "their disintegration," he noted, was one of his ultimate goals. Yet such disunity often existed beforehand. Many tribal societies lacked institutions for accommodating differences of opinion or personality. Consensus was the accepted ideal, but the failure to achieve consensus left no method of carrying on together. Unlike the national state, tribal society was not organized to compel the unwilling to perpetual conformity.[19]

The Teton Sioux and the Northern Cheyennes in the post–Civil War period provide examples of the kinds of tensions that could turn tribesmen and allies against each other, and the way in which whites could take advantage of these divisions for military and other ends. Some testimony is available from both tribes which had not previously been evaluated by historians, particularly in connection with the motives of Indian scouts. Some of these scouts indicated quite rational and pragmatic reasons for serving the army. A brief examination of the history and society of these tribes is necessary for full understanding.

The people the whites called Sioux were certainly conscious of kinship of language and culture, but at no historic period were they united in action. The Yankton Sioux displayed their willingness to fight other Sioux during the Civil War, when they already had a history of friendly relations with whites. Those Sioux who became "the Sioux" to most whites were the Teton Sioux, or Lakota, dwelling on the Plains west of the Missouri in the nineteenth century. They had seven major divisions that were further divided into bands. Edwin Denig noted that the "soldier" societies gave considerable force to the decisions of chiefs, but that the personality of a band chief largely determined the actions and character of that band. Other tribes confronted with the Sioux advance had not been able to make any lasting peace with them because of the lack of unity; no agreement with one band, or several, was binding on all. The United States would encounter the same problem. The Tetons' confrontation with the United States, however, exposed weaknesses in the system which had never appeared as such in conflict with other Indians.[20]

The Cheyennes and Arapahoes, being much smaller tribes, exhibited somewhat greater unity. Both spoke Algonkian languages and they became close allies in the eighteenth century, probably as much for practical military reasons as because of distant kinship of language. The two became allies of the Sioux in the early nineteenth century, and there was some intermarriage. In the 1860s, this triple alliance became the major obstacle to white travel and settlement on the central and northern Plains.[21]

However it may have appeared to the whites, this alliance was neither monolithic nor free of internal tension. Disagreements that arose from cultural conflict and white pressure existed both within the separate tribes and between the tribes. In the latter 1860s, major portions of the Brulés and Oglalas, ranging on the North and South Platte, were seeking accommodation; Spotted Tail of the Brulés was their most prominent figure. The effort to establish forts and a major travel route on the Bozeman Trail helped to consolidate resistance, but Spotted Tail remained the advocate of peace. He was fully aware that the whites' power could not be resisted successfully.[22]

While most of the Oglala Sioux—Red Cloud's folk—were involved in hostilities with the army along the Bozeman Trail in 1867, a few were apparently seeking accommodation, and were even ready to assist the soldiers. In the spring of that year, the commanding officer of Fort Sedgwick, Colorado Territory, on the South Platte, reported that " 'Red Bead' the friendly Sioux encamped near this post." Red Bead was leader of a small band of Oglalas, perhaps among those who for some years had shown a preference for living near the Oregon Trail forts, where certain luxuries were available. At the end of June, Red Bead undertook to guide a small detachment under Lieutenant Lyman Kidder, carrying orders to Custer and the Seventh Cavalry, encamped somewhere on the Republican. This party never arrived, and Custer himself conducted a search. His Delaware scouts found the remains of the whole party on Beaver Creek, where they had all been killed and mutilated by hostile Sioux. Red Bead's body had been less mutilated than the other corpses; his scalp had been removed, but was left lying by his side.[23]

The Northern Cheyennes had also given indication that they wanted peace, whatever the attitude of their Sioux allies. Several chiefs, included the respected Dull Knife, met with Colonel Carrington in June 1866 to discuss peace; they declined Carrington's suggestion that they become his allies, saying that they were not strong enough to fight the Sioux, but indicated they were prepared to be neutral if there were no further white encroachments. Soon after leaving Carrington these chiefs met a large party of Sioux warriors, who struck the Cheyenne leaders with their bows as if counting coup on an enemy; thus they displayed their anger at what they considered to be betrayal, a breaking of the united front they were trying to maintain. This action was a supreme insult, but the Cheyennes were too far outnumbered to do anything about it. Dull Knife and other Cheyennes were prominent in the defeat of William Fetterman the following December.[24]

After the Treaty of 1868, the Sioux and Cheyennes hardly presented a solid front to the whites. Large numbers were located at agencies eventually established near Fort Robinson, in northwest Nebraska, and on the Missouri River. A large minority persisted in the nomadic life in Dakota, Montana, and Wyoming territories, refusing to accept any penetration of the region. Sitting Bull of the Hunkpapas was their most prominent figure, the symbol of irreconcilability. These "winter roamers" were joined in the summer by a large proportion of the agency bands; the "summer roamers" preferred the relative certainty of government rations during the winter months. Red Cloud the Oglala was the prominent figure among this group, which of course was regarded by civil agents and the military as a disturbing element. Spotted Tail was the leading man among those remaining at the agency the year around. The basic policy of the government was always aimed at making reservation Indians of all these groups.[25]

An episode at Red Cloud agency in October 1874 suggests the division of attitudes among the Indians there, and has significance in relation to later events. An attempt by the agent to raise the United States flag over the agency aroused vehement demonstrations of opposition by the Indians, many of them "summer roamers" who had come in for the winter. The agent requested help from Fort Robinson, and Lieutenant Emmet Crawford arrived with twenty-two cavalrymen to find several hundred belligerent warriors apparently eager for a fight. When violence seemed imminent, Young-Man-Afraid-of-His-Horse and other chiefs at the head of a number of agency warriors intervened to protect the soldiers and to make it clear that they would not have any clashes with the army. According to a secondhand account, a young Oglala leader named Three Bears also played an important part in the rescue of the detachment, and Crawford later treated Three Bears as a good friend. Three Bears's part in this affair is particularly significant in light of his later role as a leader of scouts.[26]

There are clear indications from this same period, the early and middle 1870s, that there were strains and antagonisms within the Sioux-Cheyenne alliance; the close relationship of the two tribes generated ambivalent feelings among the weaker party, the Northern Cheyennes. In the early 1870s, Fort Fetterman, Wyoming, was a de facto agency for the Northern Cheyennes, who received their government rations there. Colonel George Woodward, the post commander, became well acquainted with the "old man chiefs" Dull Knife and Little Wolf, and learned something of their attitudes toward the Sioux. They strongly professed a desire for peace and a separate reservation on the Yellowstone, and Woodward understood that they preferred to be apart from the Sioux. They thought their more numerous allies imposed upon them, and they found Sioux sexual mores less strict than their own. The chiefs were probably telling Woodward what they thought he would like to hear, and stressing their independence of the more belligerent bands that were rallying around Sitting Bull. Yet the attempt to make peace with Colonel Carrington in 1866, and the horse-whipping of the Cheyenne chiefs by Sioux warriors that followed, lend substance to Woodward's understanding of the situation.[27]

There are other indications of the tensions in the alliance, existing alongside close and comradely relations. In 1865 the Southern Cheyennes, visiting their northern brethren after Sand Creek, were of the opinion that the northerners had become much like the Sioux. Many members of the Dog Soldier society had intermarried with the Sioux; this group had become virtually a separate division of the tribe. Such acculturation is often disturbing to conservatives, especially older people who have seen the changes taking place. Among many differences, the Cheyennes were notably strict in their rules regarding premarital chastity for women; the Sioux were by no means indifferent to such matters, but were less demanding than the Cheyennes. Probably this was the matter to which Dull Knife and Little Wolf alluded in conversation with Woodward. The Cheyenne warrior Wooden Leg tells us that Little Wolf did not speak Sioux and did not care to associate with the Sioux too much; the Sioux therefore did not know him well, and as a result he would be placed in an embarrassing situation in 1876. At the same time Wooden Leg, member of a younger generation than Little Wolf's, does not seem to have shared his feelings.[28]

The 1876 campaign against the Sioux, intended to force the last recalcitrants onto the reservation, exposed a number of weaknesses in the army; at the same time, it also exposed the divisions and antagonisms among the Teton Sioux and the Sioux-Cheyenne-Arapaho alliance. The events of that year subjected these people to severe pressures as they sought a course of action that would allow them to survive on acceptable terms.

At the beginning of the summer campaign, it appeared that the Sioux and Cheyennes were in fact unified. Crook tried to recruit allies from among the Sioux and Cheyennes at the Nebraska agencies. He had no luck, a fact he attributed to the opposition of the civil agents. Within a few months a substantial portion of those at Red Cloud agency had moved out to join the designated hostiles for the summer hunt in the Yellowstone country. It seems unwise to assume that they would have been willing to enlist except for the agents' opposition. If they had enlisted, however, they would have constituted a considerable advantage for the army. Some chiefs had expressed willingness. Crook told them that the soldiers would do the fighting, while the Sioux scouts would find the hostiles and "gobble up the ponies"; it would be better, he suggested, for the reservation Sioux to get the "bad Indians'" horses than somebody else. If the Sioux did not sign up, he would have to call on the Crows, their hated enemies. Bourke notes that the Sioux allies would have been hostages for the good behavior of those remaining on the reservation, and that a sharp line of separation would have been drawn between friend and foe. Their enlistment would also have cut off the supply of guns and ammunition that the army was convinced flowed from the agencies to the hostiles. Failing to recruit these Sioux and Cheyennes, Crook did call upon the Crows and Shoshones, who accompanied him to the Rosebud.[29]

The victory of united Sioux and Cheyennes over Custer would seem to be evidence of their solidarity, yet incidents connected with that very battle indicate that the Sioux were not taking the loyalty of their allies for granted; in fact, these incidents suggest suspicion and distrust. Five young Arapahoes had left the Fort Robinson area on a little raid against the Shoshones. At this time virtually all their people were at the agencies and were having no part of the current conflict. In the Bighorn region the five ran into the assembling Sioux, who accused them of scouting for the army; vouched for by the Cheyenne leader Two Moon, they fought in the battle against Custer to demonstrate their good faith.[30]

The other incident on the Little Bighorn is even more revealing. As the battle was closing, Little Wolf arrived at the campground with his small personal band. The aroused Sioux accused him and his warriors of being enemy scouts; Little Wolf angrily pointed out that he would hardly bring women, children, and camp equipage with him on such a mission. Other Cheyennes vouched for Little Wolf, and there the matter ended. Obviously the hostiles were in a highly suspicious mood, even before their erstwhile allies enlisted as scouts against them. Undoubtedly some of these Sioux had been at Red Cloud agency when Crook made his offer; they clearly found it quite conceivable that the offer had been accepted by some men.[31]

In fact, some Sioux were serving with the troops that summer, but they constituted a rather special case. With Custer's Arikara scouts rode five Sioux, apparently Hunkpapas married to Arikara women. This may seem surprising, in view of all that has been said about the long hostility between these two tribes. Yet the two peoples had long held periodic truces for trade; a sort of mutual dependence seems to have existed that could not be broken, even by bitter hostilities. Western reminiscences contain frequent references to individual members of one tribe living with some other tribe, apparently adults who had made the choice rather than captives taken in childhood. Marriage was a common reason, for many western tribes were matrilocal—that is, the husband lived with his wife's family. With or without the attractions of the exotic woman, many such men may have been restless or discontented, perhaps misfits in their own society, looking for greener pastures elsewhere. Some of them may also have been outcasts who had offended their own people or were fleeing a blood feud. This speculation seems to challenge the usual generalizations about the closeness of kinship and other ties in a tribal society, and about the ethnocentrism of such societies. Some persons, however, may have found these ties a little too binding. It is not entirely surprising to find such men serving as scouts, if they were indeed restless and adventuresome.[32]

One might think that these Sioux scouts faced a moral dilemma. There is no indication that any of them failed to do what was asked of him, any more than the Arikaras. There is no way of ascertaining whether or not they anticipated having to go against the Sioux when they enlisted for the current six-month period, or whether they had any misgivings or scruples. W. H. C. Bowen, a former frontier officer, wrote that in his experience the men of the Plains tribes were always to be depended on for the term of enlistment, and that he had never heard of a case of treachery. Whites experienced with Plains Indians often remarked that Indians were rigid in expecting fulfillment of promises; nothing should be promised that was not certain of fulfillment. No people find it easy to live up to their highest ideals, but these Sioux with Custer probably believed that their honor was involved in their oath of enlistment. The actions of one are suggestive. Left Hand's enlistment ran out in the course of the expedition, and he left the column after his discharge. After the Little Bighorn, his dead body was discovered in the abandoned hostile campsite. Perhaps his own people killed him, but it is more likely that he was killed fighting the whites. The end of his hitch had apparently released him from a moral conflict.[33]

It was in the fall of 1876 that the army really began to attach Sioux, Cheyennes, and Arapahoes to its own cause. Acting on his belief that the bands at Red Cloud agency were supplying both men and munitions to the designated hostiles, Crook surrounded the camps of the bands of Red Cloud and Red Leaf and took away both their arms and their horses. Then he again offered to enlist men of the Sioux, Cheyennes, and Arapahoes as scouts. He got almost the entire strength of the agency Arapahoes, but only five Cheyennes; the most interesting aspect of the affair, however, was that most of the sixty Sioux scouts who signed up were from Red Cloud agency, especially from the bands who had just been disarmed and dismounted. Relatively few came from the trusted "friendlies" under Spotted Tail.[34]

Fortunately, we have some good evidence as to the motives of the men who enlisted, knowing they might have to fight other Sioux. William Garnett, who interpreted for these scouts during their service with the army, later explained their motives as he gathered them from their conversations and conferences with Crook. The younger men, including Three Bears, concluded after the army's crackdown that fall that Red Cloud's policy of obstruction had only put their people in bad odor with the government. They hoped that by serving with the whites they could acquire favor and better treatment for their bands. They were particularly concerned about an Interior Department plan to transfer them to the Indian Territory. Discussing matters with Crook at Fort Fetterman before marching against the hostiles, they told him that they did not want to be moved to some strange place, but to have a reservation in their own country. They wanted Crook to use his influence against the Indian Territory scheme. Crook had, in fact, already registered a protest on this matter and he would continue to support Spotted Tail's and Red Cloud's resistance to agencies on the Missouri River. John Bourke's diary version of the same conference indicates that the Indians did indeed express their concern over the removal proposal, indicating particularly that they wanted nothing done or decided about the matter while they were away fighting. According to Bourke, the scouts also had much to say about being given captured horses (one of the necessities of life) and about proper rationing for their families while they were away.[35]

Three Bears's presence as first sergeant of the Sioux contingent is significant, in light of his role in protecting Emmet Crawford's detachment at the agency in 1874. Garnett described Three Bears and the other scouts as younger men, evidently representing the opposition to Red Cloud at the agency. Red Cloud had lost considerable support for his resistance to the agents in 1873 and 1874, simply because many agency Sioux had decided that cooperation was likely to produce better results than obduracy. Crook sought to encourage these more cooperative leaders by keeping them on the rolls as scouts—with official status and pay—even in the face of economizing directives from Washington.[36]

Here is evidence, of a more direct sort than is usually available, of the motives of Indian scouts for operating against their fellow tribesmen; while the desire to regain horses and weapons after a humiliating deprivation may have played a part, it seems evident that the Sioux scouts were rationally calculating what course of action would be most beneficial to them. Their first thought, obviously, was for their immediate bands, not for those bands that still refused to surrender. They had concluded that they could best serve the interests of those to whom they owed their first loyalty by gaining the favor of the more powerful whites. While their emotions as trained fighting men were undoubtedly involved, the testimony of Garnett and Bourke suggests that the scouts were deliberately taking advantage of the army's evident need for their skills in the hope of averting the dreaded removal and improving conditions on the reservation.

It seems certain that they knew what they were getting into and were prepared to face it for the results they wanted to obtain. Crook sought to ease their possible scruples by assuring them that his primary purpose was not to kill the hostiles but to "make them behave themselves." He particularly ordered that women and children should not be killed deliberately, but taken prisoner. Sergeant Fast Thunder observed that this was all very well, but that the hostiles would not know this, and "will make hard work for us." Clearly the scouts expected to have to face the hostiles in battle and had compelling reasons for agreeing to do so.[37]

A few years later an earnest humanitarian reformer, George W. Manypenny, claimed that the scouts in this campaign in the autumn of 1876 had actually been deceived as to the intended enemy. Crook had told them, Manypenny claimed, that they would be fighting not against their own people, but against the "Northern Indians." While Manypenny was decidedly hostile to the army, there is no reason to doubt his sincerity. It is most unlikely, however, that these scouts could have been so deceived after the war had been going on for months, and after Crook had made a previous attempt to enlist scouts at Red Cloud agency. The term "Northern Indians" was frequently used by the army at this time to designate the nonagency bands. The practical difficulties of such a deception are obvious, even if we did not have the testimony of the scouts that they knew quite well what the situation was.[38]

Those Cheyennes who signed up as scouts in this or subsequent campaigns could assume that they were more likely to be fighting the more numerous Sioux than their fellow Cheyennes. In early 1877, Nelson Miles put White Bull, a respected Cheyenne medicine man, in uniform almost immediately after the Indian surrendered. He and the Sioux chief Hump soon helped Miles locate the camp of the Sioux leader Lame Deer; when surrender negotiations broke down, White Bull saved Miles's life.[39]

The most prominent Cheyenne to serve as a scout, however, was Little Wolf; his case suggests the readiness of former hostiles to become scouts, yet not all Cheyennes approved his actions. Little Wolf served as a scout under William P. Clark in

1877, after surrendering at Fort Robinson. The government's decision to send the Northern Cheyennes to Indian Territory resulted in the flight of Dull Knife's and Little Wolf's bands back to the north, and prompted Crook's bitter comment that the government seemed to have forgotten the services that many of these Cheyennes had rendered. Yet after reaching Montana and surrendering to their old friend "White Hat" Clark, Little Wolf let Nelson Miles persuade him to enlist, with most of his warriors, as scouts once more. This enlistment probably afforded a means by which the army could keep them out of the hands of the Interior Department. There was an irony in the situation which the Cheyennes did not fail to appreciate. Years later one of them told George Bird Grinnell, "My friend, I was a prisoner of war for four years, and all the time was fighting for the man who captured me." Some must have recalled those years fondly; years later James Tangled Yellow Hair enlisted as a scout because "I had heard our old men make such good talk about Bear Shirt [Miles]."[40]

Yet not all the Cheyennes saw it the same way. Wooden Leg was highly critical of those who, like White Bull, helped the soldiers to "kill friends"; it "showed a bad heart." He did not like to hear stories told by the scouts about their adventures. His brother had died at the hands of soldiers, and he wondered if some Cheyenne had guided the white men who killed him. Years later he enlisted in Edward Casey's company at Fort Keogh; apparently conditions had altered so much by that time that he saw no inconsistency in his actions.[41]

The lack of a single Cheyenne attitude on scouting, and on their former allies, also emerges from another conflict of testimony. Some whites asserted that the Cheyennes, when they began surrendering in early 1877, were eager to enlist to fight Crazy Horse; supposedly the Oglala leader had refused to aid the impoverished Cheyennes who fled from the Red Fork battle. Wooden Leg and other Cheyennes flatly denied this story. If the whites who made these assertions reported in good faith, then the difference must lie in the particular attitudes of the Cheyennes with whom they spoke. Both whites and Cheyennes may have been rationalizing.[42]

The question of why Indians would enlist to fight fellow tribesmen or former allies leads to complexities of human behavior under stress. Men trained to war, accustomed to regard horses and weapons as the accoutrements of manhood, probably preferred such a life to the confinement and boredom of the reservation. Undoubtedly the whites played on factions and antagonisms within tribal groups to turn tribesmen against each other.

Yet one cannot assume that the scouts simply reacted to white manipulation of their emotions and prejudices. The testimony of the Sioux scouts, in particular, is that of men making a rational calculation of ends and means. They had certain specific things they hoped to gain for themselves and their bands, and they told the whites what these things were. James Cook, on the basis of a wide acquaintance among the Sioux, characterized scouts as "men who had been endowed with sense enough to see that there was absolutely no use in the Indians' fighting against the white soldiers."[43] Since the army gave strong indications of wanting and needing their services, the scouts tried to use this need to extract as much advantage as they could from the situation. It may be that they overestimated the gratitude of Washington, or the influence the army leaders had with the government, but they acted on the best information they had at the time.

Clearly the Indians who enlisted as scouts and the leaders who favored such a step gave first consideration to their immediate bands, collections of kinfolk and familiar associates. Indeed, band chiefs in many cases must have considered this their first obligation. In the absence of a centralized, hierarchical state, they were responsible to the people directly in their charge.

There were of course many factors that allowed men to rationalize and accept what another member of the same culture regarded as betrayal. Fast Thunder explained to Crook that they could bring the "Northern Indians" in to the agencies "and they will learn after a while that we will do what is right by them."[44] There is no reason to doubt his sincere conviction that the scouts were serving the long-range interests of their whole people in reconciling them to the new order. His words suggest not betrayal, but the clear realization that only a few choices were open.

Chapter Nine

The Pawnee Wolves

Many Plains tribes called a scout a "wolf," and the sign language terms for the two were the same. Many tribes also referred to the Pawnees as "wolves," and their designation in sign language was the same gesture: two fingers held up, on one hand or two, near the head to indicate the ears of the wolf. The term was apparently one of respect and not of contempt. As George Bird Grinnell noted, there is no reason to suppose the Indians regarded wolves with contempt or hatred, any more than they did other animals. The Pawnees were wolves because of their skill as horse thieves and their ability to disguise themselves as wolves and imitate the animal's cry. Thus the name was a reluctant tribute from their enemies. It was not inappropriate, then, that one of the most successful and long-serving of scout units was the Pawnee Scout battalion led by Frank North. They furnish a notable example of Indian-white military cooperation, and an example of how the white military exploited intertribal animosities and, however unintentionally, the Indians themselves.[1]

Unlike most of the nomadic tribes, the Pawnees had lived on the great Plains in what is now Nebraska and Kansas for centuries before European contact. They were of the Caddoan language family and had close ties with the Arikaras in Dakota. Traditionally they were sedentary farmers, living in earth-lodge villages along the Republican, Platte, and Loup rivers. As was the tendency among village tribes, their social structure and government were more hierarchical and possessed more authority than those of the nomads. The acquisition of the horse, beginning in the seventeenth century, gave a greater degree of freedom from the villages and made them partially nomadic. The villages and fields remained the focus of their lives, but they spent long periods in winter and summer on communal hunts for buffalo. Their warriors engaged in the horse raids common to the Plains tribes, ranging far to the south and even into New Mexico. Yet the central Plains remained their homeland; sites important to their religious and ceremonial life were located in what is now central Nebraska and northern Kansas. The French called the Loup (Wolf) River for the Skidi band, and the Americans called the Republican River after the supposedly republican form of government of the Pawnees who lived on its banks. The Skidi band apparently came first to the region, and they retained a sense of separateness from the other three bands—Chaui, Pitahauerat, and Kitkehahki. The Skidis were among the few American Indians north of Mexico to practice regular ceremonial human sacrifice.[2]

The nineteenth century was a series of disasters for the Pawnees. The opening of white travel routes through the Platte Valley brought the whites' diseases, so disastrous to the Indians. The attacks of other Indians made life increasingly hazardous. The Sioux, Cheyennes, and Arapahoes intruded ever more seriously into their hunting grounds, especially the buffalo range along the Republican. In 1859 the Pawnees signed an agreement with the federal government to accept a reservation in east-central Nebraska, along the Loup; the whites were now to assert an ever increasing control over their lives. The fortified villages they established along the Loup were increasingly subject to heavy Sioux raids; at the same time they found it ever more dangerous to hunt along the Republican. Yet hunt they must, for the government did not provide enough food to sustain them, no more than it provided protection from their enemies. More than one prominent Sioux warrior took the name Pawnee Killer as an honor. Outnumbered and losing population, the Pawnees were on the defensive; they still adroitly made off with other people's horses, but only to lose them to the Sioux. Their relations with the whites were uneasy, marked by accusations of thievery and war scares, but they could not afford another powerful enemy.[3]

In the meantime their government agents tried to civilize them by putting their children in school and teaching the men to farm in the white man's fashion. These innovations were not attractive; farming was traditionally a woman's activity, and the school demonstrated a complete disregard for the children's culture or their difficulties of adjustment. The pressures to which they were subjected by white settlers as well as Indian enemies were not conducive to assimilation. The coming of the Civil War initially meant only that there was even less hope of white protection from the Sioux. Yet the war was also to bring a dramatic, if temporary, adjustment in the situation.[4]

The hostility of the nomadic tribes along the Platte River road became desperate by 1864. Conventional generals like Robert Mitchell, and their volunteer troops, found the enemy elusive, yet travelers could move only in large bodies and way stations required garrisons and fortifications. In other words, the whites were now in much the same predicament the Pawnees had been in for years. It may have been this new community of interest that prompted the higher military authorities to use the skills of the Pawnees. There is some discrepancy in accounts of the origin of the scout unit,[5] but the idea apparently came from General Samuel Curtis, a volunteer officer commanding on the central Plains at the time. Curtis authorized a company of Pawnees under Joseph McFadden, an interpreter at the agency, with Frank North as second in command. Agent B. F. Lushbaugh was reluctant to have the agency left undefended, but Curtis allowed a company of volunteer cavalry to be stationed there—an indication of the Pawnees' relative military value in the general's view.[6]

The Pawnee company was part of an uneventful march by Curtis into Kansas; they encountered no hostile Indians. Curtis was not pleased with McFadden's lack of control over the Indians, but Frank North made a favorable impression on him; he authorized North to enlist a new Pawnee company to serve as Nebraska volunteer cavalry, with North as captain. North encountered some initial difficulties in enlisting his men in the fall of 1864; having collected 100 men at the agency, he had to journey to Omaha on horseback to satisfy bureaucratic requirements imposed by General Mitchell. On returning to the agency, he found that his men had departed for their winter hunt. North heard that local whites had sabotaged him by telling the Pawnees that they would be sent south "to fight the Negroes," a conflict in which they had no personal interest. North rounded up his men again and, as he put it, "returned good for evil" by having the Pawnees credited against the draft quota for Platte County, Nebraska Territory. The white opposition may have been from persons opposed to arming these Indians, but it may also have originated in the conviction that the presence of the Pawnees was a protection to local settlements.[7]

Frank North, born in Ohio in 1840, had come to Nebraska in the 1850s with his parents. After his father's death in a blizzard in 1857, the family established itself in Columbus, a frontier settlement east of the Pawnee reservation. As a boy North had been handicapped by asthma, for which the medical science of the day had virtually no treatment. After moving to Nebraska he became an extremely active and daring young man, perhaps in compensation. His acquaintance with the Pawnees began soon after they were established on the Loup in 1859, and apparently he acquired fluency in their language over the next few years. At the time Curtis decided on a Pawnee company, North was working at the trader's store at the Pawnee agency. From his subsequent career it is evident that he was on terms of friendship and mutual respect with the tribe. He was tall and thin (like Charles Gatewood), and all accounts describe him as a modest, unassuming, likable man, who did not seek publicity and who let others take credit for his achievements. Obviously something is lacking from these rather conventional tributes to tell us how North was able to function so effectively as leader of the Pawnees. In a private letter written a few months after the Red Fork battle, however, Luther North tells how the Cheyennes' fire became so heavy that the Pawnees (and Luther) felt like running: "Frank straightened himself up on the old black horse and said very quietly, 'the first one of my men that runs I shall kill.' They didn't run."[8]

This incident seems inconsistent with what has been said previously about the relationship between Indian scouts and their leaders. It sounds more consistent with the harshest and most rigorous school of regular officers. Some things that are known about the nature of Pawnee society, however, may illuminate the nature of North's control over his men. As mentioned, Pawnee society was hierarchical to an extent not seen among the nomads. The class structure was not immutable, but the lines were well recognized and not easily crossed. Chieftainship was incontestably hereditary in certain leading families. Wealth and family determined status; there was a strong emphasis on the giving of gifts, upward and downward, but in practice "Them as had, got." Maturity was especially respected, and the Pawnees assumed that maturity came late; one did not break into the Pawnee "establishment" through youthful aggressiveness. The hereditary chiefs did not lead their warriors in battle; rather, they appointed some prominent warrior to lead the war party, as they appointed someone else to lead the tribal police. The leading warrior was the representative of the chief's authority, and he had an arbitrary power to command that the nomads would have considered excessive, except perhaps in the military society chiefs in a few tribes. Here we may have a clue to Frank North's status. There is no evidence that any chief appointed North a war leader, but the system may well have created a mental niche into which the Pawnees could fit him. They were habituated to obey the man who led them in war. Whites, ignorant of this facet of Pawnee society, called North the "white chief" of the Pawnees. It is hard to determine the extent of North's awareness of these matters.[9]

The Pawnee scouts could march in a column of twos if the situation called for it; it was this ability that caused the Cheyennes to mistake them for regular cavalry at Plum Creek in 1867. The most notable example of the scouts' discipline, however, occurred during the expedition under Crook in late 1876. The Pawnees had to serve alongside Sioux scouts, many of whom had probably been killing Pawnees just a few years earlier; moreover, the Pawnees had just helped the army to dispossess many of these same Sioux of their horses. As they marched along the North Platte, a Sioux rode up to the Pawnee column and struck one of the scouts in the face with his coup stick. The Pawnees drew their revolvers and the obstreperous Sioux would have taken the Spirit Road if the alert North had not instantly ordered them to hold their fire. The offended scout later begged tearfully to be allowed to avenge himself, but North refused permission. A complaint to Crook led the general to speak to the entire body of scouts, urging reconciliation. There was a formal shaking of hands and exchange of gift horses, but Luther North was convinced that the animosity lingered.[10]

Two other episodes illuminate North's status, both as a respected friend and adviser and as an outsider. During the 1865 expedition under Connor, one Pawnee accidentally shot and killed another. The dead man was a Chaui, or Grand Pawnee, while the other was a Skidi; the Chaui scouts were suspicious and there was potential for a split that would cripple the organization. North investigated and found no evidence of bad feeling between the two men, so he concluded that the killing was indeed accidental. Apparently all parties accepted his word as final.

During the summer hunt of 1866, the Skidis took meat from a cache left by the other bands. On return to the reservation the other bands demanded payment. A tribal council was unable to reach agreement, and tempers were rising. Finally all sixteen Pawnee chiefs called on Frank North, who was putting up hay in one of his fields near Columbus. They all sat in a circle in the hayfield, smoked a pipe, and examined the matter, agreeing that North's decision would be final. North decided that the Skidis should return the meat, and appointed a committee of chiefs from each band to determine the amount taken.[11]

These episodes demonstrate the respect the Pawnees had for North's integrity and good judgment. Yet at the same time, it was important that he was an outsider; he was not clearly identified with a particular band, as he would have been if he had married a Pawnee and lived among them, as McFadden had done. The two incidents clearly illustrate the extent to which the Skidis, after centuries of association with the other three bands, were still a separate people. On the Loup River reservation, in spite of the need to unify the villages for defense, the Skidi village was still half a mile distant from the other three bands.[12] These bands had not lived in such close proximity until a few years earlier, when the reservation was established; the meat cache affairs suggests that they had not had time to develop a mechanism for settling such interband disputes. There is no need to assume that they turned to North as a "Great White Father," a member of a superior race. It was convenient to have a friend whose judgment was trusted and whose goodwill extended equally to all bands. At the same time, it should be noted that they did not turn to their agent, or any other white person on the reservation; also, despite the value they placed on maturity, they consulted a man who was only twenty-six. North was no "white chief," but he clearly held a special place in the Pawnees' regard.

While the chiefs held North in high regard, there is reason to believe that the scouts themselves represented a rather different group within the tribe, and a different set of motives. Within the tribe was a large social group called the "Boys." These were men, not all of them young, who refused to concern themselves with wealth and status, preferring a life of war and adventure. Having dropped out of the accepted class system, they were not considered fully mature. Yet they made up the war parties and performed such useful functions as scouting for enemy raiding parties and simply providing a helping hand when needed. Because they preferred freedom and excitement to prestige, wealth, and responsibility, they were to some extent a disturbing element. The kindred Arikaras had the same class, and the chiefs found them a rebellious lot, tempted by the more egalitarian life of the nomads. The Arikaras sometimes banished Boys who became too independent; among the Pawnees, long hunts and horse raids may have provided the safety valve that Edwin Denig found lacking among the sedentary Arikaras. It seems more likely that the Pawnee Boys furnished a large portion of the recruits for the scout battalion.[13]

Another group that furnished recruits consisted of former students at the agency school. Years of indoctrination intended to make them into imitation whites had alienated them from their people. By serving with the scouts they gained status as warriors and were reintegrated into the tribe. Knowledge of English and a greater understanding of the whites' thinking and values must have been of use to them in their military service, but that had not been the intention of the educational program. To the educators, this running off to fight Sioux and collect scalps was simply a reversion to savagery; reintegration as Pawnees was the last thing they wanted for their pupils. Thus we see again the conflict of aims, in the short run, between the civil and military agencies in dealings with the Indians. The army advanced its purpose, and the ultimate purpose of government control over the Indians, by exploiting the aspects of Indian culture the assimilationists were most eager to extirpate.[14]

While the assimilationists lamented the army's encouragement and perpetuation of the bad old ways, the Pawnee elders worried about the extent to which the scouts were becoming divorced from the traditional way of life. The chiefs had thought enough of North to ask him to serve as an arbitrator between the bands. As time went on, however, they apparently had second thoughts about the effects of scout service on their society. The scouts had served intermittently for about five years when North sought to reenlist men in early 1870. Agent J. M. Troth then reported to his superiors that the chiefs "earnestly desired" that the young men not be permitted to enlist, so that they would stay home and learn to farm. The reasons given in the record were these:

> *They are found after being engaged in that service to be less tractable than the other Indians.*
> *They associate with bad white men, and learn to drink and gamble, which unfits them for useful occupations and has an unfavorable effect on others.*
> *The long-standing feud between the Pawnees and the Sioux is by this means kept up and peaceable relations between them rendered almost impossible.*

It is unfortunate that we do not have the exact words of the chiefs themselves. The order and phrasing of these objections must reflect the priorities of the white administrators as much as or more than those of the chiefs, especially since the alleged effects of scout service on the young warriors were exactly those that antimilitarists of the time believed military service had on all soldiers. Undoubtedly the agent was much concerned over the tractability of his charges; it would not be surprising if the chiefs, accustomed to authority, had the same concern. It is certainly possible that the scouts had acquired habits of drinking and gambling, to which traditionalists were opposed. One may doubt the validity of the idea that all would be well between Sioux and Pawnees if only there were no Pawnee scouts; one of the bloodiest attacks by the Sioux on the Pawnees occurred on the Republican in 1873, when there had been no Pawnee Scouts serving for over two years. The chiefs had opposed enlistments in 1869, but ostensibly only until some action was taken on a complaint about some soldiers who fired on a party of discharged scouts who were returning home.[15]

Agent Troth and his immediate superior were Quakers; under no circumstances could they honestly approve of the activities of the scouts. If the parallels with the Arikaras are valid, however, the Pawnee chiefs may well have found the scouts a disturbing element, disrupting their own control and hastening cultural change. North and his organization provided an alternate source of authority and prestige, outside the traditional social structure, and allowed young men to escape the bounds of the structure for long periods.[16]

The Indian Bureau's opposition to enlistments distressed General C. C. Augur, the department commander, and also the officials of the Union Pacific Railroad, who made use of their influence in Washington to change the situation. The Pawnees' operations had protected the construction of the line, and the company hoped they would continue to do so. The U.P.'s general superintendent, O. G. Hammond, wrote to Congressman Oakes Ames, the company's friend and virtual agent in Washington, asserting that the Pawnees found the pay they received as scouts helpful to the whole tribe. He believed that having the scouts in service would mean less, rather than more, trouble for the Pawnee villages, since the Sioux would be kept busy elsewhere. Hammond had consulted with General Augur, who said that the scouts' enlistment would be both desirable and economical, costing nothing but their pay. Augur denied that the scouts were learning to drink. The adjutant general of the army informed the commissioner of Indian affairs that the Union Pacific was eager to have the scouts enlisted "on account of apprehended Indian hostilities." Clearly Augur was using the railroad's political influence to get around the Interior Department's opposition to the scouts' enlistment; it was another skirmish in the two federal agencies' long war over control of the Indians. Two companies enlisted in September of that year and patrolled the Union Pacific line until the following January.[17]

The Union Pacific had some reason to value the services of the Pawnees. Their activities in 1865–66 have been noted; in 1867 the army authorized North to enlist a battalion of four companies, giving him the nominal rank of major. There were 200 men in the scouts that year, the greatest strength the unit achieved. North chose the officers, all officially civilian scouts like himself, from his friends and relatives in Columbus, includ-

ing his young brother Luther. The latter 1860s were the time
when the number of officially recorded engagements with Indians reached a peak. The transcontinental railroad was under
construction across the Plains, and the construction crews suffered harassment from Sioux and Cheyennes. The Pawnees
patrolled the rail line from central Nebraska to southeastern
Wyoming, skirmishing with raiding parties and recovering
stolen horses and mules.[18]

General Augur, the department commander, was so pleased
with the Pawnees that he wanted a greatly expanded scout organization in case hostilities continued the next year. He proposed
to raise three 400-man battalions from the friendly tribes in his
department. Aside from the military value of the idea, "it opens
to these people a useful career, renders them tractable and obedient, and educates and civilizes them more effectually than can
be done any other way." Augur further observed that the Pawnees "are hardly ever sick, and never desert, and are careful of
their horses," a statement that suggests the state of the regular
cavalry at that time. Having marched with them on an inspection tour, he had never seen one drunk, nor had he ever seen
"more obedient or better behaved troops."[19]

At the end of the scouts' 1867 service, however, an incident
occurred which illustrated some of the problems of handling Indian scouts, and which must have strained Augur's favorable
opinion a bit. He had intended to discharge them in December,
so they could spend the winter with their families. For some bureaucratic reason they were required to wait for some time at
Fort Kearny, Nebraska, for discharge. Naturally they saw no
point in waiting, and grew bored with inactivity. When North
disciplined one of his men, they all decamped for home without
discharge. Augur chose to react in accordance with common
sense and not by "the book." He sent North a bunch of blank
discharge forms so he could fill in the names; the paymaster
went to the reservation and paid the scouts off. What would
have been mutiny and desertion in regular troops had to be regarded in a different light with Indian scouts who were not
versed in the fine points of military law; they had simply gone
home when their work was done for the season. From all evidence, the episode did not affect North's future relations with
the scouts or Augur's high opinion of their military value.[20]

In 1868 an episode occurred that points out the close personal relationship of Frank North with the whole Pawnee tribe, and how different his attitude was from that of a professional officer. The army had authorized two companies of fifty men each for the year. There were several skirmishes along the railroad, though nothing so spectacular as the Plum Creek affair in 1867. In July the Department of the Platte received warning that large numbers of Southern Cheyennes and Arapahos were moving north to the Republican to attack the Pawnees on the summer hunt. North decided to join the tribe on the hunt with twenty-five men from each company; he apparently did so without orders, leaving his superiors in the dark as to his whereabouts. The command left Wood River station, Nebraska, accompanied by a party of wealthy Chicagoans seeking sport, and joined the Pawnee tribe on the Little Blue River. The hunt on the Republican was successful, but North found himself in what he later considered the tightest spot of his career. While he was hunting with less than a dozen scouts, a large party of Sioux attacked. Simultaneously the Sioux attacked the main Pawnee camp. The main body of scouts and Pawnee warriors beat them off and then relieved North's little party after two had been killed. A witness described the scouts as "crazy with joy" to see North alive. North reported very briefly on the deaths of the two scouts after his return to the rail line; apparently no one asked him to account for his actions, which had resulted in the deaths of two army enlisted men. On his own initiative he had provided the Pawnees the protection that the government had not. Apparently he conceived of himself as the friend and protector of the whole Pawnee tribe, not just the commander of a military unit. Moreover, he judged the Pawnees to be as worthy of protection as white railroad builders. Knowing of their danger, he took personal responsibility without concern for the chain of command. The two men killed were the only Pawnee scouts ever lost in combat.[21]

In 1869 the army went on the offensive on the central and southern Plains. Major Eugene Carr received orders to drive the hostiles out of the Republican River buffalo range; the particular object of attention was the Cheyenne Dog Soldier society, which had become virtually a separate band, intermarrying with the Sioux. Carr's command comprised eight companies of the Fifth

Cavalry and three companies of Pawnee scouts. Carr was not at first impressed by the scouts; they did not do things the army way, and Luther North, in charge of them at first, was not properly respectful to his commander. Carr would have preferred about one company of Indians for scouting and more cavalry. After Frank, who had been enlisting another company at the Pawnee agency, joined the command, the situation improved.[22]

As they moved up the Republican, the Pawnees skirmished with the Dog Soldiers almost every day. The Cheyennes later gave the Pawnees credit for the damage inflicted by this expedition. "They always showed up first and the Cheyennes mistook them for friendly warriors." The Dog Soldiers moved north to escape the soldiers, but not quickly enough. At Summit Springs in Colorado, near the South Platte River, Carr caught up with them on July 11. The engagement was unusual in that an Indian camp was surprised in broad daylight, and the cavalry, with scouts in the lead, made an old-fashioned, shoulder-to-shoulder charge. The Cheyennes recalled that the Pawnees did most of the killing and captured most of the horse herd. Tall Bull, the Dog Soldier chief, died protecting his wives. Fifty-two Indians were reported killed, many apparently women and children. A captive white woman was rescued; another had been killed by her captors. The Dog Soldiers never recovered from the blow.[23]

Carr's report shows that his opinion of the Pawnee scouts had altered considerably: "The Pawnees under Major Frank North were of the greatest service to us throughout the campaign. This is the first time since coming west that we have been supplied with Indian scouts—and the result has shown their value."[24] The whole command was thanked by the Nebraska Legislature, and one Pawnee received the Medal of Honor. The name on the citation was that of Sergeant Mad Bear (Co-rux-te-chod-ish), cited for riding out after a raiding party on July 8, and being wounded and his horse killed by "friendly fire." Luther North later insisted that the medal was intended for Traveling Bear (Corux-a-Kah-Wadde) for bravery at Summit Springs, and that the latter actually received the medal.[25]

There were further expeditions in 1869, with less notable results. In the following year, despite the opposition noted earlier, two companies of scouts guarded the railroad without any dramatic incidents. They were mustered out in January 1871 and were not to be called on again for over five years, and then in very different circumstances. North spent much of that time working as guide, interpreter, and scout at various posts in Nebraska. The early 1870s saw a slackening, though hardly a cessation, of Indian–white hostilities on the northern Plains. The Platte Valley, with its railroad, became quite peaceful. This state of affairs, as much as opposition from chiefs and Indian agents, put an end to the Pawnee Scouts.[26]

For the Pawnees the next few years were anything but easy or peaceful. The Loup River reservation was virtually surrounded now by white settlers, who resented the Indians' presence and coveted their land. White intruders regularly stole timber from reservation land, while the Indians were accused of stealing horses and other property from whites. Certainly they begged, and they probably did steal on occasion, for the food supplied by the government continued to be inadequte and their farming efforts had variable success. The agents' efforts to stamp out horse-stealing expeditions against other tribes contributed to the discontent of the Boys. Some, like the great horse thief Big Spotted Horse, spent much of their time in Indian Territory visiting the Wichitas, fellow Caddoans with many cultural similarities. White pressure for the Pawnees' removal from Nebraska thus coincided with a growing belief among Pawnees that it was impossible to live a satisfactory life in the old homeland.[27]

This conflict was not a simple one between conservatives and "progressives," as white officials may have believed. Both those who opposed removal and those who favored it were traditionalists in their own ways, and none of them wholeheartedly wanted to adopt the white way of life. Big Spotted Horse had spent some time in jail for stealing horses from the Cheyennes in Kansas; he hoped that in Indian Territory he would be able to continue the sort of life a warrior should live. Frank White (Li-heris-oo-la-shar), a prominent scout who advocated assimilation, also favored the move. The opposition was led by the hereditary chiefs. Their culture and religious life were closely tied to Nebraska, yet the thought that something more like the good old days might be possible to the south was tempting. Both the corrosion of old values by white influence and nostalgia for what had been were in operation. There were conservatives on both sides of the question, but some were trying to conserve the village social order, while others wanted to hold onto the horseback warrior's mode of life.[28]

The crowning blow came on the summer hunt of 1873, when the main Pawnee hunting party was attacked on the Republican by a large force of Sioux. It was one of the last great purely intertribal battles, and yet it occurred in a sense under government auspices. Both groups were on leave from their agencies for the hunt; the Pawnees were under military escort, although the troops were nowhere near when the attack occurred. Outnumbered and caught in a canyon leading down to the Republican valley, the Pawnees suffered heavy losses; the highest estimate was 156, many of them women and children. This disaster was the final blow to the Pawnees' morale. The next year, despite continued opposition from many chiefs, portions of the tribe began to move to Indian Territory. One chief, Pitelesharu, died in what may have been a shooting accident, but Luther North suspected that the death was related to his stubborn opposition to removal.[29]

Big Spotted Horse and some others found new opportunities for scouting in the Red River was of 1874. Otherwise the removal had far different results from those hoped for. The land the Pawnees received was small and hardly of the same quality as the land they had surrendered in Nebraska. The climate was unfamiliar, disease (particularly malaria) attacked them, and the death rate soared. Their shattered morale probably did not support a strong will to live. It was not possible, after all, to carry on the old, free, horse-stealing life. George Bird Grinnell visited them at this time and found their condition "most miserable"; their old spirit was gone, and they had become a sad, serious people, seldom laughing.[30]

For a few of them a temporary reprieve came in 1876. The unexpected difficulties of the Sioux war prompted a new call for their services. Frank North, still working as a government guide and interpreter, received an order to report to the division commander, General Sheridan, at Chicago. Sheridan personally ordered him to recruit a company of 100 Pawnees for service in the north; Frank wanted to raise a battalion, which would have given him his old nominal rank and pay of a major, but Sheridan vetoed the idea. North's asthma was again troubling him, and he was in poor condition for campaigning, but he and Luther journeyed immediately to Indian Territory. The brothers found the Pawnees in "a most deplorable condition," but glad to see them. They "fairly climbed over each other" to get at Frank, shouting his Pawnee name—Pani La-shar, Pawnee Chief.[31]

There was no difficulty in getting men; although many were suffering from malaria, 100 signed up within an hour, insisting they were well enough to service. Many others followed the departing contingent for miles, in the hope that some of the ailing would drop out and they could take their places. Even though some were shaking so badly they could hardly keep up, they insisted that they would be all right when they got to Nebraska. Luther recalled that this proved true, except for two who died at Sidney Barracks. The Norths had no doubt that, for all their affection for Frank, the rush to enlist was due most of all to eagerness to return to "their beloved Nebraska."[32]

This band of shaking, malarial men, with a commander who could hardly breathe, might have seemed both pathetic and ludicrous, setting out to recapture past glories. For a few months, however, they did just that. Outfitted and mounted at Sidney, Nebraska, they marched for Fort Robinson in October. Crook had decided that the Sioux at Red Cloud agency, near the fort, had manifested too much sympathy for the active hostiles, for whom they were suspected of providing recruits. Mackenzie and the Fourth Cavalry having arrived from Texas, Crook ordered them to surround and disarm the bands of Red Cloud and Red Leaf, and to take their horses. Deprived of mobility, they would be powerless to aid the hostiles, if such was their intention. The operation was the usual early-morning surprise, except that no blood was shed; the Sioux made no resistance. The Pawnees contributed greatly to the silent approach and the swiftness of the final dash to drive off the horses. Years later, Luther North discussed the episode with elderly Sioux at Pine Ridge reservation. Although he strove to express goodwill, he found many of them still bitter, and not ready to forgive the Pawnees. One old man declared that the soldiers could not have taken the horses without the Pawnees; in fact, the soldiers had brought the Pawnees along to protect them. The thought of 40 Pawnees (in his immediate detachment) protecting 500 soldiers gave Luther some amusement. Yet this old man's memory suggests again that, paradoxically, the Sioux respected their hated Indian enemies in a way they refused to respect the whites. Defeat being undeniable, it was preferable to credit it to other Indians, however bitterly hated.[33]

In the subsequent campaign under Crook, which culminated in the Red Fork battle, the Pawnees distinguished themselves. Relations with the Sioux scouts, many of them from the same bands unhorsed by Mackenzie a few weeks earlier, were strained. The Norths were not pleased with Crook's informal methods of command, nor did they believe that the general's efforts to reconcile the different tribal contingents were wholly successful. John Bourke noted that the Pawnees and Shoshones scalped the dead Cheyennes, while the Sioux, Cheyenne, and Arapaho scouts did not, "respecting the wishes and prejudices of the white soldiers." Luther North was undoubtedly right in observing that in fact the Pawnees and Shoshones were long-standing enemies of the Cheyennes, while the others had until recently been their allies; the white men's notions had nothing to do with it. Luther's own prejudices at the time are illuminated by a letter to George Bird Grinnell in which he expressed the hope that Mackenzie would command in any subsequent campaign rather than Crook; Mackenzie wanted to fight, "while Crook is forever trying to make peace." At that period Luther's feelings about the Sioux apparently did not differ much from those of his Pawnee friends. This tribal prejudice, not shared by Crook, prevented his seeing that the general was aiming at something beyond military victory. Close friendship for one group of Indians did not necessarily entail empathy with "the Indians" in general.[34]

For the Pawnee Scouts, however, there were to be no subsequent battles. They were stationed at Sidney Barracks for some weeks, and gave evidence of assimilation by forming a baseball team to play the white soldiers. Crook wanted them retained until he knew definitely if the bulk of the hostiles would surrender. With the congressional appropriation nowhere in sight, however, Sheridan ordered him to discharge them. Crook expressed a high opinion of the services they had rendered, and granted Frank North's request that he be allowed to accompany them back to their reservation. Since they would have to travel through settled areas in Kansas, Frank wanted to be sure they would not suffer from trigger-happy whites.[35]

Although North remained active, the few remaining years of his life were anticlimactic. He engaged in business with Buffalo Bill Cody, operating a Nebraska ranch and later supervising the Indians in Cody's Wild West show. During troubles with the Colorado Utes in 1879, he expressed the expectation, or hope, that he would be asked to recruit his scouts again, but the conflict never reached such proportions. A few Pawnees individually acted as scouts in Colorado. Frank's health continued to deteriorate, and he died at age forty-five in 1885. His last years symbolized the transformation of the frontier life he had known into a myth for the entertainment of an increasingly urbanized nation.[36]

For the Pawnees the struggle with a changing world continued. They suffered most of the ills of reservation Indians. By one means or another, much of their new land passed into the hands of white settlers. Although they intermarried with whites to some extent, they did not disappear. In the second decade of the twentieth century, when their population was less than 700 people, the birth rate began to overtake the deaths. A few years later, a number of young Pawnees visited the old homeland in Nebraska, driving late-model cars, and dropped in on Luther North in Columbus. Luther was pleased that the tribe still remembered him, but noted that while they spoke better English than he, not one could speak Pawnee.[37]

George E. Hyde concludes that the Pawnees' poor showing against the Sioux in the 1880s could be accounted for by poor leadership. When the Norths provided leadership, the Pawnees showed superior quality as fighting men. Modern weapons and the support of the army, however, must also have accounted for much of the difference.[38]

From one point of view the story of the Pawnee Scouts was one of consistent success—an outstanding example of Indian-white cooperation. From another standpoint, it was an example of the exploitation of intertribal animosities, and of Indians themselves, for the purposes of an alien people. The Norths and their military superiors had a point, for the Pawnees had every reason to wish to strike back against their enemies, and to desire an alliance with the stronger power that could make retaliation possible. They had received no favors from the Sioux and had no reason to expect any. The scouts enjoyed adventure, suffered few casualties, recovered self-esteem battered by both Sioux and "civilization," and obtained economic benefits for themselves and their people. These things were meaningful to them in ways their would-be civilizers could not imagine.

The Quaker agents had their point, too. The way of life in which such values were functional was doomed, and the scouts, although they could hardly realize it, hastened its demise. In truth, they were between the hammer and the anvil.

It would hardly have served the Pawnees' interests to resist the whites. In a situation in which options were few, those who served as scouts chose a course that seemed both attractive and sensible, and performed as well as could be asked. If intertribal warfare was ultimately self-defeating, it was also an unavoidable condition of the Indians' situation in the nineteenth century.

Chapter Ten

"More Formidable Indians":
The Apache Scouts

No Indian scout units achieved more contemporary and historical fame or generated more controversy than the Apache scouts
of Arizona. They have been the subject of more detailed study
than other scout units, and have figured prominently in histories of the Indian wars. They furnish probably the best-
documented example of two of the most striking features of the
Indian scout phenomenon: the way in which formerly hostile Indians became instruments of white conquest and assimilation,
and the readiness of some Indians to serve against their own people. It was this latter feature that generated acute doubts in the
minds of whites about where the real loyalties of the scouts lay.
The only Indian scouts who ever turned on their white allies in
battle were Apaches, and many military men could never forget
that fact. Since an Apache was simply an Apache to all but a few
whites, who could guarantee that they would not rejoin their
own people at some moment most inconvenient for the army?

The statement that the Apache scouts served against their
own people is not incorrect, but it should be modified and clari-
fied in the light of historical and anthropological information
now available.

The Apaches have become an American myth; both formal
history and popular entertainment have depicted them as fierce,
cruel, implacably warlike, and diabolically cunning. Army officers, not without admiration, credited them with superhuman
powers of endurance, elusiveness, mobility, and mastery of
guerrilla tactics. Even George Crook, who discerned their humanity better than most, depicted them as supremely proficient
individual fighters and as "tigers of the human species."[1]

Such a legend inevitably obscures human individuality and weakness. Moreover, the designation of all these people by the single word "Apache," with all its fearsome connotations, perpetuates the concept of a single, indistinguishable horde, all dedicated to unending hostility.

One finds something different in turning to the Apache of the anthropologists, especially in the works of Morris E. Opler and Grenville Goodwin. The people called Apache (apparently from a Zuñi word for "enemy") were of the Athapaskan language family, scattered over the Southwest from Texas to Arizona. West of the Rio Grande were two major groupings, now designated as Chiracahua and Western Apaches; the former ranged over what is now southwestern New Mexico and southeastern Arizona and an area astride the Continental Divide in the Mexican states of Sonora and Chihuahua. The Western Apaches lived primarily in present Arizona, west and north of the Chiricahuas. Both of these groupings were further divided into "subtribal groups," divisions, bands, and large family groups. There were clans that cut across these divisions to some extent. Government was highly decentralized; chieftainship was basically hereditary in certain families, but to be chief of a body as large as a subtribal group was a matter not of formally constituted authority, but of the influence of prestige and personality. This point applies to such famous figures as Mangas Coloradas, Cochise, and Victorio. So notable a man as Geronimo, of the Southern Chiricahuas, was never formally a chief but enjoyed great influence because of leadership abilities in war and shamanistic powers such as second sight.[2]

All these peoples were certainly similar in culture and language and were conscious of kinship. Yet the evidence about the degree to which this awareness precluded competition and conflict is less clear. The most northwesterly branch of the Western Apaches were called the "brainless people" by other Apaches; the Spanish translated this term into Tontos (fools), which name was taken up by the Anglo-Americans. Such a description at best suggests a less than perfect sense of solidarity among all "Apaches." Apache witnesses have indicated that it was not considered wrong for Chiricahuas to fight the Tontos, and the reverse undoubtedly applied.[3]

Reminiscent accounts by Apaches leave an inescapable impression of a tendency to squabbling and even feuding, even to the point of violence. The impression is necessarily unfair, since no people are free of such difficulties. But the Apaches lacked a mechanism or authority that could override such animosities and kinship ties, and reach an adjustment that all must accept. In the case of homicide and various other personal injuries, as among many Indian peoples, justice rested with the kin of the injured party, not with impersonal authority. A man not of chieftain stock, such as Geronimo, might exercise great influence, and a chief might exercise influence outside his own band; thus many possibilities existed for factional conflict, complicated by personality and kinship ties. Men who married outside their group customarily lived with the wife's people, but were always outsiders to some degree, however long their residence. This situation further complicates the question of who served against "his own people."[4]

In the later eighteenth century the Spanish military found it possible to recruit Chiricahua Apaches to fight against the Mimbreños (Ojos Calientes), another part of the Chiricahua "nation."[5] Even after the Spanish alliances disintegrated under Mexico, the "Apaches Mansos" (literally, "tame Apaches") living near Tucson scouted for the Mexican and United States forces. According to Mrs. Andrew Stanley, a White Mountain Apache, her people were always suspicious of any one of their own who had been held captive and returned; such a one might be leading the enemy to their camp.[6]

In the eyes of both military and civilians the Apache scouts were closely identified with General George Crook, even though he was not their only begetter. Crook's belief in them, and his heavy reliance on them, led to conflicts with civilian critics and his military superiors, and created a division of opinion within the army which long outlived him. The impression persisted, even among the soldiers, that Crook had originated the whole practice of using Apache scouts.

Aside from the Apaches Mansos, the army was able to begin cooperation with Western Apaches with the arrangements made between Major John Green and Chief Miguel of the White Mountain Apaches in 1869, and the subsequent establishment of Fort Apache. Obviously Crook, who took command in Arizona Territory in 1871, was not the originator of this cooperation; rather he was the consistent and earnest advocate of the fullest use of the Apache scouts. In the early part of his Arizona operations, he enlisted Pimas, Papagos, Yavapais, Walapais, and anyone else available and willing to fight the hostile Apaches, but he found the Apaches themselves to be the most effective scouts. At first Crook asked them to act only as guides and trackers, finding the hostiles for the small, fast columns. They soon demonstrated, however, their willingness to fight effectively alongside white soldiers. They made possible the success of Crook's campaigns in central Arizona from 1872 to 1875, which put the majority of Arizona Apaches on reservations.[7]

As John Bigelow noted, Crook did not seek to make his scouts into soldiers so much as to make them "more formidable Indians." By this means he took away many of the advantages formerly enjoyed by the hostiles and partially bestowed them on his own forces. No longer could the Apaches rest secure in their mountains. Contrary to custom, they could no longer spend winter in the warm lower altitudes. Surrender and the reservation became the only alternative to destruction. Some bands were willing to deliver the heads of particularly recalcitrant leaders to Crook in return for permission to surrender and ensure the safety of their families. Twenty-two Medals of Honor were awarded for the winter campaign of 1872–73, and ten of them went to Apache scouts. Obviously they were willing to participate in combat, and Crook was making a special effort to reward and encourage them. By 1874 it was possible for Chief Desaline to lead a body of scouts without white supervision, and bring about the surrender of a large number of hostiles.[8]

Dan L. Thrapp, the most thorough student of the Apache wars, has divided them into two types of campaigns. One was the persistent guerrilla warfare of many small bands which intensified in the 1860s and persisted into the early 1870s, when Crook's massive campaign made warfare intolerable for the majority of the Western Apaches. This phase was succeeded, in the latter 1870s, by spectacular affairs in which relatively small bodies of Apaches who would not or could not accept reservation conditions eluded large bodies of troops on both sides of the Mexican border for extended periods. In these affairs leaders like Victorio, Nana, Juh, and Geronimo gained renown among the whites, but their exploits were really only last-ditch efforts to live where and how they pleased.[9]

In the first phase, the scouts enabled the troops to find and attack the various hostile bands, while increasingly joining in combat. In the latter phase the hostiles demonstrated even greater mobility and covered great distances; the scouts became ever more important in trailing, pursuit, and attack. The more difficult it became to overhaul and strike the elusive enemy, the more the scouts' role eclipsed that of the regular troops. By 1876 General August Kautz was convinced that one company of Apache scouts was more effective than six companies of cavalry in heading off forays from the reservation. In the campaign of 1879–80 against Victorio, the Apache scouts from Arizona struck the most effective blows against the hostile leader.

The White Mountain Apaches served quite willingly against Victorio. There was bad blood between the two groups because of earlier killings of various persons, including some of Victorio's band and a White Mountain chief. Also scouting against Victorio was a band of Chiricahuas led by Chief Chihuahua; these men were not officially enlisted but had come along anyway. James Kaywaykla, then a child with Victorio's band, later expressed great resentment of Chihuahua's actions; he thought the Chiricahuas had acted from a desire to escape reservation boredom and to possess arms and ammunition again.[10]

By the time of this campaign, there were among the younger scouts men such as John Rope, who had never been on the warpath except as government scouts. Rope's account is the best we have from an Apache scout, showing these notorious warriors as wholly recognizable human beings. He admits that the White Mountains regarded the Chiricahuas as especially formidable; if he had been older and more knowledgeable he would not have been so eager to take the lead in trailing them. Returning from one of their expeditions, the scouts found their people were not camped at the usual place on the reservation; the scouts feared that their people had gone on the warpath, placing them in a dilemma. "Even if they had gone on the warpath, we were still scouts and would have to fight for the white man." Fortunately their people had only moved in closer to Fort Apache to be safer from marauding hostiles.[11]

If Rope's statement is correctly translated, it offers a significant indication as to the loyalty of the scouts. The loyalty—or loyalties—of Apache scouts became a matter of concern to whites other than those who simply would not trust any Indian. Augustus Tassin, commanding a scout detachment in the late 1870s, sought diligently after the Southern Chiricahua leader Juh, without overtaking him. Tassin's first sergeant of scouts was a man who answered (for whites) to the name Tizwin, after an Apache home brew. Tassin learned a lot from Tizwin, but his most educational experience came some time after this fruitless expedition, when Juh came in to reside on San Carlos reservation for a time. In comradely fashion, Tizwin introduced his former commander to his brother-in-law—none other than Juh himself. Tassin was now able to understand his lack of success in pursuit of Juh. As for Tizwin, he was no doubt in an awkward position, caught between his kinship loyalty and his pledged word as a scout.[12]

The greatest cause for doubt of the scouts' loyalty was the so-called Cibicu mutiny of 1881, in which Apache scouts actually turned on their white comrades on the field of battle. It was this affair especially that whites thought of when they asserted that Apache scouts were "always treacherous," whatever might be the case with Plains Indians. The incident grew out of a religious-cultural revival movement not unlike the later Ghost Dance messianic movement. A medicine man or shaman named Noch-ay-del-klinne, reportedly a former scout, began to hold dances and to commune with the dead. The agent at San Carlos became deeply disturbed that so many of his charges were sojourning in the mountains with the medicine man, and rumors circulated that a great uprising was in the making. Various prominent leaders supposedly saw the spirits of Mangas Coloradas, Cochise, and Victorio rise from the earth at the medicine man's call. Apparently there was disagreement as to whether their message to the living was a call for war or for accommodation with the whites, and one cannot help thinking that the reports were decidedly inadequate.[13]

The department commander, Colonel and Brevet Major General Orlando B. Willcox, ordered Colonel Eugene Carr, Sixth Cavalry, commanding at Fort Apache, to arrest the medicine man. Carr was uncertain whether his scout company, composed of White Mountain Apaches, could be depended on if Noch-ay-del-klinne's followers, many of them kin to the scouts, resisted the arrest. The stories of unrest had led Carr to disarm his scouts for a time earlier; with hindsight this display of mistrust seems unwise. Crook had always insisted that no fear of the Indians' power be shown. Yet Carr would need nearly all the fort's small garrison to effect the arrest, and he could hardly leave a scout company of doubtful loyalty behind with the soldiers' families. He telegraphed to Willcox for authority to discharge the current scouts and enlist others of no relation to the supposed malcontents; the telegraph line was down, however, and Carr was not prepared to take the responsibility on himself.[14]

Carr had consulted his scout commander, Lieutenant Thomas Cruse, now in charge of what had been Charles Gatewood's old company. Many years later, Cruse remembered telling Carr that it would be a "terrible test" to ask the scouts to participate in this action. In view of the breakdown in communications, however, Carr decided to take the scout company with him. He moved out of Fort Apache on August 29, 1881, with two companies of cavalry and the scout company. The actual arrest of the medicine man took place the next day without violence, but on the return journey large numbers of Apaches followed the column. When Carr camped in the evening by Cibicu Creek, the Indians, with faces painted, moved in closer. When Carr ordered them back, shooting started, and the scouts joined in, firing on the soldiers. Cruse said later that he had his back turned to his men at the moment the firing began, and could not testify himself to their actions. He always believed that the scouts had no preconcerted plan to turn on the troops, but that religious excitement and family ties had "swept them off their feet" in the moment of crisis. He was sure that the man who began the firing was a former scout called Sanchez, the only man Cruse thought should have been hanged for his connection with the affair; in fact, Sanchez came to no harm, and later served as a scout again under Crook.[15]

Eight whites were killed or mortally wounded at the Cibicu, although Cruse thought that enough Apaches were present to have finished them off if they had had a real leader. The medicine man was killed at Carr's orders when the fighting started. First Sergeant Mose did not join the other scouts, but guided the command back to the fort in the dark. In the course of subsequent campaigning, most of the defecting scouts were killed or captured, or surrendered. Three were tried by court-martial, convicted of mutiny, and hanged: Sergeants Dandy Jim and Dead Shot and Corporal Skippy. Several others went to Alcatraz for a time. Cruse regretted these deaths, especially that of Dead Shot, whom he regarded as a "fine, upstanding" man; Cruse recalled with satisfaction that his testimony did not contribute to the executions.[16]

By strict military law the scouts who had mutinied were enlisted men, and the executions were legally justified. Yet the scouts can hardly have seen the matter in that light. They could not be sure what would happen to Noch-ay-del-klinne now that he was captured. Once their friends and kinfolk were engaged with the soldiers, their decision to fight was not surprising. No doubt it would have been better not to place them in a position where they had to decide between conflicting loyalties, although Carr was also placed in an awkward situation by Willcox's order and the break in the telegraph line. Carr may have recalled that the scouts had arrested fellow tribesmen before, though under less trying circumstances, without the exacerbation of intense religious excitement. Carr's earlier service with the Pawnees and other Indian scouts may have influenced him, but he was experienced enough to have learned that not all Indians, individually or as tribal groups, would react alike. A court-martial censured Carr for certain tactical decisions, but not for bringing the scout company along. Joyce Mason notes that there were no further mutinies of scouts. Any who were seriously discontented simply deserted; scouts were rarely severely punished for desertion. The executions may have contributed to this result, but scouts were seldom placed in such a position again. Yet for some whites, civilian and military, it would remain an established fact that Apache scouts were "always treacherous" and could not be trusted.[17]

Other, accidental factors may have contributed to the Cibicu debacle. Lieutenant Charles Gatewood was not present with his old command because he was on leave at the time. Many of the men who had served with him against Victorio, the men he regarded as the best company he had commanded, including Dead Shot, were enlisted in Company A at the time of the mutiny.

Not present was the subchief Alchesay or Alchise, Gatewood's first sergeant and a Medal of Honor winner in Crook's earlier campaigns. Alchesay was later accused of participation in some of the hostilities that immediately followed the Cibicu fight and was imprisoned for a brief period, but he was later very much in General Crook's confidence. We can only conjecture whether matters would have been different if Gatewood and Alchesay had been with their old comrades at the moment of crisis at Cibicu.[18]

The complaints of certain Apache chiefs to General Crook, who returned to the Arizona command in 1882, suggest the importance of personal relationships in Indian-white relations, and the Apache regard for military leaders as opposed to civil agents. The chiefs expressed distrust of the officers now in Arizona, whom they feared might attack them for no good reason; this fear arose from the Cibicu affair and certain episodes that followed it. Yet they recalled officers of the earlier days, men they had fought both with and against, with affection. Men like "old John Green" and Major George Randall had fought them, had administered their affairs after surrender, and had led them against the hostiles. They might be strict, but they did not steal, and they did as they said, qualities the Apaches found preferable to uncertainty and vacillation. Of Randall, Alchesay said, "When he promised a thing he did it; when he said a word he meant it." Here was a part of the reason many of the White Mountains had preferred to be under the military at Fort Apache. Latter-day stereotypes to the contrary, many Indians did regard the military with a degree of respect and trust not given to most civil agents.[19]

The Cibicu mutiny certainly did not end the need for or the dependence on Apache scouts, although Willcox and Carr were determined to punish the mutineers. The secretary of war gave special permission to double the size of scout companies until the unrest subsided, although Sherman wanted their role reduced to trailing, not combat. Unease about Apaches did lead to the enlistment of Walapais, Yumas, and Mohaves, whose effectiveness Thomas Cruse summed up in two words: "no good." Charles Gatewood, having commanded Yumas and Mohaves, agreed; they were discharged shortly and replaced with White Mountain Apaches. Quality, after all, was as important as numbers; Willcox wanted Gatewood to enlist "Chiricahuas and other choice Indians." Gatewood's own writings, however, suggest that he felt the greatest rapport with his old friends the White Mountains.[20]

In subsequent difficulties with the southern Chiricahuas, operating out of the Sierra Madre range in Mexico, the scouts again struck the most effective blows. A raid on the San Carlos reservation in 1882 carried off most of the Chiricahuas who lived there; how willingly they went with the raiders is unclear. The fugitives held off pursuing troops by effective rear-guard actions, but just below the border a small force of scouts and cavalry under Captain Tullius C. Tupper, with Al Sieber present, took the Chiricahuas by surprise and inflicted serious losses, including the running off of the horses.[21]

When Crook returned to Arizona, replacing Willcox as department commander in September 1882, he pursued a policy that differed considerably from that of his predecessor. Alchesay, though accused of hostile acts by the agent at San Carlos, was consulted by the general and given every evidence of renewed trust. Sanchez, considered by Cruse to be the real troublemaker at Cibicu, was made a sergeant of scouts. Cruse later claimed that Crook's action in Sanchez's case antagonized many Sixth Cavalry officers who remembered the Cibicu. Crook's actions here undoubtedly were a part of his general policy of winning over former hostiles and attaching them to his cause by means of scout service. In regard to Cibicu, he was prepared to let bygones be bygones. Perhaps he had his doubts about the substance of some of the accusations. Some of his statements and orders at this time suggest that his actions were an indication of his own verdict on the Cibicu and those involved.[22]

To solve the problem of the hostiles in Mexico, Crook determined on an expedition into the Sierra Madre, with the permission of the Mexican government. His force consisted of 192 Apache scouts, commanded by Captain Emmet Crawford, and one company of the Sixth Cavalry comprising 42 men. The proportion of scouts indicated the value Crook placed on them. Al Sieber was chief of scouts, and Charles Gatewood and scout John Rope were among those present. Alchesay of the White Mountains accompanied the expedition as a civilian scout and adviser to the general. Some of the scouts were pessimistic about the prospect of success; a sergeant from San Carlos told Crook that the Chiricahuas would never be caught because they could hide like coyotes and smell danger a long way off. This statement constituted an acknowledgment of the powers of the Chiricahuas by an expert judge. Crook, however, had a prisoner who was acquainted with the mountain hideaways of the hostiles; this was Tsoe, a Cibicu Apache nicknamed Peaches, who had been married to a Chiricahua woman. Following her death, he had deserted during the raid into Arizona, was captured on San Carlos reservation, and was now willing to guide Crook's column.[23]

Crook's hopes were justified. The scouts were able to locate the hostile camp and take it by surprise when most of the fighting men were absent on a raid. With most of the women and children prisoners, the hostile warriors watched the column but were unable to find an opening for attack. From Rope's account, Crook personally took the risk of meeting with the hostile chiefs to discuss surrender terms. Once the Chiricahuas had been alerted, chances of surprising them again were slight; Crook would have had to withdraw and wait for another opportunity. Yet the Chiricahua men now knew that their Mexican sanctuary was vulnerable, and they preferred to be with their wives and children. They agreed to surrender, although Geronimo and some others came in in their own good time, months later.[24]

Once the Chiricahuas were on the San Carlos reservation, Crook followed standard procedure: he enlisted as many of them as he could, putting the whole band under Lieutenant Britton Davis. The subchief Chato became Davis's first sergeant, and the officer regarded him highly. James Kaywaykla, on the other hand, denounced Chato as a traitor to his people. Yet Kaywaykla acknowledged that men whose tribal loyalty was undoubted, such as Chihuahua, also enlisted. Kaywaykla understood their reasons: "Ours was a race of fighting men—war was our occupation. A rifle was our most cherished possession . . . there was not a man who did not envy the scout his rifle." Some men, however, such as Geronimo and Kaytennae, Kaywaykla's stepfather, held aloof from enlistment offers.[25]

This division among the Chiricahuas, despite the small numbers involved, provides a well-documented instance of factional conflict among Apaches. Kaywaykla and Eve Ball's other informants presented a bitter assessment of their tribesmen who enlisted as scouts. They charged Chato, in particular, with betrayal, lying, and intriguing against the chiefs to gain power. They charged that Chato, Tsoe, and the mixed-blood interpreter Mickey Free habitually misrepresented the intentions of Geronimo, Kaytennae, and others to get them in trouble with Lieutenant Davis—who himself is depicted as well intentioned and well liked by the Chiricahuas, but misled by those on whom he relied. These intrigues, Ball's friends assert, were what caused Kaytennae to be arrested and sent to Alcatraz for some months; Davis had been deceived into believing that Kaytennae intended to assassinate him and lead an outbreak.[26]

Ball presents her accounts as "the Chiricahua viewpoint." Yet if one compares them with accounts obtained years earlier by anthropologist Morris Opler, it becomes evident that each researcher became involved with a faction among the Chiricahuas, and that there were two viewpoints, at the very least, on the scouts and their enemies. Opler's informants, sons of Chiricahua scouts, describe them as sensible men who knew it was impossible to fight the whites and who believed that as scouts they were serving their people's best interests. From their viewpoint Geronimo was the troublemaker who caused all the Chiricahuas to suffer misery and misfortune. They also blamed Western Apaches for acting as secret agents and for telling stories about the Chiricahuas that got them into trouble. This tribal feud must be a major cause of the unfavorable characterizations of both Chato and Geronimo, although the tales about the latter have had wider circulation.[27]

The final Chiricahua outbreak, generally called the Geronimo campaign, demonstrates these differing viewpoints clearly. In May 1885, about 140 Chiricahuas fled the reservation for Mexico. They included 35 men and 8 boys old enough to fight, constituting about one-third of the fighting strength of the tribe, according to Crook's estimate. Eighty Chiricahua men remained on the reservation, and 50 promptly enlisted as scouts. Most of the leading men were with the fugitives, including Naiche, Cochise's son and hereditary chief of the central Chiricahuas. Geronimo, though not formally a chief, was especially influential, and the whites regarded him as the hostile leader.[28]

Chato had finally driven off the natural leaders by turning Davis against them, while frightening the chiefs by telling them they would be executed or imprisoned. This, at any rate, was the viewpoint of the hostile faction. Geronimo insisted for the rest of his life that he fled because he feared arrest, and there is sufficient evidence to support his sincerity in this belief. The tribal leaders knew, of course, that if anyone would be arrested for wartime actions, they would be the ones. Geronimo's spiritual powers included a ceremony for predicting the actions of the enemy. Samuel Kenoi, one of Opler's informants, believed that the ceremony caused Geronimo's suspicions to reach a climax. The ceremony, as Opler remarks, was "the servant of his fears." The immediate occasion of the outbreak was a dispute with Davis over the making of home brew and the beating of wives, two practices the whites were determined to eradicate. The hostiles insisted that Chato and Mickey Free had aggravated the problem by misrepresentation and false interpretation.[29]

Immediately after the outbreak, more Chiricahua men enlisted as scouts than had fled with the hostile leaders. This should be remembered in connection with contentions that the "Chiricahua viewpoint" is that of the 1885 hostiles. One son of a scout, another of Opler's informants, concluded that the Chiricahuas who went out were simply more scared than those who remained on the reservation. He viewed the scouts as realists who "knew what life was like" and made friends with the whites. Instead of betraying those who left the reservation, the scouts in his view were trying to save as many fugitives as possible. This conclusion may seem like a later rationalization, but it assumes significance in light of arguments among the military as to whether the scouts were willing to fight and kill their hostile tribesmen.[30]

In the campaign against Geronimo, Crook carried his faith in scouts to the logical extreme by making them the striking arm of his whole command; battalions of scouts, supported by pack trains, conducted offensive operations below the border in the Sierra Madre. An increasing force of regular troops remained in Arizona and engaged in largely defensive duties. The 1883 expedition had persuaded Crook that the regular cavalry was more of a hindrance than a help, and that only Apaches could catch

Apaches in the dry, barren, and rugged sierra. Indeed, he concluded that Chiricahuas had the best chance of catching other Chiricahuas, and enlisted them immediately. Not only were they best acquainted with the Mexican mountain country, but they were "matchless" as scouts. The White Mountain Apaches were nearly as good, for they were also natives of high mountain country, but the Chiricahuas had been hostile more recently; they still had that "keen edge" which had been dulled somewhat in those who had been at peace for a decade or more. White troops, in any case, lacked the Apaches' superb physical conditioning and ability to endure the hardships and privations of campaigning in the sierra. Of the scouts' loyalty, Crook insisted, he had no doubts.[31]

Crook's conclusions were not acceptable to many whites, who thought that the long-drawn-out campaign confirmed their own distrust of Apache scouts. The clear statement that regulars could not cope with either the country or the Chiricahuas was offensive to many of the general's colleagues. In addition, the enlistment of Chiricahuas seemed to be an unwise trusting of treacherous savages. Surely the Cibicu affair proved that Apache scouts could be trusted only to a limited extent.

Unfortunately for Crook and the scouts, General Sheridan, now commanding general of the army, shared the widespread distrust of Apaches. When Sheridan visited Crook in November 1885, he suggested that the reservation Chiricahuas ought to be removed from Arizona entirely, to deprive the hostiles of potential help and recruits. Both Crook and Captain Emmet Crawford, one of the general's most trusted "Indian thinkers," opposed the idea as "inopportune." Crawford was about to leave for Mexico with a battalion of 200 scouts, many of them Chiricahuas, who could hardly be expected to fight if their families were carried off as prisoners. Seeing that the men on the spot held such definite opinions, Sheridan put off his proposal. Crook and Crawford both expressed great confidence in the scouts, but Sheridan's doubts did not go away.[32]

Crawford knew, and probably pointed out to Sheridan, that during the previous July, Chato and a detachment of scouts had captured fifteen women and children of the hostiles in Mexico. Scout battalions under Crawford and Captain Wirt Davis had achieved whatever limited success had been gained up to the time of Sheridan's visit. The Chiricahuas were in Crawford's battalion, since he was acquainted with them from reservation days.[33]

Crawford headed south into the Sierra Madre once again in November. The battalion sergeant major was Noche, who was considered without equal as a guide; Chato was not along this time. Weeks of hard marching convinced the officers that the Apaches were masters of scouting, and that white troops could neither have kept up the pace nor carried out the movements skillfully enough. The scouts neglected no possible precaution and the officers let them do things their own way; any impulse to interfere was dampened by the thought that many of these men, the Chiricahuas within the last few years, had killed whites. Finally, a long, hard night march enabled them to surprise the hostile camp. Lieutenant William Shipp was disappointed that the scouts did not charge right into the camp; he reflected that soldiers might have done so, but that soldiers would never have managed the approach well enough to achieve surprise.[34] The attack itself became largely an exchange of fire, proving virtually bloodless, and all of the hostiles escaped, leaving considerable baggage behind. The next day Mexican troops attacked the scouts, ostensibly by mistake, while Geronimo and his followers observed with interest from the nearby hills. Crawford was mortally wounded, as was the Mexican commander. The surviving officers, Lieutenants Marion P. Maus and Shipp, managed to halt the firing; unfriendly discussions with the Mexican officers demonstrated that the Mexican forces were nearly as suspicious of the scouts as they were of the hostiles, and it was deemed wisest to withdraw to the border. Crook and even Sheridan were convinced that Crawford, who died on the journey north, would have brought about the surrender of Geronimo in a short time, if it had not been for this unfortunate affair.[35]

Geronimo did indeed make a surrender offer soon after, and Crook went south to meet personally with the hostiles in Mexico in March 1886. Among those who accompanied him were Kaytennae, now returned from Alcatraz, and Alchesay of the White Mountains. Crook believed Kaytennae was now quite subdued and ready to serve the whites, but James Kaywaykla asserted that his stepfather went along to keep the interpreters honest and to keep Chato in check. No one else, however, indicates that Chato was present on the occasion. Geronimo told Crook of the fears that had caused him to run; Crook was skeptical. Alchesay, on the strength of his own record of service, pleaded for good treatment for the Chiricahuas. The hostiles surrendered with the understanding that they would be sent out of the country for a few years and then allowed to return to San Carlos. The hostiles and scouts marched north together, but the hostiles camped separately and retained their weapons. Just before crossing the border, Geronimo broke away with about twenty men and a number of women and children and fled back into Mexico.[36]

This episode was the last straw for Sheridan. He telegraphed Crook that he could not see how the escape could have been made without the connivance of the scouts. It now seemed to him that Crook should go over to the defensive, covering important points with troops and patrolling the border with cavalry. Crook replied that such a policy could not possibly succeed against Geronimo's elusive raiders. Crook remained convinced that only offensive operations with scouts against the Mexican refuges of the hostiles could end Geronimo's incursions and quiet unrest on the reservation. Crook then submitted a request to be relieved, which could be construed as a demand to be allowed to do it his way or not at all. Sheridan later commented that he had for some time been uneasy about Crook's "policy of operating almost exclusively with Indian scouts," but that he could not well force a commander of Crook's experience to change his methods while continuing in command. The request for relief gave Sheridan an out; he transferred Crook to the Department of the Platte and replaced him with General Nelson Miles.[37]

Miles had used Indian scouts, including recently surrendered hostiles, extensively on the northern Plains. He was too experienced, however, to assume that all Indians would be the same, and he knew of Sheridan's disapproval of the Chiricahuas and of Crook's reliance on scouts. Observing the reservation Chiricahuas, he noted that they had never given up their arms or horses, for Crook believed that disarming them would only lead to further difficulties. Miles thought the Chiricahuas "a more turbulent and dissipated body of Indians" than he had ever seen before, and he was sure they were in communication with the hostiles, plotting a further outbreak. Lieutenant Marion Maus, who had commanded Miles's Cheyenne scouts in the Nez Perce campaign and had been with Crawford on his last expedition, was of the same opinion, and his judgment undoubtedly carried weight with Miles. Naturally, he immediately discharged the Chiricahua scouts.[38]

No one denied the indispensability of Indians as trailers. Miles continued to use Apaches of groups other than the hostiles, as well as Indians of other tribes. Charles Gatewood, now in failing health, was stationed on the border for a time with a company of Navajos; he considered them "loafers" and hoped for their discharge. Miles, however, knew that Sheridan wanted the regulars to play a larger role in the campaign, and he was receiving similar urgings from his division commander, General Howard. He therefore placed Captain Henry Lawton, Fourth Cavalry, in command of a force of white soldiers especially selected for physical fitness, and sent them in pursuit of Geronimo's little band in the sierra. Meanwhile other commands patrolled or guarded strategic points such as waterholes.[39]

Crook's partisans noted with pleasure that Lawton's command kept on the trial until virtually every man was exhausted, but never came in contact with or killed a hostile. Ultimately Miles selected Gatewood and two Chiricahuas to go to Geronimo and persuade him to surrender. The mission emphasized the importance of personal relationships; with Crook gone, Crawford dead, and Britton Davis having resigned from the army, Gatewood was the only officer with whom Geronimo was well acquainted and whom he would trust. Moreover, the two Apaches, Kayitah and Martine, were related to various members of Geronimo's band, and he would probably trust their word. After certain confusions, Geronimo and company did indeed surrender to Miles and were shipped off to Florida. Later there were various unedifying squabbles within the army over who was entitled to the greatest share of credit for the results. Not surprisingly, Chiricahua testimony gives Martine and Kayitah, rather than Gatewood, the starring roles in the surrender negotiations.[40]

Before Geronimo's surrender Miles had taken a step that generated lasting controversy. He ordered the reservation Chiricahuas, including former scouts, arrested and shipped to Florida. Several leading men, including Chato, had been in Washington conferring with the president and other officials; on the return trip they were arrested at Fort Leavenworth, then sent to St. Augustine to join the others. Eventually, former scouts, hostiles, and all were united in imprisonment at Mount Vernon Barracks, Alabama—including Martine and Kayitah, who had facilitated the final surrender. Naturally the former hostiles took considerable pleasure in the plight of the scouts.[41]

Miles based his action, undertaken with the full support of Sheridan and the Cleveland administration, on the belief that the reservation Chiricahuas, scouts included, were in league with the hostiles, rendering them aid and comfort in various ways. All of these officials believed that the only way to end the repeated outbreaks was to imprison the whole tribe. To Crook and his supporters the arrest and removal was a blatant injustice to faithful soldiers and peaceful Indians who were trying to adapt to a new way of life.

Sheridan believed that the Chiricahua scouts were willing to try to capture the hostiles or induce them to surrender, but would not try to kill them. Crook pointed out that with two exceptions, all of the hostiles killed during the whole campaign were killed by scouts. (The exceptions were one hostile killed by a reservation Apache and one by a cowboy.) As if tacitly acknowledging that there might be some substance to Sheridan's charge, Crook asked whether the purpose of the campaign was simply to kill a certain number of Indians or to bring peace and preserve lives in the most effective manner. Allowing for the fact that Crook was pleading his own case, there is a clear indication that the two generals differed significantly on the army's duty in the West. Sheridan saw the soldier's duty as the destruction of a clearly defined enemy. Crook, despite a personal dislike of Geronimo, was no longer so sure of the rights and wrongs of the matter. If the scouts could secure the end of the fighting without much bloodshed, that was acceptable to him.[42]

Lieutenant Shipp also thought that the Chiricahua scouts were not eager to kill their kin, but for him this lack of enthusiasm did not amount to "treachery," for he asserted that the scouts were above that. The White Mountain scouts had no such scruples about killing Chiricahuas, he thought, but were dominated and intimidated by their Chiricahua comrades. Since Opler's informants indicated that the scouts were trying to bring

the hostiles in for their own good, there may well be substance
to this view.[43]

Lieutenants Maus and Gatewood made a more serious charge.
They asserted that the Chiricahua scouts were giving or selling
ammunition to the hostiles, at least during the surrender negotiations in early 1886. The charge seemed plausible because
many of the hostiles carried captured military arms of the same
caliber as those issued to the scouts. Other whites, though not
those most closely associated with the scouts in this campaign,
charged that Chato and others had hindered operations and were
nearly mutinous at times. The recollections of the hostiles make
no reference to aid of this sort. They regarded the scouts as the
only enemy they really feared, because of their knowledge of the
country and their ability to move rapidly. The hostiles' bitterness toward the scouts is the strongest evidence that Crook's
confidence was not misplaced.[44]

The imprisonment of the scouts and their families reflected
on Crook's military judgment and offended his sense of justice.
For both these reasons he sought to rectify the situation. At first
he quietly established contact with the Indian Rights Association, urging its members to study the situation and agitate for
the release of the Chiricahuas. After Sheridan's death in 1888
and his own promotion to major general—a rank higher than
Miles's—Crook openly associated himself with the Indian
Rights Association in a movement to have the Chiricahuas
transferred to some western reservation where they could begin
to farm and support themselves. The agitation opened a public
controversy over the Geronimo campaign, with Miles and
Crook as the protagonists.[45]

Inevitably the discussion centered on Crook's conduct of the
campaign and the loyalty of the Chiricahua scouts. If Crook was
right, Chato and the scouts had suffered a great injustice; if
Miles was right, the Chiricahuas deserved no better, and their
transfer to the West might result in another guerrilla war. Crook
particularly favored the tribe's removal to the region of Fort Sill,
Indian Territory, where the climate was more like that of their
homeland. Public opinion in Arizona was decidedly opposed,
even though Fort Sill was over 700 miles from the San Carlos
reservation; certainly this opposition was a tribute to the impression made by the long-range raids of Victorio, Geronimo,

and others in the past. Miles was now opposed to the Fort Sill transfer, even though he had himself suggested this course at the time of the removal from Arizona.[46]

Crook visited the prisoners in Alabama in January 1890, and reported officially to the secretary of war. Naturally he painted the gloomiest picture possible of their condition. Crook attributed the high death rate among them to "homesickness, change of climate, and the dreary monotony of empty lives." Their recent experience, he thought, was a striking example of the difficulties encountered by Indians who tried to live at peace and follow white ways. He took Chato as a particular example. Chato had taken up farming after his surrender in 1883, had planted crops, raised sheep, and acquired several horses and mules. He had refused to join the 1885 outbreak—at the risk of his life, according to Crook—and had served loyally as a scout. Given a medal by the president, he had been arrested while returning from Washington, and was now confined with the men he had helped to run down. Showing Crook the medal Cleveland had given him, Chato asked, "Why was I given that to wear in the guard-house?" Crook submitted that Chato had not really been given much encouragement in his efforts to become a "self-sustaining citizen."[47]

Although the Geronimo campaign was "fought over again at the Capitol," there was no immediate result. Crook died suddenly in March 1890, and the matter was shelved for the time being. In 1894 the Chiricahuas finally moved to Fort Sill and were able to begin farming. Ironically, most of the men were enlisted as scouts, an action that gave them a small income and placed them under military authority. Geronimo and other leaders ranked as sergeants, so that they had official authority to keep order. In later years, confronted with rumors that he was instigating unrest, the old raider indignantly answered that he was a soldier, wearing the uniform of the United States, and that such accusations hurt his honor. In 1912, three years after Geronimo's death, the government gave the Chiricahuas the choice of remaining in Oklahoma or moving to the Mescalero Apache reservation in New Mexico; the majority chose the latter course. Among them was Chato, who died in 1934, in a manner symbolic of the Apaches' painful transition from one world to another. Driving his own automobile while intoxicated, he ran off the road.[48]

The Chiricahuas' story, however, was only part of the history of the Arizona Apaches. Several thousand had lived more or less quietly on San Carlos and Fort Apache reservations since their surrender to Crook in the 1870s. Striving to adjust to a new way of life, they had been as vulnerable to the depredations of the relatively few hostiles as the white population. Increasingly their attitude toward the "broncos" or "renegades" seems to have converged with that of their white neighbors. The scouts continued in service, their duties becoming increasingly like those of the reservation police. Indeed, the Apaches made no distinction in their language between the two organizations. Occasionally individuals were unable to adjust to reservation life, or became involved in homicide or other crimes against their own people; they usually fled into the mountains and lived as outlaws, raiding the reservation as well as the whites for supplies, ammunition, and women. Singly or in groups of less than a dozen, they were still being hunted down by scouts in the 1890s. Massai and the Apache Kid, the most notorious, operated alone; both were former scouts. Experienced scouts considered these pursuits more dangerous than the bigger campaigns of earlier years; these renegades were desperate men, with nothing to lose.[49]

The scouts continued on the government payroll long after the turn of the century. A contingent was sent to accompany General John Pershing's punitive expedition against Pancho Villa in 1916. It was probably their last serious employment, and it was the first time the army made serious use of aerial reconnaissance. Even in this changing military world, the officer in charge of the scouts was impressed by their abilities; middle-aged and unimpressive in full olive drab, they were still unsurpassed in reconnaissance and ambush. In later years, scout enlistment was a sinecure for aging men, most of whom were still too young to have scouted for Crook in the "good old days." Their feelings were hurt when the increasingly mechanized army could find no role for them. The army pensioned off the last of them in 1943.[50]

A reasonable conclusion would be that the Apache scouts made the best of a bad situation. Individually and in groups they made their peace with the whites, and most of them kept it. Scouting enabled them to continue in a line of work for which they were qualified, and to live a life of adventure and travel that was more attractive by far than unmitigated reservation life. By accommodating to white ways in a fashion that suited them, they eased their difficulties of adjustment; they were able, at first, to take the part of the "white man's road" that suited them. Unyielding resistance, it must be remembered, meant eventual annihilation, not just for warriors but often for women and children. Tribal and band differences that seemed insignificant to whites eased the scouts' consciences in serving against people of basically similar language and culture. Generally speaking, the closer the ties of kinship, the more reluctant they were to go the full route in fighting. Yet divided opinions could bring them into the field against old friends and relatives. Some of them may well have believed that they could help these friends and relatives best by compelling them to surrender.

Chapter Eleven

For some military commanders a major benefit of Indian scouting service was that it facilitated the Indians' assimilation into white culture and society. Such assimilation was the avowed aim of official government policy in the post–Civil War period, and the fond hope of humanitarians and missionaries. A number of military commanders also hoped earnestly for assimilation as an alternative to extermination or slow disappearance, which were disturbing to their sense of right, the more so as they had to witness them at first hand. Of course, for the army assimilation was a by-product of the military usefulness of Indian scouts, not the first consideration. But in convincing military and civil superiors that Indian scouts were a good investment, some of the commanders could readily point out the ways in which military service could facilitate the ultimate, peaceful end.

Military service would be many Indians' first intensive contact with white ways. It was inevitable that they would be influenced in some way, for good or ill, by the experience. The military naturally preferred to believe that the influence of military life would be for the good.

The first benefit, in the eyes of the military, was that scout service provided work for reservation Indians; like its civilian contemporaries, the army believed that idle hands became the devil's playthings. Work prevented the Indians from brooding over their wrongs, or from turning to activities disapproved by whites to relieve boredom. George Crook, who has been called the most original thinker in the Indian-fighting army, was the earnest advocate of this idea, but not the only one. As early as 1867, General Christopher Augur concluded that scouting "opens to these people a useful career, renders them tractable and obedient, and educates and civilizes them more effectually than can be done in any other way." This was an admirable capsule statement of the military assimilationist philosophy, on which others would only expand. A more limited view, but one that must have had wide appeal, was that of General Irvin McDowell, writing in the same year. McDowell simply wanted some of the more unruly Indians in his Department of California enlisted and taken off to campaign somewhere away from home so that they could not make trouble for the army.[1]

Enlisted scouts received the same pay as white soldiers, and were issued rations. These allowances helped to supplement the supplies issued to reservation Indians by the Indian Bureau. The inadequacy of these reservation rations was a major source of discontent among western Indians; it was also one of the army's principal weapons in its fight with the civil agency, providing substance to the military charges of corruption and incompetence within the bureau. In this, as in other ways, the army believed itself to be doing what the bureau was supposed to do, by keeping the Indians reasonably satisfied and preventing human suffering.[2]

Beyond these immediate benefits, thoughtful officers hoped for more radical, long-term changes leading to assimilation. They believed that military service would wean the Indian scout away from dependence on tribal ties and lead him to think and act individually. The authority of tribal chiefs would thus be eroded, at least that of chiefs perceived as reactionaries who retarded the progress of their people. It is likely that many scouts did in fact acquire a new source of authority and identity outside the traditional society. Such a transformation was highly desirable to the army, since the respect and authority were transferred to the military, but the chiefs might have another opinion. This is suggested by the opposition of the Pawnee and the Arikara chiefs, long friendly to the whites, to the enlistment of scouts.[3]

In the contest over authority and policy with the Bureau of Indian Affairs, the enlistment of scouts often served as a legal means of removing at least some Indians from the control of the rival agency. Army officers often encountered frustration when they complained of civilian mismanagement of Indians; it frequently seemed, as Crook once complained, that Washington did the very opposite of what they recommended. Enlistment, in their view, provided one means of protecting the Indians. After the flight of Little Wolf's Cheyennes from Indian Territory to Montana, the men of this band enlisted as scouts at Fort Keogh. Military leaders had expressed strong disapproval of the policy of removing these people to the southern Plains, which had resulted in bloodshed for which the army was blamed. Enlistment of these Cheyennes as scouts provided a means of thwarting further attempts to move them. When civil agents attempted to move three bands of White Mountain Apaches from Fort Apache, Arizona to the reservation at San Carlos, they ran into the fact that the men of these bands were enlisted scouts. The Indians remained under military jurisdiction while being introduced to farming and other facets of the new life.[4]

In such situations, of course, the Indian bands were under direct military control. All scouts, as enlisted men, were subject to military law and discipline. To the army officers the scouts' military status had the obvious advantages of enabling them to control malcontents and punish violators of the whites' rules. Even so, experienced and sensible officers were aware that Indians could not automatically be held responsible for strict adherence to unfamiliar rules. Desertion, for instance, was seldom punished as severely among scouts as among regular troops.[5]

Conversely, the enlistment of scouts, particularly recently surrendered hostiles, served to convey the army's trust and respect for the Indians. It suggested both that their quality as warriors was valued by the "soldier chiefs" and that the officers trusted their sense of honor to hold them to their promises. When Colonel Nelson Miles wanted to enlist Little Wolf's Cheyennes, he worked on the reluctant chief by praising the band's fighting qualities and achievements. William White, a former enlisted man, later ventured the opinion that Miles acted more out of diplomacy, attaching the Indians to the army and finding some occupation for them, than from any belief in their military value. Miles's own recollections, however, indicate that he had both the "public relations" and the more narrowly military end in view. Certainly his display of respect must have eased both the pride of the warriors who had had to surrender and their fears of being returned to the hated Indian Territory.[6]

Miles earnestly recommended that the Cheyennes and Sioux in his custody at Fort Keogh be allowed to remain in the area and be furnished with agricultural implements. This plan was in accord with the assimilationist philosophy of both civilian reformers and soldiers of humanitarian inclination. Hardly any person of influence, civilian or military, whose concern with the "Indian question" went beyond the equating of good Indians with dead ones imagined any other way of helping Indians than making them over in the white image. The concept of doing so under military control and discipline may now suggest "brainwashing"—forcibly imposing new patterns of behavior on captives and encouraging submissive, dependent attitudes toward their captors. Yet a really intensive, conscious effort of this kind would seem to be precluded by the qualities necessary in Indian scouts, and the kind of relationship of whites and Indians required by such service, except in so far as all military training tends to produce such effects.[7]

One clear example linking military service for Indians with a prison atmosphere may have broken the Indians' will to resist and induced them to identify with their captors. In 1875 a group of southern Plains warriors, mostly Cheyennes, Kiowas, and Comanches, were arrested for alleged crimes and depredations during the Red River war of 1874–75 and sent to prison at Fort Marion, St. Augustine, Florida. They were under the control of Lieutenant Richard Pratt, already an experienced commander of Indian scouts. Pratt, committed to a belief in equality and the assimilability of Indians, put the incarcerated warriors in uniform, drilled them, and set them to doing guard duty over themselves. He found them much more efficient and conscientious than the white soldiers on duty at the fort. Pratt's tractable captives were the start of his school for Indians in Carlisle, Pennsylvania, and his lifelong commitment to Indian education and assimilation. The sincerity of Pratt's belief that he was doing the Indians good is unquestionable; so are the respect and affection with which many of his erstwhile prisoners regarded him throughout their lives. Yet the eagerness with which many of them took up the military routine and the later educational program suggests their need for activity and self-respect, and their feeling of helplessness in the grip of powerful forces. It was also a tribute to their adaptability. Pratt was encouraged by the thought that the prisoners, supposedly among the most savage and incorrigible of their tribes, could make such progress. It apparently did not occur to him that the "worst" Indians, by white standards, the notable warriors and raiders, might be the best by the standards of their own society: the ambitious, intelligent, persevering, and enterprising.[8]

By the 1880s, as the Indian wars themselves were waning, a school of thought had emerged within the army which saw military service on a large scale as the answer to the problem of what to do with the Indians. Experience of the horsemanship and general fighting abilities of many western tribes turned various officers' thoughts to their potential value as cavalrymen; the example of the British "irregular" cavalry regiments in India seemed an encouraging precedent. Watching Chief Washakie drill his Shoshones in mounted maneuvers, John Bourke could only think "what fools we were not to incorporate these nomads —the finest light cavalry in the world—into our permanent military force." In 1880 *The United Service*, one of the first professional military journals in the United States, featured an article by Captain H. C. Cushing, "Military Colonization of the Indians." The idea gained popularity over the next decade, and Lieutenant George S. Wilson and Majors William Powell and Ezra P. Ewers produced similar articles advocating the idea. Frederic Remington seconded them in the more widely circulated *Harper's Weekly*, even including a sketch of his own idea for an Indian uniform, blending buckskin and frontier military style.[9]

Cushing's article, the first, was also the most elaborate, and it summed up most of the ideas of the military assimilationists. Condemning U.S. Indian policy and administration to date, Cushing suggested that Indian campaigns thus provoked were enormously expensive and likely to become more difficult as the Indians acquired better arms and better knowledge of the whites' military methods. The answer to both the moral and the practical problems posed by the current state of affairs, Cushing urged, was "military colonization," based on the example of ancient Rome. The western Indians were barbarians who loved war; they would not become Christian farmers by a sudden transformation. Instead of attempting to force them into an alien mold, he suggested organizing various bands or tribes as military colonies, enlisting the men as soldiers, and putting them under officers specially selected for ability to work with Indians and subject to replacement if they fell short in any way. At first nomadic wandering would continue, but now it would be under military supervision. Cushing may have been aware that the Plains tribes did indeed organize tribal buffalo hunts in a disciplined fashion very much like a military expedition, although he did not mention the practice. Gradually the officers would introduce more military regularity and formal discipline, in such small increments that the Indians would hardly be aware of it. Step by step the officers would diminish the chiefs' authority and the men's identification with the tribe, making each Indian more aware of himself as an individual. Eventually the tribe would become more sedentary, spending more time at its home post-cum-village, where the Indians could also learn crafts and skills as they built their own housing. Farming and cattle raising could be introduced in easy stages, encouraged by the army's purchase of supplies from the Indian farmers. In the meantime, the Indian regiments would serve as the means of discouraging other tribes from going to war, and the Indians' fighting qualities would thus be used for the benefit of "civilization."[10]

The defects of this scheme are evident with hindsight. Cushing's emphasis on indirect manipulation and gradual alteration of the behavior of unsuspecting Indians almost suggests he was a disciple of Jean-Jacques Rousseau's theories on the education of children. This emphasis should make clear the degree of paternalism involved in his thinking, and his assumption that any direct appeal to the Indians' reason was useless. The military assimilationists generally shared the basic lack of respect and downright repugnance for the Indians' culture which was so evident among their civilian counterparts. They all assumed that what the Indians needed was a large dose of Christian discipline, regular habits, morality, and skills, all supposedly lacking in the Indian way of life. Even Crook, who respected Indian intelligence and reasoning ability far more than most of his contemporaries, believed that "the mere fact" that scouts were "subjected to rules and regulations" was bound to have a good effect. Where military and civilians differed was in certain assumptions about the ease with which the transition could be made and in opinions about the army and military life which were part of a wider disagreement in American society.[11]

Army officers were aware, because of personal observation, of how difficult it was for Indians to make the transition to a radically different way of life. They attributed this difficulty to savage obduracy, civilian bungling and dishonesty, or the general injustice of the whites' treatment of Indians, depending on their own individual perceptions and attitudes. A few possessed enough empathy to understand how painful such cultural change must be, and enough discernment to realize that their own society did not always present an admirable contrast to that of the "savages." Yet with things as they were, the Indians seemed to have only two alternatives—"civilization or extermination."[12]

The deeper disagreement was on the underlying value of military life and the military virtues. Aside from nineteenth-century America's general disdain for and lack of interest in the regular army and the military profession, the movement for humanitarian reform in Indian affairs included a number of Quakers and other prominent peace advocates and antimilitarists. These people doubted profoundly the very validity of the military profession and its values; in addition they were generally convinced that the army wanted control over Indian affairs in order to pursue a policy of pure force and brutality. Turn the Indians over to the army, declared Pima Indian agent J. H. Stout, "and in a very few years the complement of 'good Indians' in the happy hunting-grounds will be complete." The attitude toward the soldier was much like that which Kipling caricatured in "Tommy"; the "single men in barracks" could bring the Indians nothing but drunkenness, debauchery, and venereal disease. Military life tended only to make men demoralized, lazy, and unfit for honest work in civilian life. Besides, encouraging Indians to pursue ways of violence was only to perpetuate some of the worst features of savage life, to pander to their worst tendencies.[13]

Naturally such views were offensive and unacceptable to the army men; they rejected such reflections on their moral fiber. Most officers were not likely to consider whether it was de-

sirable to make whole Indian tribes more or less permanent adjuncts of the army, and to assimilate them into a regimented,
segregated version of white society. They were unlikely to question the validity or values of the way of life they themselves had
chosen.

One reason that these military men believed in their proposals
was that they had seen or heard of most of what they proposed
already in practice somewhere in the West, on an improvised
and temporary small scale. Apart from scout organizations pure
and simple, there were Indian groups that were long-term adjuncts of military posts, the men serving as scouts, such as the
Tonkawas at Fort Griffin and the Seminole Negroes at Fort Duncan. There were reservations placed for a time under military
control, where the officers in charge commanded the scout detachments who policed their own people, as at San Carlos. Settlements of Indians around military posts, where the commanding officer or a subordinate acted as de facto agent, sometimes
gave rise to an official reservation, as with the Northern Cheyenne reservation near Fort Keogh, Montana, or the Walapai reservation that originated at Camp Beale's Spring in northwestern
Arizona. In some cases forts established near reservations cooperated with the Indians in defense against hostile incursions, as
with Fort Custer, Montana and the Crow reservation, or Camp
Brown, Wyoming, and the Wind River Shoshone reservation;
the post was later renamed Fort Washakie in honor of the Shoshone chief. Sometimes an Indian reservation served, generally
by accident rather than official intention, as a defensive bastion
for white settlers against hostile raiders; examples were the
Brazos reservation in Texas before the Civil War, the Pawnee
reservation in Nebraska, the Blackfoot reservation in Montana,
and the Wind River reservation in Wyoming. At Fort Apache and
San Carlos the army provided agricultural equipment and encouraged farming by providing a good, capitalistic incentive—
it purchased the Apaches' hay and other surplus produce, to the
anguish of would-be white contractors. It seemed to some army
assimilationists that the possibilities inherent in such improvi-
sations needed only to be made systematic and comprehensive.[14]

In all of these proposals the paternalistic strain is obvious. It
suggests emulation of European colonial powers and a militant

assumption of the "white man's burden" to civilize the non-European—ideas that were not uncongenial to many Americans in the late nineteenth century. Yet George Crook, advocate and practitioner of assimilation through the agency of the army, was less than a complete believer in such a philosophy. By the 1880s he favored giving full citizenship and the vote to Indians within a short time, and wrote a letter to this effect for the public use of the Indian Rights Association. The Indians, he thought, were as capable of responsible and intelligent citizenship as many other groups (probably he meant immigrants and blacks) who had been granted the privilege. Here Crook differed not only with most of his military colleagues, but with many of the civilian assimilationists; certainly he differed from the tendency of the Bureau of Indian Affairs to establish authoritarian regimes in which authority and decisions rested solely with the agent and his superiors in Washington.[15]

There were other reasons for enlisting Indians besides these grand objectives. Such measures would provide justification for expanding the army, increasing the congressional military appropriation, and opening new opportunities for junior officers in a period of slow promotion. It would give the army that control over Indian affairs for which it had campaigned for years.[16]

The culmination of military assimilationism came when the Indian wars were virtually over. This was not just an example of preparing for the last war, rather than the next, but also a way of extending and justifying military control over the Indians when the most obvious reason for such control was receding into the past. From 1890 to 1894, the army tried the experiment of enlisting Indians, not as short-service scouts, but as regular soldiers serving the standard five-year enlistment in regular units. The white enlisted men in one company in each of several regular regiments were transferred or discharged, and the companies were filled up with Indians. The members of a company were generally of the same tribe, and the officers selected were generally men with extensive experience in dealing with Indians. The first such company was Edward Casey's Cheyenne unit of the Eighth Cavalry, which participated in the Ghost Dance campaign in South Dakota. This was a limited attempt to carry out the recommendations of men like Cushing, Powell, and Ewers. Only a portion of the manpower of the several tribes was used, and no new units were created. Instead, Indians replaced white soldiers in already existing regular units, and this arrangement was to be a source of discontent and opposition.[17]

While the enlistment of Indians as regular soldiers had many advocates, army opinion on the subject was decidedly divided, as it had always been. Of nine senior officers polled on the question beforehand, six opposed the idea. Among those opposed, interestingly enough, was George Crook. He judged that regular army rules and discipline were not suited to Indians and that a better policy would be to continue the less formal, short-enlistment scout units. This recommendation was consistent with opinions Crook had expressed earlier; he probably feared that the regular way of doing things would negate the very qualities of independence, initiative, and scouting skill that made the Indian scouts so valuable in the first place. In view of Crook's criticism of the army's tendency to turn the soldier into a machine, he may even have thought that the soldier should become more like the Indian, rather than vice versa.[18]

The experiment of enlisting Indians as regular soldiers had the support of Commanding General John M. Schofield, who differed greatly in this respect from his predecessor, Sheridan. Schofield expressed his belief in both the reliability of Indian soldiers and the assimilationist purpose; he doubted that Indians would be quite so efficient as white soldiers at first, but thought a few years of service would change things greatly. Yet in spite of Schofield's backing, the Indian companies lasted only a few years. Between 1894 and 1897, all such companies were mustered out. Officers who served with them judged the Indian units to have been successful, but officers in the upper echelons did not agree. They charged that too much depended on the personality of the commanding officer; a company that was happy and hard-working under a man like Casey or Hugh Scott, who were sympathetic, patient, and deeply interested in the welfare of the Indians, might go to pieces if the officers were killed or transferred. The personal leadership necessary with Indians ran counter to the army's ideal of making officers interchangeable parts. Indeed, it was a manifestation of the clash between the impersonal, mechanically functioning state and the kinship and personal loyalties that bound the Indians; the Indians would face that conflict many times in the future. Hugh Scott, who commanded a Kiowa troop of the Seventh Cavalry, believed that the officer corps opposed the experiment because white soldiers had been discharged to make room for Indians; they might have been more receptive if new Indian units had been created, thus expanding the army and opening new chances for promotion. For this reason, Scott believed, the army was determined to see the experiment fail. All the same, Scott insisted, his men were good soldiers, and the experiment had helped them to fit more easily into white society. Among other things, they had been able to save their pay and use it to build homes after leaving the army.[19]

Scott's conclusion suggests that, after all, most army officers were less enthusiastic about helping the Indians than about the advantages they thought Indian soldiers offered the army. Few had the dedication and mental breadth of Crook, Scott, Casey, and some others. For many, interest in the Indians' welfare faded as the practical benefits to the army and the officer corps became less apparent and the chance of future Indian conflicts dwindled.

Yet the Indian scouts, like the rest of the Indians, had a degree of influence on the army. When confronted with the Philippine insurrection at the turn of the century, the old Indian fighters were not wholly at a loss. As soon as possible they enlisted Filipinos to fight other Filipinos. The most prominent in this role were the Macabebes of Luzon, who had played the same role under Spain; oddly enough, they were said to be descended from Mexican Indian troops sent to the islands long ago by the Spanish. Led by General Frederick Funston, the Macabebes struck the decisive blow to end the insurrection by capturing Emilio Aguinaldo, the Filipino leader. When the army created regular Philippine units to help garrison the islands, their antecedents were clearly indicated by the name: Philippine Scouts. Even so, the army did not, institutionally, become a guerrilla fighting force; the desire and the perceived necessity to emulate European standards were too strong.[20]

The army did not become the major agency for the assimilation of the Indians, because of both external opposition and lack of commitment on the part of most of its officers. But in the course of asserting United States control over the West it played that role for a time, for many Indians, however unintentionally. The army gave many Indian men their first real introduction to the culture that would soon dominate their lives. By providing them with a mode of assimilation congenial to their inclinations, their talents, and their self-respect, scouting may have made that introduction a good deal less painful than any planned by either humanitarians or exterminationists.

Chapter Twelve

Conclusion

Evaluation of the role of the Indian scouts requires consideration of more than military effectiveness. The army found the scouts necessary in pursuing their immediate goal of subduing Indian resistance; the historian must also examine the less immediate effects on the scouts and their peoples. In fact, the scouts' contemporaries anticipated many of the questions that might be asked today.

The officer corps remained divided on the subject of military value from beginning to end. Few denied the necessity of Indians for scouting in the narrowest sense of trailing and reconnaissance; without such services, the army columns would have stumbled about aimlessly in an alien environment. On the question of the Indians' combat value, opinions varied. Some officers regarded all Indians as cowards whose only skill was in running away; some described the Indian warrior as a "first-class fightin' man" with whom the regular trooper could not possibly cope on a man-to-man basis.

From the latter judgment arose the conclusion that substantial numbers of Indians should be recruited to fight other Indians, to augment and even to replace the regular troops. Some military men bitterly opposed this conclusion, out of both pride in their service and fear of the effects on the army's prestige. The disagreement naturally raised the question of the number of scouts to be employed, which became a source of contention between field commanders and budget-conscious administrators in Washington. Commanders who wanted large forces of Indian auxiliaries sometimes had to go outside the recruiting regulations and secure allies in ways reminiscent of the earlier colonial years.

The local commanders' pleas for more scouts show how they perceived the need for Indian assistance. Indian scouts served in virtually every theater and every Indian conflict in the trans-Mississippi West. The manner and effectiveness with which they were employed varied, but seldom did the army try to do entirely without them. Frequently the scouts did a quite disproportionate share of the fighting; often they made the difference between success and frustration. Sometimes the cliché of the cavalry's arrival just in time to save beleaguered comrades or civilians was reversed, and the cavalry was rescued at the last minute by Indians.

Although the nearly universal use of scouts testifies to their effectiveness, some whites could never overcome their doubts about their loyalty, especially when the scouts employed were closely related in language and culture to the "hostiles." It was true that sometimes individual men and groups who had served as scouts were later to be found in the hostile ranks, owing to various circumstances. On one occasion, Apache scouts turned on their regular comrades on the battlefield; though some officers saw mitigating circumstances, many could never again completely trust Apache scouts. Those most closely associated with Indian scouts, however, generally testified to the seriousness with which they took their oath of enlistment and their obligations as they perceived them.

The enlistment laws and administrative requirements caused Indian scout units to be, for the most part, temporary organizations. Only in exceptional circumstances did officers and men remain together over a period of years, acquiring the degree of acquaintance, shared experience, and mutual respect that made for maximum effectiveness.

On the other hand, certain tribes or bands cooperated with the army and other whites consistently over long periods. The Tonkawas, the Warm Springs of Oregon, the Crows, the Wyoming Shoshones, and the Pawnees are prominent examples. All saw advantages to be gained from cooperation: help against more powerful Indian enemies, material gain, more favorable terms than could be won by resistance, and a chance to adjust to radically changing conditions in ways that were relatively easy and familiar. The actual benefits varied considerably, but it would be hard to demonstrate in any of these cases that resistance or noncooperation in the name of a nonexistent racial solidarity would have brought more.

Because there was no formal doctrine to guide the army in its Indian relations, the method of employing Indian scouts varied with the ideas of officers, especially department commanders. These men differed over the degree of reliance on scouts, especially for combat, the numbers necessary, whether to employ men from the same tribe as the hostiles, and on the degree to which scouts might serve such purposes as surrender negotiations. It is perhaps surprising, therefore, that there was as much uniformity as did exist.

Uniformity would have been greater if the federal government had followed a suggestion made in 1878 by Commissioner of Indian Affairs Ezra Hayt. Hayt advocated an Indian auxiliary force of 3,000 men, commanded by picked officers, held in readiness to prevent or contain outbreaks. As Robert Utley points out, such a force could also have been dispersed to serve as police in potentially dangerous situations. Moreover, the very existence of such a force would have absorbed some of the restless younger men most likely to come into collision with whites. It would have provided them with what they regarded as dignified, manly employment, and would have meant greater material comfort for their families. They would have been under white authority, but in a way many found more acceptable than the reservation system. All of these ends were indeed served by the actual Indian scouting system, though less systematically and on a smaller scale.[1]

The question of atrocities apparently did not concern the officers as much as it did their civilian contemporaries. "Atrocities" are defined here as acts that violate established European standards concerning the killing of prisoners and wounded, torture, and the status of women and children. Whites had long believed that Indians habitually killed the helpless, tortured prisoners, mutilated the dead, raped women, and generally indulged innate cruelty and blood lust. Such things certainly happened at times, but the popular perception of them made no allowance for exaggeration and took no account of circumstances or of great individual and tribal variation. "Savagery" and "civilization'' were defined as mutually exclusive opposites; this definition precluded acknowledgment that the difference might be one of degree, or that civilized whites might also commit such acts, especially in warfare against people conceived of as outside the pale of humanity. Inability to admit that such things were possible among civilized Christians meant that the Indians had to be regarded with special horror. Mutilation of the dead was widespread among the western tribes, but the horror felt by nineteenth-century whites may not be equaled in the twentieth century, when we have a wider knowledge of the things that can be inflicted on the living.

Trans-Mississippi Indians rarely took adult males prisoner. This was long-established custom; European ideas to the contrary are of relatively recent origin. Women and children were sometimes killed, but on other occasions taken prisoner and enslaved or adopted into the tribe, depending on custom, circumstances, and the emotions of the warriors. Most of the Plains tribes did not customarily practice torture of prisoners, but whites commonly believed they did. "Keep the last bullet for yourself" was a frontier aphorism. Probably groups from many tribes committed such acts when they were particularly enraged by white men's acts, or when they took revenge on a person or group particularly hated, just as many other peoples have done. "Apache" was a byword for cruelty and torture, and apparently Apaches did occasionally inflict prolonged torture on captives. Yet some Apache men preferred to absent themselves when such acts were performed. Among all peoples there are persons who seem to take pleasure in such acts whenever opportunities that make them acceptable within their particular societies arise. Men of many Plains tribes are known to have raped captive women, probably as an expression of hatred and contempt. The Apaches virtually never did so, for fear of supernatural contamination.[2]

If any such practices were customary in a particular tribe, they would not automatically cease when the warrior put on the army blue. The western volunteers, in their employment of Indian allies, may not have been unduly disturbed by this fact. In the eyes of many whites, the victims were getting what they deserved; if women and children died, one need only remember that "nits make lice." Indian allies who killed indiscriminately were adopting the thoroughgoing solution many westerners favored for the "Indian problem." Civil War volunteers and Texas Rangers often took scalps themselves, though they seem to have drawn the line at torture. This genocidal attitude was by no means univeral; Rip Ford told his Indian allies to leave an old Comanche women unmolested, but he learned later "that that is just what they didn't do."[3]

The regulars generally endeavored to control their scouts in these matters. Scalping the dead seems to have been tolerated, though not openly approved. Attempts were made to prevent indiscriminate killing in the aftermath of battle, and torture was not allowed. If scouts ever used torture to extract information, no record was kept of the fact. Killing and mutilation certainly occurred when whites were not actually present to enforce their peculiar prejudices. On the day after the Battle of the Rosebud, the Crows killed at least one wounded Sioux and mutilated the enemy dead. Reporter John Finerty observed later that "the exigencies of Indian warfare" sometimes required commanders to overlook such things, and that the Crows continued to serve the army because they did so. The same episode led John Bourke, who had just finished praising the Indian allies in his diary, to rage that the sooner the Indians ceased to be Indians and became assimilated, the better.[4]

A classic example of counterproductive violence occurred during Nelson Miles's winter campaign against the Sioux in 1876–77. A party of Sioux leaders on its way to Fort Keogh, carrying a white flag, was attacked and killed by Crow scouts within sight of the post. Naturally, surrender negotiations were delayed, although Miles dismounted the scouts as punishment. The incident did not prevent Miles from employing large numbers of Crows the following summer, under loose supervision.[5]

Officers occasionally felt helpless to protest, as when the Crows burned a Sioux near Fort C. F. Smith in 1867. The post was dependent on the goodwill and assistance of the Crows in fighting off the Sioux. In such cases the whites could console themselves with the thought that such things were common in intertribal warfare, and would happen anyway. One could assume that the victims had done the same thing themselves, or would have, given the opportunity.[6]

Some perceptive army officers were aware, however, that the

simple picture of murderous Indians and humane whites was far too simple. Few officers had such broad experience with Plains Indians as both enemies and friends as William P. Clark. He knew that the cruelties of Indian warfare often arose from what the Indians perceived as necessity; moreover, he thought such episodes as general massacres were as unusual for Indians as for whites. If Indian allies were permitted to commit acts like mutilating the dead, the whites were failing to set a better example and had no reason to be contemptuous of the Indians.[7]

The fact was that the whites' hands were not immaculately clean. The record of regular army men was probably better than that of the Civil War volunteers, but some of them were also guilty of acts that they would have regarded as savagery if Indians had committed them. The murder of prisoners, including women and children, apparently occurred in a few instances. Warfare tends to generate carelessness about human life, particularly if differences in culture and race allow one to regard the enemy as less human than oneself. This is not a subject that nineteenth-century whites cared to examine too closely. Everyone was sure that cruelty and treachery were peculiarly characteristic of Indians; the Declaration of Independence itself said so, and a great mass of popular literature and folklore agreed. These savage traits excused retaliatory violence on the one hand, and justified coercive acculturation on the other.[8]

Francis Jennings argues that the myth of the Indians' peculiar ferocity and cruelty arose in the colonial conflicts of the seventeenth century, as part of a general ideology of justification for dispossession and extermination. Well before the Civil War, as historian William Skelton has noted, many army officers distinguished "civilized" and "savage" warfare as two quite different things. Actions that would have been atrocities in the former were justified in Indian warfare as retaliation and to teach the savages a lesson. When Colonel George Wright hanged various Northwest chiefs after the 1858 war, he undoubtedly believed he was punishing criminals and forcing their tribesmen to behave themselves in the future. The whole army knew that surprise attacks on hostile camps, often the only means of striking an elusive enemy effectively, inevitably led to shooting of women and children, even if efforts were made to prevent it. Some officers reacted to humanitarian criticism by asserting that the "squaws" were the ones who committed the worst tortures and therefore deserved no sympathy.[9]

Yet many commanders issued specific orders that women and children were not to be harmed; no doubt they then hoped for the best. Crook observed that the killing of Indian noncombatants was little different from what happened in cities besieged in civilized wars; artillery bombardments killed innocent civilians along with soldiers. Crook did not think the whites had given the Apaches any lessons in chivalry to be emulated. Civil War veterans understood this well enough, just as they knew of the destruction Sherman and Sheridan had inflicted on Southern homes and food supplies in 1864–65. Most of them preferred to believe, however, that they were different from savage warriors. The nineteenth century romanticized war in a way that the twentieth finds repugnant. One could not condemn the savages so readily if one admitted that civilized warfare, including the glorious Civil War, was not really different in kind.[10]

The question of moral justification, then, rested on the larger questions of morality in war. Ending a war quickly generally means reducing the loss of life, and officers like Crook argued that the use of Indian scouts was therefore a humane measure. The army could break resistance sooner, or even head it off or contain it. If the army were indeed performing a police function, it could do so more effectively and painlessly with Indian help.[11]

Far beyond the immediate military concerns were the long-range effects of scout service on the Indians themselves, which varied greatly among individuals and groups. Two Leggings and Plenty Coups, both Crows, differed on the value to their people of their alliance with the whites. Plenty Coups rejoiced that his people had secured a large reservation in their own country; Two Leggings could see only what had been taken away.[12]

In general, the whites exploited the services and talents of the Indian scouts to promote white purposes. Whites obtained control of the West and its resources, and Indians found themselves confined to restricted areas under close supervision. This had always been the whites' basic goal, and neither resistance nor cooperation on the part of Indians turned them from it. The goal the Indians cherished was to continue the way of life to which they were accustomed, but this was impossible.

The intentions of the whites most directly involved were not necessarily exploitive. Within the context of expansion, these white men often assumed that what they were doing was best for the Indians. Some made substantial efforts to protect the Indians' interests against tribal enemies, frontiersmen, and civil authorities. Few would identify themselves with Indians against whites generally, but some clearly came to identify themselves with their Indian friends against other Indians. It was natural to regard the Indians who helped whites as good and to regard those who resisted as bad. Indians who changed sides, of course, confused these distinctions and caused a few whites, such as William P. Clark and George Crook, to have doubts about the justice of their cause.

The tendency in recent Indian history is to represent Indians as being acted upon by whites, usually disastrously. But the Indians themselves acted, both on whites and on each other. They made choices and sought answers to their problems. Their choices were shaped by situations that they did not perceive as being wholly white-created, even though the white presence was important. Some Indians chose military cooperation with whites because they sought definite benefits, immediate or long-range. Some inevitably sought immediate personal gain, while others had in mind a long-term strategy for the benefit of the group that held their primary loyalty. Their purposes were not necessarily those imagined by whites, and the Indians often acted on the assumption that whites could be used to serve Indian purposes.

Rewards varied considerably. As Crook observed about the treatment of the Northern Cheyennes, the federal government often seemed to forget the services rendered by Indians. The Tonkawas dwindled to near-extinction despite their long tradition of cooperation with whites. The Chiricahua scouts landed in prison with those whom they had fought. The Pawnees lost their homeland, though partly of their own choice. The Crows and Shoshones, on the other hand, at least gained reservations where they wanted to live, and perhaps saved themselves from destruction by the Sioux, although their lives would never again be the same. Those Sioux who cooperated with the army may have helped to head off a disastrous attempt to transfer them to Indian Territory. Military service finally made it possible for the Northern Cheyennes to live in country they could consider home. It is doubtful that resistance could have gained them more.[13]

Military cooperation with whites was divisive. Whites did not create intertribal conflict, although white exploitation of these conflicts may have made some of them worse. Whites took advantage of intratribal divisions, sometimes without being fully aware of what was going on. Dividing the Indians against themselves was intentional; breaking down traditional authority was often government or military policy, as was enhancing the authority of leaders who were cooperative. The whites thought they were encouraging and assisting good Indians against bad ones, and also helping the Indians to progress and become civilized. In many cases, indeed, the cooperating groups themselves regarded the diehard resistants as a menace—troublemakers who would bring down the whites' wrath on everyone.

Army officers often presented Indian military service as a means of assimilating Indians into white society. Opinions were divided on this point, for many humanitarians and Indian agents considered such service harmful. The humanitarians were often pacifists or antimilitary progressives. The warrior psychology was part of the savagery from which they sought to raise the Indians; scout service could only perpetuate such attitudes. The warrior continued to be glorified, and received material rewards besides. This situation worked against the desired reeducation toward agriculture and individual accumulation of property. No doubt the humanitarians also perceived such violent, aggressive activity as opposed to conversion to Christianity.

For these very reasons, scout service held attractions for men who regarded war as their proper occupation and horses and weapons as the attributes of manhood. It was possible, at least for a time, to adjust to a new and trying situation, and a changing way of life, in a more acceptable fashion than that demanded by the Indian agents. The adjustment was less drastic, and the warriors were able to meet the future at least partially on their own terms. The military, which had to regard organized violence as within the range of normal human activity, could accept aspirations and emotions that the humanitarians could not.[14]

Some of the objections from whites derived from the division of authority the enlistment of scouts created. The ultimate aims of the army and the Bureau of Indian Affairs were the same: to subject the Indians completely to white authority and make them live in a way acceptable to white cultural prejudice. Each agency doubted the motives and competence of the other. Enlistment of scouts gave the army a measure of authority over particular groups of Indians, and thus weakened the authority of civilian agents. The Indians frequently preferred the military because the soldiers did not steal and because there was less doubt about what they expected the Indians to do. Sometimes the Indians appealed to the nearest military authorities from what they considered the injustices of the civil agents. The logical extreme of this military assumption of authority is found in cases in which a band of Indians became adjuncts of a military post, with the men serving as scouts for long periods. The Indians often preferred the military, and they certainly tried to use the conflict between the army and the BIA to their own advantage. Yet the conflict of policy and shifts of control were undoubtedly confusing and aggravated the Indians' sense of insecurity.[15]

One argument used against the military was that army life and association with soldiers would corrupt the Indians and introduce them to bad habits. Some of the Indian agents were not the best men to talk about military immorality, but army life was not calculated to turn Indians into sober Protestant Christians. The Tonkawa village outside Fort Griffin, Texas, was described as a den of iniquity, and the Tonkawas had plenty of help and instruction in making it so. Wooden Leg the Cheyenne recalled that he learned to drink while serving at Fort Keogh, and many of his fellow tribesmen apparently did the same. But although the better intentioned Indian agents wanted their reservations to be hermetically sealed environments, where Indians could learn civilization without its vices, even the most isolated reservations seldom fitted this description in the later nineteenth century.[16]

Nineteenth-century whites frequently assumed that the Indians were doomed because of unwillingness or inability to change. The modern historical emphasis on the destruction of Indian cultures tends to perpetuate a more sophisticated and sympathetic version of that stereotype. But the Indians of the trans-Mississippi West often displayed great adaptability in trying circumstances, although they did not always adapt in the ways whites thought best for them. The Indian scouts took advantage of an opportunity to gain immediate and long-term benefits in changing times, in ways that worked for them. Even though their range of choices was constantly being narrowed, they insisted on choosing. They chose neither to vanish nor to become carbon copies of the whites. Individually or as groups, they violated almost every model of behavior constructed for them by whites.

Had the western Indians all chosen resistance, they would have saved neither their homelands nor their ways of life. White conquest would have been slower, more difficult, and more expensive, but the probable result would have been true genocide. In this light, we can agree with Michael Tate that the scouts probably conserved more than they destroyed.[17]

ABBREVIATIONS

DAB Dictionary of American Biography

ISC Indian Scouts, Correspondence, Letters Received, Office of the Adjutant General, 1871–80, Roll 259, Record Group 500, National Archives and Record Service, Washington, D.C.

NARS National Archives and Record Service, Washington, D.C.

NSHS Nebraska State Historical Society, Lincoln

OAG Office of the Adjutant General, Department of War, Washington, D.C.

OIA Office of Indian Affairs, Washington, D.C.

POIW John M. Carroll, ed., *Papers of the Order of Indian Wars* (Fort Collins, Colo.: Old Army Press, 1975)

RG Record Group

SDHDP Selected Documents, Headquarters, Department of the Platt, Records of U.S. Army Commands, U.S. Department of War, Record Group 94, National Archives and Record Service, Washington, D.C.

Notes

Introduction

1. Robert F. Berkhofer, *Salvation and the Savage* (New York: Atheneum, 1972), pp. vii–xv; this preface is found only in the paperback edition.

2. Francis Jennings, *The Invasion of America* (Chapel Hill: University of North Carolina Press, 1975), pp. 171–74.

3. O. G. Libby, ed., *The Arikara Narrative of the Campaign against the Hostile Dakotas, June 1876* (New York: Sol Lewis, 1973); W. A. Graham, comp., *The Custer Myth* (Harrisburg, Pa.: Stackpole, 1952); Walter Camp, *Custer in '76*, ed. Kenneth Hammer (Provo: Brigham Young University Press, 1976); George Bird Grinnell, *Two Great Scouts and Their Pawnee Battalion* (Glendale, Calif.: Arthur H. Clark, 1928); Robert Bruce, ed., *The Fighting Norths and Pawnee Scouts* (Lincoln: NSHS, 1932); Luther H. North, *Man of the Plains*, ed. Donald Danker (Lincoln: University of Nebraska Press, 1961).

4. David J. Wishart, *The Fur Trade of the American West, 1807–1840* (Lincoln: University of Nebraska Press, 1979); Arthur J. Ray, *Indians in the Fur Trade* (Toronto: University of Toronto Press, 1974).

5. James Willard Schultz, *William Jackson, Indian Scout* (Boston: Houghton Mifflin, 1926); John S. Gray, "Arikara Scouts with Custer," *North Dakota History* 35 (December 1968): 443–78.

6. Kenneth W. Porter, "The Seminole Negro-Indian Scouts, 1870–1881," *Southwestern Historical Quarterly* 55 (January 1952): 358–77.

7. Thomas H. Leforge, as told to Thomas B. Marquis, *Memoirs of a White Crow Indian* (1928; rpt. Lincoln: University of Nebraska Press, 1974), p. 272.

8. Compare Max L. Moorhead, *The Apache Frontier* (Norman: University of Oklahoma Press, 1968), and Moorhead, *The Presidio* (Norman: University of Oklahoma Press, 1975).

9. On "Native Americans," see Nancy Oestreich Lurie, "The Good, Bad, but Never Indifferent Indian," *Reviews in American History* 7 (June 1979): 167–68.

1. Indian Allies: A Long History

1. Bernal Díaz del Castillo, *The Discovery and Conquest of Mexico*, trans. A. P. Maudslay (New York: Farrar, Strauss & Giroux, 1956); Philip Wayne Powell, *Soldiers, Indians, and Silver* (Berkeley: University of California Press, 1952), and *Mexico's Miguel Caldera* (Tucson: University of Arizona Press, 1977).

2. Max L. Moorhead, *The Apache Frontier* (Norman: University of Oklahoma Press, 1968), and *The Presidio* (Norman: University of Oklahoma Press, 1975); Oakah L. Jones, *Pueblo Warriors and Spanish Conquest* (Norman: University of Oklahoma Press, 1966); Elizabeth A. H. John, *Storms Brewed in Other Men's Worlds* (College Station: Texas A&M University Press, 1975); Charles L. Kenner, *A History of New Mexican-Plains Indian Relations* (Norman: University of Oklahoma Press, 1969).

3. For broad parallels and contrasts in Indian relations on the two frontiers, see Powell, *Mexico's Miguel Caldera*, pp. 263–65.

4. Powell, *Soldiers, Indians, and Silver*, pp. 158–71; Jones, *Pueblo Warriors*, pp. 170–88.

5. William H. Prescott's histories of the conquests of Mexico and Peru, published in the 1840s, were familiar to the more literate public. Generally speaking, however, nineteenth-century Americans had little respect for Hispanic-American culture, and even less for Latin military prowess.

6. Ralph P. Bieber, ed., *Marching with the Army of the West, 1846–1848* (Glendale, Calif.: Arthur H. Clark, 1936); James H. Simpson, *Navaho Expedition*, ed. Frank McNitt (Norman: University of Oklahoma Press, 1964).

7. Francis Jennings, *The Invasion of America* (Chapel Hill: University of North Carolina Press, 1975), pp. 202–7.

8. Douglas Edward Leach, *Flintlock and Tomahawk* (New York: Norton, 1958); Leach indexes 44 references to Indian allies and spies in a 304-page work.

9. Jennings, *Invasion of America*, p. 125.

10. Ibid., pp. 124–25.

11. Francis Parkman, *A Half-Century of Conflict* (Boston: Little, Brown, 1892), and *Montcalm and Wolfe* (Boston: Little, Brown 1884); Wilbur R. Jacobs, *Wilderness Politics and Indian Gifts* (Lincoln: University of Nebraska Press, 1966); Douglas E. Leach, *Arms for Empire* (New York: Macmillan, 1973); Robert Rogers, *Journal of Major Robert Rogers*, ed. Howard H. Peckham (New York: Corinth, 1961), pp. 89–92, 98–99; Larry E. Ivers, *British Drums on the Southern Frontier* (Chapel Hill: University of North Carolina Press, 1974), especially p. 147.

12. Paul E. Kopperman, *Braddock at the Monongahela* (Pittsburgh: University of Pittsburgh Press, 1977); Parkman, *Montcalm and Wolfe*, pp. 210–11; Jacobs, *Wilderness Politics*, pp. 142–46.

13. James T. Flexner, *George Washington in the American Revolution* (Boston: Little, Brown, 1967), p. 94; Douglas Summers Brown, *The Catawba Indians* (Columbia: University of South Carolina Press, 1966), pp. 252–80; Dale Van Every, *A Company of Heroes* (New York: Morrow, 1962). Barbara Graymont, *The Iroquois in the American Revolution* (Syracuse: Syracuse University Press, 1972); James H. O'Donnell, *Southern Indians in the American Revolution* (Knoxville: University of Tennessee Press, 1973).

14. Bert Anson, *The Miami Indians* (Norman: University of Oklahoma Press, 1970), p. 126; Reginald Horsman, *Matthew Elliott, British Indian Agent* (Detroit: Wayne State University Press, 1964) and *The War of 1812* (New York: Alfred E. Knopf, 1969); Richard C. Knopf, ed., *Anthony*

Wayne (Pittsburgh: University of Pittsburgh Press, 1960), pp. 274, 347.

15. Horsman, *War of 1812*, pp. 215–49; Angie Debo, *The Road to Disappearance* (Norman: University of Oklahoma Press, 1941), pp. 78–83; Thurman Wilkins, *Cherokee Tragedy* (New York: Macmillan, 1970).

16. Mary Whately Clark, *Chief Bowles and the Texas Cherokees* (Norman: University of Oklahoma Press, 1971); David Lavender, *Bent's Fort* (New York: Doubleday, 1954); Annie Heloise Abel, *The American Indian as Slaveholder and Secessionist* (Cleveland: Arthur H. Clark, 1915) and *The American Indian as Participant in the Civil War* (Cleveland: Arthur H. Clark, 1919).

17. John K. Mahon, *History of the Second Seminole War, 1835–1842* (Gainesville: University of Florida Press, 1967).

18. Francis Paul Prucha, *The Sword of the Republic* (New York: Macmillan, 1969), especially pp. 152, 335, 354, 362. See also Willis B. Hughes, "The First Dragoons on the Western Frontier, 1834–1846," *Arizona and the West* 12 (Summer 1970): 115–38.

19. Prucha, *Sword of the Republic*, pp. 155–57, 177.

20. Grant Foreman, *Advancing the Frontier, 1830–1860* (Norman: University of Oklahoma Press, 1933), pp. 150–51, and *Indians and Pioneers* (Norman: University of Oklahoma Press, 1936).

21. The basic work on the period is Robert M. Utley, *Frontiersmen in Blue* (New York: Macmillan, 1967).

22. On the northwest wars, see Robert Ignatius Burns, *The Jesuits and the Indian Wars of the Northwest* (New Haven: Yale University Press, 1966). On California, see Robert F. Heizer, ed., *The Destruction of California Indians* (Sante Barbara: Peregrine Smith, 1974); George Crook, *General George Crook: His Autobiography* (Norman: University of Oklahoma Press, 1946), pp. 3–82; Utley, *Frontiersmen in Blue*, pp. 56–57.

23. Utley, *Frontiersmen in Blue*, pp. 70–77, 81–84, 108–11; Frank McNitt, *Navajo Wars* (Albuquerque: University of New Mexico Press, 1972); Michael L. Tate, "Frontier Defense on the Comanche Ranges of Northwest Texas, 1846–1860," *Great Plains Journal* 2 (Fall 1971): 41–56.

24. Utley, *Frontiersmen in Blue*, pp. 56–57; Foreman, *Advancing the Frontier*, pp. 274–78; Percival G. Lowe, *Five Years a Dragoon* (Norman: University of Oklahoma Press, 1965), pp. 185, 199, 223; Randolph B. Marcy, *Thirty Years of Army Life on the Frontier* (New York: Harper, 1866), pp. 56–76.

25. Burns, *Jesuits and the Indian Wars*, pp. 117–242; Alvin M. Josephy, *The Nez Perce Indians and the Opening of the Northwest* (New Haven: Yale University Press, 1965), pp. 333–85; Lawrence Kip, *Army Life on the Pacific* (New York: Redfield, 1859); U.S. Congress, Senate, Senate Executive Document no. 32, "Topographical Memoir of Colonel Wright's Campaign," by Lieutenant John Mullan, 35th Cong., 2d sess. (1859); Erasmus D. Keyes, *Fifty Years' Observations of Men and Events, Civil and Military* (New York: Scribner's, 1884), pp. 265–85; Clifford M. Drury, *Chief Lawyer of the Nez Perce Indians, 1796–1876* (Glendale, Calif.: Arthur H. Clark, 1979), pp. 133–64.

26. McNitt, *Navajo Wars*, especially pp. 48–51, 157–68; Simpson, *Navaho Expedition*, pp. lxxvii–lxxix, 35, 67–73; Annie Heloise Abel, ed., *The Official Correspondence of James S. Calhoun While Indian Agent at Santa Fe and Superintendent of Indian Affairs in New Mexico* (Washington, D.C.: Government Printing Office, 1915), pp. 36, 56–57; George Archibald McCall, *New Mexico in 1850*, ed. Robert Frazer (Norman: University of Oklahoma Press, 1968), pp. 84–180; Joseph K. F. Mansfield, *Mansfield on the Condition of the Western Forts*, ed. Robert Frazer (Norman: University of Oklahoma Press, 1963), p. 8; James H. Quinn, "Notes of Spy Company under Col. Cooke . . . April 3, 1854, to May 2, 1954," MS, New Mexico Higlands University, Las Vegas, N.M., courtesy Robert M. Utley; Hamilton Gardner, "Philip St. George Cooke and the Apache, 1854," *New Mexico Historical Review* 28 (April 1953): 115–32; Dale F. Giese, ed., *My Life with the Army in the West* (Santa Fe: Stagecoach Press, 1967), pp. 31–36.

27. Walter Prescott Webb, *The Great Plains* (Boston: Ginn, 1931), pp. 160–67, and *The Texas Rangers* (Austin: University of Texas Press, 1965), pp. 1–16; T. R. Fehrenbach,

Comanches (New York: Alfred A. Knopf, 1974), pp. 263–67, 293–333.

28. Fehrenbach, *Comanches*, pp. 311–12; Noah Smithwick, *The Evolution of a State* (Austin: Gammel, 1900), pp. 213–21. The Lipans first notified the Texans of the presence of the Comanches because they (the Lipans) were not strong enough to fight the Comanches alone.

29. Webb, *Texas Rangers*, p. 71; James Pike, *Scout and Ranger*, ed. Carl L. Cannon (Princeton: Princeton University Press, 1932), pp. 74–122; Smithwick, *Evolution of a State*, pp. 221–24, 232–33, 244–50; John Henry Brown, *Indian Wars and Pioneers of Texas* (Austin: L. E. Daniel, n.d.), pp. 25–26, 69–70, 73–74, 80–84; Kenneth F. Neighbours, "José María, Anadarko Chief," *Chronicles of Oklahoma* 44 (Autumn 1966): 254–74; James K. Greer, *Colonel Jack Hays* (New York: Dutton, 1952).

30. John S. Ford, *Rip Ford's Texas*, ed. Stephen B. Oates (Austin: University of Texas Press, 1963), pp. 219–40; Dorman H. Winfrey and James M. Day, eds., *The Indian Papers of Texas and the Southwest*, 5 vols. (Austin: University of Texas Press, 1966), pp. 231–39; Frederic Remington, "How the Law Got into the Chaparral," in Harold McCracken, ed., *Frederic Remington's Own West* (New York: Dial, 1960), pp. 114–16.

31. The removal of the Indians is described in Kenneth F. Neighbours, *Indian Exodus* (n.p.: Nortex, 1973); Pike, *Scout and Ranger*, pp. 20–21, 24, 71–72; James B. Barry, *A Texas Ranger and Frontiersman*, ed. James K. Greer (Dallas: Southwest Press, 1932), pp. 111–13; Ford, *Rip Ford's Texas*, pp. 439–56.

32. Ford, *Rip Ford's Texas*, p. 453; Mildred P. Mayhall, "The Battles of Wichita Village and Crooked Creek," *True West* 19 (February 1972): 12–16; U.S. Congress, House, Commissioner of Indian Affairs, *Annual Report, 1858*, pp. 533–34, and Secretary of War, *Annual Report, 1858*, 1: 267–78; L. S. Ross's personal account in E. E. White, *Experiences of a Special Indian Agent* (Norman: University of Oklahoma Press, 1965), pp. 263–66.

33. Mayhall, "Battles," pp. 17, 66–67.

34. W. W. Newcomb, *The Indians of Texas* (Austin: University of Texas Press, 1961), pp. 133–53, 343–46, 353, 359; W. Arens, *The Man-Eating Myth* (New York: Oxford University Press, 1979), questions whether any society ever practiced cannibalism regularly or sanctioned it. For eyewitness accounts of Tonkawa cannibalism, see Smithwick, *Evolution of a State*, pp. 245–46; Pike, *Scout and Ranger*, pp. 95–96; John Holland Jenkins III, ed., *Recollections of Early Texas* (Austin: University of Texas Press, 1958), pp. 77–78. On the Tonkawas' relations with other tribes, see Marcy, *Thirty Years of Army Life*, pp. 149–52.

35. Kip, *Army Life on the Pacific*, pp. 35, 45–46, 54, 60, 69, 85; Secretary of War, *Annual Report, 1858*, 1:365,383, 390; Mullan, "Topographical Memoir," p. 31. Wright, a veteran of the Seminole War, must have been aware of the role of Indian allies in that conflict. The Nez Perces insisted on being issued full uniforms; one reason is suggested by Wright's order warning his troops not to shoot them by mistake, perhaps issued at the Indians' request.

36. Grant Foreman, ed., *Adventure on Red River* (Norman: University of Oklahoma Press, 1937), pp. 55–56; U.S. Congress, Senate, *Report of the Secretary of War, Communicating the Report of Captain George B. McClellan, (First Regiment United States Cavalry,) One of the Officers Sent to the Seat of War in Europe, in 1855 and 1856*, 35th Cong., spec. sess., Senate Executive Document no. 1 (1857), pp. 324–25 (hereafter cited as McClellan, *Report*). McClellan was closely associated with Marcy from 1852 on, so a direct influence on his thinking is quite possible.

37. Burnet to David G. Burnet, September 15, 1859, in "Lieutenant William E. Burnet Letters," ed. Raymond Estep, pt. 2, *Chronicles of Oklahoma* 38 (Winter 1960):360–61; Richard F. Burton, *The City of the Saints*, ed. Fawn M. Brodie (New York: Knopf, 1963), pp. 43, 53–54. McClellan warned that it would be necessary to restrain the Indians' "tendency to unnecessary cruelty," which he apparently took for granted (McClellan, *Report*, p. 125). See also Chris Emmett, *Fort Union and the Winning of the*

Southwest (Norman: University of Oklahoma Press, 1965), p. 204, for recommendations of Lieutenant Alexander Macrae in 1857.

2. The Amateurs Take Over: The Influence of the Civil War

1. See Robert M. Utley, *Frontiersmen in Blue* (New York: Macmillan, 1967), pp. 214-15. Robley D. Evans, *A Sailor's Log* (New York: Appleton, 1901), pp. 16-17, describes the destruction of buffalo along the Platte Valley in 1859.
2. This interpretation, suggested by Charlton Ogburn, *The Marauders* (New York: Harper, 1956), p. 212, contrasting American and Chinese soldiers in Burma in World War II, does not seem irrelevant to America's first total war; Jacob P. Dunn, *Massacres of the Mountains* (New York: Harper, 1886), pp. 366-67, offers a contemporary's analysis of frontier attitudes.
3. Ogburn, *Marauders*, p. 91: "We conceived of the Japanese as a pestilence that infected the land"; Utley, *Frontiersmen in Blue*, pp. 217-18; Dunn, *Massacres*, pp. 364-66.
4. Alvin M. Josephy, *The Nez Perce Indians and the Opening of the Northwest* (New Haven: Yale University Press, 1965), pp. 348-73; Robert Ignatius Burns, *The Jesuits and the Indian Wars of the Northwest* (New Haven: Yale University Press, 1966), p. 140; Kent Richards, "Isaac I. Stevens and Federal Military Power in Washington Territory," *Pacific Northwest Quarterly* 63 (July 1972): 81-86. For mountain men and Indians, among many sources, see Warren A. Ferris, *Life in the Rocky Mountains*, ed. Paul C. Phillips (Denver: Old West, 1940); Washington Irving, *The Adventures of Captain Bonneville, U.S.A.*, ed. Edgerly W. Todd (Norman: University of Oklahoma Press, 1961); William C. Hamilton, *My Sixty Years on the Plains* (Norman: University of Oklahoma Press, 1962); Frances Fuller Victor, *The River of the West* (Hartford: Bliss, 1870), especially p. 142. The many studies of white attitudes toward Indians tend to rely on elite

literary sources and generalize very broadly about fron-
tiersmen; see Roy Harvey Pearce, *Savagism and Civiliza-
tion* (Baltimore: Johns Hopkins Press, 1965); Robert H.
Berkhofer, *The White Man's Indian* (New York: Alfred A.
Knopf, 1978); Louise K. Barnett, *The Ignoble Savage*
(Westport, Conn.: Greenwood Press, 1975); the exception
is Lewis O. Saum, *The Fur Trader and the Indian* (Seattle:
University of Washington Press, 1965).

5. Reginald S. Craig, *The Fighting Parson* (Los Angeles:
Westernlore, 1959), pp. 33–35. On Pfeiffer, see Frank
McNitt, *Navajo Wars* (Albuquerque: University of New
Mexico Press, 1972), pp. 354n, 377n, 403–8; Lawrence
Kelly, ed., *Navajo Roundup* (Boulder: Pruett, 1970), p. 156.
For Healy, see Paul F. Sharp, *Whoop-Up Country* (St.
Paul: University of Minnesota Press, 1955), p. 115. See
also Richard Slotkin and James K. Folsom, eds., *So Dread-
full a Judgment* (Middletown, Conn.: Wesleyan Univer-
sity Press, 1978), pp. 370–91.

6. On white concepts of Indian cruelty, see Pearce, *Savagism
and Civilization*, especially pp. 163–88; on Parkman, see
Berkhofer, *White Man's Indian*, pp. 6–10, 147–48; Francis
Jennings, *The Invasion of America* (Chapel Hill: University of North Carolina Press, 1975), pp. 146–70.

7. Aurora Hunt, *Major General James Henry Carleton,
1814–1873* (Glendale, Calif.: Arthur H. Clark, 1958);
Utley, *Frontiersmen in Blue*, pp. 233–35; Harvey Lewis
Carter, *"Dear Old Kit"* (Norman: University of Oklahoma Press, 1968), including a well-annotated version of
Carson's autobiography; Kelly, *Navajo Roundup*, pp. 18–19
and the following letters therein: Carleton to Carson, April 11, 1863, pp. 30–31; Carson to Carleton, July
24, 1863, pp. 31–32; Carleton to Carson, August 18, 1863,
pp. 76–77; Carson to Captain Ben C. Cutler, December 6,
1863, pp. 162–73.

8. *War of the Rebellion: Official Records of the Union and
Confederate Armies* (Washington, D.C.: Government
Printing Office, 1880–1900), ser. 1, vol. 41, pt. 1, pp. 139–
43; pt. 3, pp. 400, 742; pt. 4, pp. 99, 151, 422, 496; George
H. Pettis, *Kit Carson's Fight with the Comanche and
Kiowa Indians* (Santa Fe: New Mexico, 1908), by a par-

ticipant. The opinion of George Bent, son of trader
William Bent and the Cheyenne Owl Woman, is in
George E. Hyde, *Life of George Bent, Written from His
Letters*, ed. Savoie Lottinville (Norman: University of
Oklahoma Press, 1968), p. 246. Bent, a participant on the
Indian side in various campaigns of the period, was not ad
Adobe Walls, but he certainly knew Indians who were.

9. Dunn, *Massacres*, pp. 335–41; Ray C. Colton, *The Civil
War in the Western Territories* (Norman: University of
Oklahoma Press, 1959), pp. 134–35; *War of the Rebellion*,
ser. 1, vol. 33, pt. 2, pp. 200–203; U.S. Congress, House,
Secretary of War, *Annual Report, 1867*, 1:153–55; Daniel
Ellis Conner, *Joseph Reddeford Walker and the Arizona
Adventure*, ed. Donald J. Berthrong and Odessa Davenport
(Norman: University of Oklahoma Press, 1956), especially
pp. 73–74, 219–21; Clara T. Woody, ed., "The Woolsey
Expeditions," *Arizona and the West* 4 (Summer 1962):
157–76; J. Ross Browne, *Adventures in the Apache Coun-
try*, ed. Donald M. Powell (Tucson: University of Arizona
Press, 1974), p. 111; Dan L. Thrapp, *The Conquest of
Apacheria* (Norman: University of Oklahoma Press, 1967),
pp. 33–34; Constance W. Altschuler, ed., *Latest from
Arizona* (Tucson: Arizona Pioneers' Historical Society,
1969), pp. 136, 142.

10. The Warm Springs of Oregon should not be confused, as
has been done, with the Warm Springs, or Ojo Caliente,
Apaches, otherwise the Mimbres, of western New Mex-
ico. John M. Drake, "Cavalry in the Indian Country,
1864," ed. Priscilla Knuth, *Oregon Historical Quarterly* 65
(March 1964):48–49, 118; Keith Clark and Donna Clark,
eds., "William McKay's Journal, 1866–67: Indian Scouts,"
Oregon Historical Quarterly 79 (Summer–Fall 1978);
W. R. Parnell, "Operations against Hostile Indians With
General George Crook, 1867–68," *United Service* n.s. 1
(May–June 1889); Keith Clark and Donna Clark, eds.,
Daring Donald McKay (Portland: Oregon Historical Soci-
ety, 1971), p. xx.

11. Stan Hoig, *The Sand Creek Massacre* (Norman: University
of Oklahoma Press, 1961), p. 121.

12. C. M. Oehler, *The Great Sioux Uprising* (New York: Oxford University Press, 1959); Gabriel Renville, "A Sioux

Narrative of the Outbreak in 1862, and of Sibley's Expedition in 1863," *Collections of the Minnesota Historical Society* 10, pt. 2 (St. Paul, 1905):611; Thomas Hughes, *Indian Chiefs of Southern Minnesota* (Minneapolis: Ross & Haines, 1969), pp. 121–27.

13. U.S. Congress, Senate, Committee on Indian Affairs, *General Alfred Sully's Company of Yankton Sioux Indian Scouts*, 57th Cong., 1st sess., Senate Executive Document no. 298 (1901).

14. *War of the Rebellion*, ser. 1, vol. 41, pt. 1, pp. 140–50, 163–64; David L. Kingsbury, "Sully's Expedition against the Sioux in 1864," *Collections of the Minnesota Historical Society* 8 (St. Paul, 1898); John Pattee, "Dakota Campaigns," *South Dakota Historical Collections* 5 (Pierre, 1910).

15. George Bird Grinnell, *The Fighting Cheyennes* (Norman: University of Oklahoma Press, 1955), pp. 137–64; Hyde, *Life of George Bent*, pp. 164–222. Eugene F. Ware, *The Indian War of 1864*, ed. Clyde C. Walton (Lincoln: University of Nebraska Press, 1960), pp. 355–57, describes the setting of the "Great Prairie Fire" and asserts it burned well into Kansas; George Bent asserts that he was in the region at the time and saw nothing of the fire (Hyde, *Life of George Bent*, pp. 176–77).

16. George E. Hyde, *Red Cloud's Folk* (Norman: University of Oklahoma Press, 1937), p. 119; Jacob Lee Humfreville, *Twenty Years among Our Hostile Indians* (New York: Hunter, 1903), p. 469.

17. Utley, *Frontiersmen in Blue*, pp. 322–32. Many relevant documents, including those from *War of the Rebellion*, ser. 1, vol. 48, are in Leroy R. Hafen and Ann W. Hafen, eds., *Powder River Campaigns and Sawyers Expedition* (Glendale, Calif.: Arthur H. Clark, 1961). Grenville M. Dodge, *The Battle of Atlanta and Other Campaigns, Addresses, Etc.* (Council Bluffs, Monarch: 1911), pp. 79–108; Hyde, *Life of George Bent*, pp. 223–43.

18. On Connor, see *DAB* 4 (New York, 1932):352–53; Fred B. Rogers, *Soldiers of the Overland* (San Francisco: Grabhorn Press, 1938); U.S. Department of War, Company Muster Roll and Record of Events, 1865–66, Company "A," Pawnee Scouts, RG 500, NARS (microfilm, NSHS); Records,

OAG, Regimental Record Books, Volunteer Organization
(Civil War) Omaha and Pawnee Scouts, 1865–66, NARS
RG 94 (microfilm, NSHS); OAG, *Official Army Register
of the Volunteer Force of the United States Army* . . . (Washington, D.C.: Government Printing Office, 1867), n.p.
For Little Priest, see Hughes, *Indian Chiefs*, pp. 147–58.

19. *War of the Rebellion*, ser. 1, vol. 48, pt. 2, pp. 117–21,
355, 1048–49; Connor to Dodge, August 19, 1865, in
Hafen and Hafen, eds., *Powder River Campaigns*, p. 46;
Robert B. David, *Finn Burnett, Frontiersman* (Glendale,
Calif.: Arthur H. Clark, 1937), pp. 72–76; Hyde, *Life of
George Bent*, pp. 227–28. Bent's stepmother, Yellow
Woman, was among those killed.

20. Jim Bridger claimed to see with the naked eye camp
smoke that Connor and his officers could not see with
field glasses. Although skeptical, Connor sent the
Pawnees to investigate. At least one officer still refused to
believe that Bridger had seen smoke even after the camp
was discovered. The old scout was simply a trained observer, like experienced Indian trailers or modern interpreters of aerial photographs. The author's brother, an Air
Force intelligence officer, has compared this incident with
the reluctance of untrained viewers to believe trained photo
interpreters' statements as to what they see. Hafen and
Hafen, eds., *Powder River Campaigns*, pp. 46–48, 125–26;
Alfred Sorenson, ''A Quarter of a Century on the Frontier,
or, the adventures of Major Frank North, the 'White Chief
of the Pawnee,' The Story of His Life as Told by Himself
and Written by Alfred Sorenson,'' MS and typescript,
Frank J. North Papers, NSHS, pp. 96–102.

21. Utley, *Frontiersmen in Blue*, p. 330; Hafen and Hafen,
eds., *Powder River Campaigns*, pp. 148–49.

22. Hafen and Hafen, eds., *Powder River Compaigns*, pp.
337–39.

23. Ibid., p. 214 (Finn Burnett's account, given in 1931, sixty-six years after the event). The Chivington remark is traditional; it is consistent with remarks attributed to him
by his friendly biographer, Craig (*Fighting Parson*, pp. 187,
190). In any case, the remark was proverbial years
before Sand Creek. Barnett, *Ignoble Savage*, p. 131, gives
an example from 1851; Harold D. Langley, ed., *To Utah*

with the Dragoons and Glimpses of Life in Arizona and California, 1858–1859 (Salt Lake City: University of Utah Press, 1974), p. 101.

24. Utley, *Frontiersmen in Blue*, pp. 332–33; Dodge, *Battle of Atlanta*, pp. 96–97.

25. Finn Burnett to Grace R. Hebard and E. A. Brininstool, March 6, 1919, in Heband and Brininstool, *The Bozeman Trail* (Cleveland: Arthur H. Clark, 1922), 1:261. Burnett, a muleskinner on the expedition, does not state when he heard Connor make this pronouncement.

26. Clark and Clark, eds., "William McKay's Journal," pp. 128–31; Secretary of War, *Annual Report, 1867*, 1:153–55, quotes a report of Captain Guido Ilges, April 30, 1867, which notes that the scouts were not really under his control, an indication that they were still Arizona militia or free agents; Sorenson, "Quarter of a Century," p. 116; OAG, muster rolls, Pawnee Scouts and Omaha Scouts, RG 500, NARS; William E. Unrau, ed., *Tending the Talking Wire* (Salt Lake City: University of Utah Press, 1979), pp. 319–20; Hughes, *Indian Chiefs*, pp. 156–58; Robert A. Murray, *Military Posts in the Powder River Country of Wyoming, 1865–1894* (Lincoln: University of Nebraska Press, 1968), pp. 17, 19, 50–52, 73–74.

27. Margaret Carrington, *Ab-sa-ra-ka, Land of Massacre* (Philadelphia: Lippincott, 1878), pp. 94–95.

28. Among many studies of the history of Fort Philip Kearny, see Hebard and Brininstool, *Bozeman Trail*; Hyde, *Red Cloud's Folk*, pp. 134–61; Robert M. Utley, *Frontier Regulars* (New York: Macmillan, 1973), pp. 97–114; Murray, *Military Posts*, pp. 11–12, 19–101.

29. Carrington, *Ab-sa-ra-ka*, pp. 132–33; U.S. Congress, Senate, *Papers Relative to Indian Operations on the Plains*, 50th Cong., 1st sess., Senate Executive Document no. 33 (1887), pp. 20–21, 23. On the Fetterman affair, see Jesse W. Vaughn, *Indian Fights* (Norman: University of Oklahoma Press, 1966), pp. 14–90; Robert A. Murray, *The Army on the Powder River* (Fort Collins, Colo.: Old Army Press, 1972), pp. 1–10.

30. *Papers Relative to Indian Operations*, pp. 31–35; SDHDP, 1866–67 (microfilm, NSHS), especially N. C. Kinney to Assistant Adjutant General, February 9, 1867, and H. W.

Wessels to Assistant Adjutant General, June 18 and June
23, 1867; Michael J. Koury, *Military Posts of Montana*
(Bellevue, Nebr.: Old Army Press, 1970), p. 15, calls Fort
C. F. Smith "the nation's most isolated post" at that
time. James D. Lockwood, *Life and Adventures of a
Drummer Boy* (Albany: John Skinner, 1893), pp. 131–91
(the recollections of a member of the C. F. Smith garrison); Merrill J. Mattes, *Indians, Infants, and Infantry*
(Denver: Old West, 1960), pp. 143–72; William H. Bisbee,
as told to W. R. Bisbee, *Through Four American Wars*
(Boston: Meader, 1931), p. 171.

31. L. P. Bradley to Assistant Adjutant General, July 27, 1867,
SDHDP; Lockwood, *Life and Adventures*, pp. 176–81;
Vaughn, *Indian Fights*, pp. 91–116; Mattes, *Indians, In-
fants, and Infantry*, pp. 134–37; David, *Finn Burnett*,
pp. 161–93. Anthony McGinnis, "Economic Warfare on the
Northern Plains," *Annals of Wyoming* 44 (Spring 1972):
62, notes that trading between hostile tribes, such as that
which excited Bradley's suspicions, was not uncommon.
See William White, as told to Thomas B. Marquis,
Custer, Cavalry, and Crows (Fort Collins, Colo.: Old
Army Press, 1975), pp. 63–64, on Sioux peace attempts
with the Crows.

32. Lockwood, *Life and Adventures*, pp. 160–75; George H.
Palmer, "'We Do Not Know What the Government In-
tends to Do . . .': Lt. Palmer Writes from the Bozeman
Trail, 1867–68," ed. Jerome A. Greene, *Montana* 28 (July
1978):21, 26, 31–33; William Murphy, "The Forgotten
Battalion," *Annals of Wyoming* 7 (October 1930):396–97.

33. McGinnis, "Economic Warfare," pp. 66–67; Hyde, *Red
Cloud's Folk*, pp. 160–67.

3. Regularization

1. Francis A. Walker, *The Indian Question* (Boston: J. R.
Osgood, 1874), pp. 22, 64–65, 81, 147.

2. Robert M. Utley, *Frontier Regulars* (New York: Macmillan, 1973), pp. 12, 16–17; William A. Ganoe, *History
of the United States Army* (New York: Appleton, 1924),
pp. 306–9, 324, 348–51; U.S. Congress, House, Secretary

of War, *Annual Report, 1869,* 1:23-24; Samuel P. Huntington, *The Soldier and the State* (Cambridge: Harvard
University Press, 1957), pp. 222-30.

3. General Orders no. 56, August 1, 1866, OAG, RG 94,
NARS.

4. Utley, *Frontier Regulars,* pp. 12, 16-17.

5. Wiley Britton, *The Union Indian Brigade in the Civil War*
(Kansas City: Franklin Hudson, 1922); Dudley Taylor
Cornish, *The Sable Arm* (New York: Longmans, Green,
1956), pp. 69-78.

6. Hubert Howe Bancroft, *History of Oregon* (San Francisco:
History Co., 1888), 2:530-31; Keith Clark and Donna
Clark, eds., "William McKay's Journal, 1866-67: Indian
Scouts," *Oregon Historical Quarterly* 79 (Summer-Fall
1978), pt. 1, pp. 128-29; the editors note that civilians
favored the measure because it "offered the advantages of
practicality, economy, and the substitution of Indian risk
for white risk."

7. Clark and Clark, eds., "William McKay's Journal," pp.
132-37 and passim; George Crook, *General George
Crook: His Autobiography,* ed. Martin F. Schmitt (Norman: University of Oklahoma Press, 1946), pp. 142-58;
Azor H. Nickerson, "Major General George Crook and the
Indians," unpublished MS, Huntington Library, San
Marino, Calif., pp. 9-13; John Gregory Bourke, *With General Crook in the Indian Country* (Palo Alto: Lewis Osborne, 1968), pp. 20-31; Oliver Knight, *Following the Indian Wars* (Norman: University of Oklahoma Press,
1960), pp. 39-57; W. R. Parnell, "Operations against Hostile Indians with General George Crook, 1867-68,"
United Service n.s. 1 (May-June 1889):485, 489, 492-93.

8. Halleck's and Steele's reports are in U.S. Congress,
House, Secretary of War, *Annual Report, 1867,* 1:73-
74, 79.

9. The actual order is not extant. Clark and Clark, eds.,
"William McKay's Journal," discusses the subject in detail (pt. 1, pp. 130-31; McKay's entries, pp. 149-50, 152-
53; pt. 2, Appendix B, including Darragh's report, pp. 328-
33, and McKay, p. 301), indicating prisoners were
taken. On restraint in warfare among "primitive"
peoples, see Harry H. Turney-High, *Primitive War*

(Columbia: University of South Carolina Press, 1949),
pp. 205-26. See also Francis Jennings, *The Invasion of
America* (Chapel Hill: University of North Carolina Press,
1975), pp. 151-52, 211-12, 220-23.
10. Parnell, "Operations against Hostile Indians," pp. 492-93.
11. Ibid., pp. 634-35.
12. Robert G. Athearn, *Forts of the Upper Missouri* (Engle-
wood Cliffs, N.J.: Prentice-Hall, 1967), pp. 211-59; Joseph
Henry Taylor, *Frontier and Indian Life and Kaleidoscopic
Lives* (Valley City, S.D.: Washburn's 50th Anniversary
Committee, 1932); Roy A. Meyer, *Village Indians of the
Upper Missouri* (Lincoln: University of Nebraska Press,
1977), p. 127; Philip Régis de Trobriand, *Army Life in
Dakota*, ed. Milo M. Quaife (Chicago: Donnelly, 1941),
pp. 50-51, 277-78; Ben Innis, *Bloody Knife!* (Fort Collins,
Colo.: Old Army Press, 1973), on the most famous Arikara scout; O. G. Libby, ed., *The Arikara Narrative of the
Campaign against the Hostile Dakotas, June 1876* (New
York: Sol Lewis, 1973); Walter Camp, comp., *Custer in
'76*, ed. Kenneth Hammer (Provo: Brigham Young University Press, 1976), pp. 180-94; James Willard Schultz, *William Jackson, Indian Scout* (Boston: Houghton Mifflin,
1926). On the hat, see Randy Steffen, *The Horse Soldier,
1776-1943*, 4 vols. (Norman: University of Oklahoma
Press, 1978), 2:38-42.
13. *Record of Engagements with Hostile Indians within the
Military Division of the Missouri, from 1868 to 1882,
Lieutenant-General P. H. Sheridan, Commanding* (Washington, D.C.: Government Printing Office, 1882), p. 33.
14. Secretary of War, *Annual Report, 1869*, 1:122; 3:544-48;
Ralph H. Ogle, *Federal Control of the Western Apaches,
1848-1886* (Albuquerque: University of New Mexico
Press, 1970), pp. 74-79; John Gregory Bourke, *On the
Border with Crook* (1891; rpt. Lincoln: University of Ne-
braska Press, 1971), pp. 436-37.
15. Text of "An Act Concerning the Employment of Indian
Scouts," approved August 12, 1876, and memo to Adjutant General, April 7, 1876, both in ISC (microfilm,
NSHS).
16. Utley, *Frontier Regulars*, pp. 1, 28; Ganoe, *History of the
United States Army*, pp. 302-7, 324-25, 348-50.

17. Utley, *Frontier Regulars,* p. 29; request of General August Kautz, Department of Arizona, and General O. O. Howard, Department of the Columbia, 1877; Sherman to Chairman, House Committee on Military Affairs [late summer 1876], both in ISC.

18. Sheridan to Adjutant General, April 7, 1876, and attached memo; Sheridan to Sherman, January 24, 1877, both in ISC; Secretary of War, *Annual Report, 1876,* 1:72; *Record of Engagements,* pp. 5–6. Sheridan's Military Division of the Missouri, the army's largest geographical division, included everything from the Mississippi to the present-day western borders of New Mexico, Utah, Wyoming (with Idaho east of 114° west longitude), and Montana.

19. Customarily department commanders enlisted scouts from tribes within their own departments; sometimes scouts were physically transferred from one department to another, but this practice was the exception.

20. August Kautz to Irvin McDowell, June 27, 1876; Adjutant General to McDowell, August 3, 1876; Kautz to Adjutant General, February 20, 1877; McDowell to Sherman, April 22, 1877; Sherman to McDowell, April 23, 1877; McDowell to Adjutant General, June 27, 1877, all in ISC.

21. Adjutant General to Sheridan, April 19, 1876; Richard Drum, Assistant Adjutant General, Military Division of the Missouri, to Alfred H. Terry, Commanding General, Department of Dakota, December 11, 1876; Adjutant General to Paymaster General, April 24, 1877; Adjutant General to John Pope, Commanding General, Department of the Missouri, June 20, 1877; OAG memo to Sherman, March 16, 1877, with accompanying table, all in ISC.

22. Innis, *Bloody Knife!,* p. 118; Edward Hatch to Acting Assistant Adjutant General, District of New Mexico, April 27, 1880, and Hatch to Assistant Adjutant General, Department of the Missouri, May 26, 1880, both in Secretary of War, *Annual Report, 1880,* 1:107, 109.

23. Captain Guido Ilges's report, April 30, 1867, in Secretary of War, *Annual Report, 1867,* 1:153–55. On the Camp Grant massacre, see Don Schellie, *Vast Domain of Blood* (Los Angeles: Westernlore, 1968).

24. Richard H. Pratt to Acting Assistant Adjutant General, Fort Sill Column, November 29, 1874, in Joe F. Taylor,

ed., "The Indian Campaign on the Staked Plains, 1874–
1875: Military Correspondence from War Department
Adjutant General's Office, File 2805—1874," *Panhandle-
Plains Historical Review* 34 (1961):121; John Gregory
Bourke, Diaries, 5:405, U.S. Military Academy Library,
West Point, N.Y. (microfilm, NSHS); Grace R. Hebard,
Washakie (Glendale, Calif.: Arthur H. Clark, 1930),
pp. 165–205; Anson Mills, "The Battle of the Rosebud," in
POIW, pp. 3–12; Joe DeBarthe, *Life and Adventures of
Frank Grouard*, ed. Edgar I. Stewart (Norman: University
of Oklahoma Press, 1958), pp. 110–22.

25. Ganoe, *History of the United States Army*, p. 348; Nelson
Miles to J. S. Brisbin, April 5, 1877; Miles to Gustavus C.
Doane, April 5, 1877; Special Field Orders no. 6, April 12,
1877; Doane to Post Adjutant, Tongue River Cantonment,
May 22, 1877; Doane to Acting Assistant Adjutant Gen-
eral, Yellowstone Command, June 13, 1877, all in
Gustavus G. Doane Papers, courtesy Merrill G. Burlin-
game, Bozeman, Mont.; William White, as told to
Thomas B. Marquis, *Custer, Cavalry, and Crows* (Fort
Collins, Colo.: Old Army Press, 1975), pp. 115–32; J. I.
Allen's account in Mary Allen Phinney, *Jirah Isham Allen,
Montana Pioneer* (Rutland, Vt.: Tuttle, 1929), pp. 78–90;
Thomas H. Leforge, as told to Thomas B. Marquis, *Mem-
oirs of a White Crow Indian* (1928; rpt. Lincoln: Uni-
versity of Nebraska Press, 1974), pp. 280–87, 314;
Hugh L. Scott, *Some Memories of a Soldier* (New York:
Century, 1928), pp. 56–68.

26. Scott, *Some Memories*, p. 57.

27. A. L. Kroeber and C. B. Krober, *A Mohave War Reminiscence, 1854-1880* (Berkeley: University of California
Press, 1973, pp. 34–39, 78–87; U.S. Congress, Senate,
Walapai Papers, 74th Cong., 2nd sess., Senate Document
no. 273 (1936), pp. 41–91.

4. Military Attitudes toward Indian Scouts

1. *Chronological List of Actions, etc., with Indians, from
January 1, 1866, to January 1891* (Washington, D.C.:
OAG, 1891), p. 15. See James H. Wilson, *The Life and*

Services of Brevet Brigadier General Andrew Jonathan Alexander, United States Army (New York, 1887), pp. 102–3.

2. Cf. entry for October 17, 1867; Wilson, *Life and Services of . . . Alexander,* p. 9, and Carl C. Rister, *Fort Griffin on the Texas Frontier* (Norman: University of Oklahoma Press, 1955), p. 73; 45 cavalry and 22 Tonkawas were engaged with the hostiles, but the first source does not mention the scouts. See also Rister, *Fort Griffin,* pp. 74–76, and *Chronological List,* pp. 10, 24.

3. In February 1880 Sergeant T. B. Glover with eight troopers and eleven scouts (probably Cheyennes) pursued some Hunkpapas near the Yellowstone and forced their surrender (*Chronological List,* p. 49; *Record of Engagements with Hostile Indians within the Military Division of the Missouri from 1868 to 1882, Lieutenant-General P. H. Sheridan, Commanding* [Washington, D.C.: Government Printing Office, 1882], p. 93).

4. George A. Custer, *My Life on the Plains* (Norman: University of Oklahoma Press, 1962), pp. 230–39; *Chronological List,* p. 16; *Record of Engagements,* p. 15 (only the latter mentions the Osages). *Chronological List,* pp. 15–16, 18–19, refers to Price's campaign against the Walapais in Arizona, but without mentioning participation by Indian allies. For the Geronimo campaign statistics, see Dan L. Thrapp, *The Conquest of Apacheria* (Norman: University of Oklahoma Press, 1967), p. 350; Angie Debo, *Geronimo* (Norman: University of Oklahoma Press, 1976), p. 237. Other statistics are based on *Chronological List.*

5. Samuel P. Huntington, *The Soldier and the State* (Cambridge: Harvard University Press, 1956), pp. 226–30, emphasizes the army's isolation from the values of the nation in this period. Yet the assimilationist hopes of many officers were basically similar to those of the reformers. John Morgan Gates, *Schoolbooks and Krags* (Westport, Conn.: Greenwood Press, 1973), pp. 54–75, argues that many officers were "progressives in uniform."

6. U.S. Congress, House, Secretary of War, *Annual Report, 1867,* 1:73–74 (Halleck's report); ibid., *1869,* 1:24 (Sherman's report); August Kautz to Irvin McDowell, June 27, 1876, in ISC.

7. McDonald's account of his defeat is given in George Forsyth, *Thrilling Days in Army Life* (New York: Harper, 1900), pp. 87–104. James Parker, *The Old Army Memories, 1872–1918* (Philadelphia: Dorrance, 1929), pp. 156–57, 167; but on p. 153 Parker notes that scouts urged on the soldiers, who they thought were too slow. Powhatan Clarke, "A Hot Trail," *Cosmopolitan* 17 (October 1894): 706–16; James M. Watson, "Scouting in Arizona, 1890," *Journal of the U.S. Cavalry Association* 10 (June 1897): 128–35 (the scout commander's view of the same episode).

8. James B. Gillett, *Six Years with the Texas Rangers, 1875 to 1881* (New Haven: Yale University Press, 1925), pp. 64–66, 200–210; these Pueblos were from Ysleta del Sur, near El Paso, the only Pueblo Indian community in Texas, founded by Pueblo people removed from what is now New Mexico by the Spanish at the time of the Pueblo revolt of 1680. On Navajos, see Charles B. Gatewood to wife, June 25, 1886, in Charles B. Gatewood Collection, Arizona Historical Society, Tucson; Charles B. Gatewood, "Campaigning against Victorio in 1879," *The Great Divide*, April 1894, p. 102; S. W. Fountain, "Lieutenant Fountain's Fight with Apache Indians . . . ," in *POIW*, pp. 83–89. See Camillo C. C. Carr, " 'Days of the Empire'—Arizona, 1866–1869," *Journal of the U.S. Cavalry Association* 2 (March 1889):20, on Pimas and Maricopas.

9. Parker, *Old Army Memories*, pp. 40–41, admits that he had a poor opinion of Indians in general, and he obviously assumes the reader will share this attitude; William Henry Bisbee, *Through Four American Wars* (Boston: Meader, 1931), pp. 192, 229. Robert G. Carter, *On the Border with Mackenzie* (Washington, D.C.: Eynon, 1935), presents himself consistently as an old war horse. Eugene B. Beaumont, "Over the Border with Mackenzie," *United Service* 12 (March 1885):286, refers to "human *lice*" in a context that includes all Indians.

10. George Crook, *General George Crook: His Autobiography*, ed. Martin F. Schmitt (Norman: University of Oklahoma Press, 1946), p. 213.

11. Clarke, "Hot Trail," pp. 714–15. Inspector General Randolph B. Marcy quoting Acting Adjutant Inspector Gen-

eral, Department of Arizona, in Secretary of War, *Annual Report, 1877,* 1:54.

12. Anton Mazzanovich, *Trailing Geronimo* (Hollywood: privately printed, 1926), pp. 248–49.

13. Sheridan to Robert Lincoln, Secretary of War, in U.S. Congress, Senate, Committee on Indian Affairs, *Report of the Committee on Indian Affairs on the Advisability of a Military School for Indians . . .* , 48th Cong., 2d sess., Senate Report no. 348 (1884), pp. 1–2. The committee chairman, Benjamin Harrison, endorsed Sheridan's opinion.

14. See Robert M. Utley, *Frontier Regulars* (New York: Macmillan, 1973), pp. 20–26, 67–69, on army pride and resentment of Congress. See Harold McCracken, *The Frederic Remington Book* (Garden City, N.Y.: Doubleday, 1966), 1966), pp. 120, 135, on dress in the field. Many regular officers seem to have a prejudice against special combat units that perform special tasks. The British military writer C. E. Callwell, *Small Wars* (London: His Majesty's Stationery Office, 1906), p. 345, writing about irregular warfare in general, concludes that it would be undesirable to form special units for scouting; all soldiers should be trained in such duties. He made an exception in favor of Gurkhas, whom he acknowledged to be unsurpassed in mountain scouting.

15. Philip Régis de Trobriand, *Army Life in Dakota,* ed. Milo M. Quaife (Chicago: Donnelly, 1941), pp. 46–47.

16. Joyce Evelyn Mason, "The Use of Indian Scouts in the Apache Wars, 1870–1886," Ph.D. dissertation, Indiana University, 1970, pp. 214–16; my interpretation follows Mason.

17. O. O. Howard to Nelson Miles, June 10, 1886, in Secretary of War, *Annual Report, 1886,* 1:181.

5. The Role of Scouts in Indian Warfare

1. C. E. Callwell, *Small Wars* (London: His Majesty's Stationery Office, 1906), refers frequently to American wars with the "Red Indians," but relates only a few specific instances. He is concerned primarily with techniques, not

with types of troops. He rather reluctantly admits that some individual "primitives" might be superior in some respects to some European soldiers, but like his American contemporaries, he believes that European discipline and persistence more than compensate for any individual shortcomings.

2. Jean Gottman, "Bugeaud, Galliéni, Lyautey: The Development of French Colonial Warfare," in Edward Meade Earle, ed., *Makers of Modern Strategy* (Princeton: Princeton University Press, 1943), pp. 247, 253; Callwell, *Small Wars*, pp. 350–52; Cyril Falls, *A Hundred Years of War* (London: Duckworth, 1953), pp. 117–18; Ross E. Dunn, *Resistance in the Desert* (Madison: University of Wisconsin Press, 1977), pp. 205–6; C. G. Gordon, *The Journals of Major-General C. G. Gordon, C.B., at Khartoum*, ed. A. Egmont Hake (London: Kegan Paul, Trench, 1885), p. 89.

3. John G. Bourke, *On the Border with Crook* (1891; rpt. Lincoln: University of Nebraska Press, 1971), p. 338; Richard F. Burton, *The City of the Saints and Across the Rocky Mountains to California*, ed. Fawn M. Brodie (New York, Knopf, 1963), p. 53; Ruth Miller Elson, *Guardians of Tradition* (Lincoln: University of Nebraska Press, 1964), pp. 73–75; Roy Harvey Pearce, *Savagism and Civilization* (Baltimore: Johns Hopkins Press, 1965), pp. 224–25.

4. John C. Ewers, *Indian Life on the Upper Missouri* (Norman: University of Oklahoma Press, 1968), pp. 75–90; James Parker, *The Old Army Memories, 1872–1918* (Philadelphia: Dorrance, 1929), pp. 38–39; Grant Foreman, ed., *Adventure on Red River* (Norman: University of Oklahoma Press, 1937), pp. 162–63; Superintendent F. W. Lander to Commissioner of Indian Affairs, February 11, 1860: ". . . some of the Eastern Snakes having been led to believe that the whites are very few in number" (Dale L. Morgan, ed., "Washakie and the Shoshoni: A Selection of Documents . . . ," pt. 5, *Annals of Wyoming* 27 [October 1953]:200).

5. S. E. Whitman, *The Troopers* (New York: Hastings House, 1962), pp. 26–27; figures as of 1877.

6. James S. Brown, *Life of a Pioneer* (Salt Lake City: Cannon & Sons, 1900), pp. 357–59.

7. John F. Stover, *American Railroads* (Chicago: University of Chicago Press, 1961), pp. 77, 80–84, map p. 85.

8. *Outline Descriptions of the Posts in the Military Division of the Missouri*, 2d ed. (Fort Collins, Colo.: Old Army Press, 1969), pp. 11, 164.

9. The lack of aerial reconnaissance and electronic communication meant that the army's capabilities in these matters could be no better than the Indians'. It would be immensely more difficult today to carry on guerrilla warfare on the treeless Plains.

10. Kenneth M. Hammer, *The Springfield Carbine on the Western Frontier* (Bellevue, Neb.: Old Army Press, 1970); John S. duMont, *Custer Battle Guns* (Fort Collins, Colo.: Old Army Press, 1974); Randy Steffen, *The Horse Soldier, 1776–1943*, 4 vols. (Norman: University of Oklahoma Press, 1978), 2:75–77, 100–102, 153–56; R. H. Pratt to Assistant Adjutant General, Department of Texas, September 9, 1873, and endorsement by Chief Ordnance Officer, Department of Texas, in Post Records, Fort Griffin, RG 393, NARS.

11. Richard I. Dodge, *Our Wild Indians* (Hartford: Worthington, 1883), pp. 449–51, 475–77, 488–89; Crook's observations in Dan L. Thrapp, ed., *Dateline Fort Bowie* (Norman: University of Oklahoma Press, 1979), p. 120; John Gregory Bourke, Diaries, 14:1485 U.S. Military Academy Library, West Point, N.Y. (microfilm, NSHS); Parker, *Old Army Memories*, pp. 36–37; Jesse W. Vaughn, *With Crook at the Rosebud* (Harrisburg, Pa.: Stackpoles, 1956), pp. 130–31, and photographs of reloaded casings found on the battlefield.

12. These points have been questioned in regard to Indians other than Apaches, but they are evident in both the contemporary literature and accounts of engagements; see Dodge, *Our Wild Indians*, pp. 420, 449–53, 475–77, 489, 491; James S. Brisbin, ed., *Belden, the White Chief* (Cincinnati: C. F. Vent, 1870), pp. 120, 130; William McElwee, *The Art of War* (Bloomington: Indiana University Press, 1974), pp. 120–46. See especially the chapter on skirmishing in Edward S. Farrow, *Mountain Scouting* (New York: privately printed, 1881), pp. 239–48. For earlier Indian adaptation to the tactical effects of muzzle-

loading firearms, see Francis Jennings, *The Invasion of America* (Chapel Hill: University of North Carolina Press, 1975), p. 166; Frank R. Secoy, *Changing Military Patterns on the Great Plains* (Seattle: University of Washington Press, 1953). On Apache camouflage, see John C. Cremony, *Life among the Apaches* (San Francisco: John H. Carmany, 1868), pp. 189–90; W. E. Shipp, "Captain Crawford's Last Expedition," *Journal of the U.S. Cavalry Association* 5 (December 1892):352. Farrow, *Mountain Scouting*, p. 89, suggests drab clothing. See also James S. Hutchins, "Mounted Riflemen: The Real Role of Cavalry in the Indian Wars," *El Palacio* 69 (Summer 1962):85–91.

13. John Ellis, *The Social History of the Machine Gun* (New York: Pantheon, 1975), pp. 79–109; he quotes Hilaire Belloc: "Whatever happens, we have got / The Maxim gun, and they have not." See also Paul Wahl and Don Toppel, *The Gatling Gun* (New York: Arco, 1965); Robert M. Utley, "The Gatlings Custer Left Behind," *American West* 11 (March 1974):24–25; Oliver O. Howard, *Nez Perce Joseph* (Boston: Lee & Shepard, 1881), pp. 43–44.

14. See Ellis, *Social History*, pp. 65–76, on military resistance to the machine gun. For engagements in which the Gatling gun figured indecisively, see Sarah Winnemucca Hopkins, *Life among the Piutes* (1883; Bishop, Calif.: Sierra Media, 1969), pp. 175–78; William H. Leckie, *The Buffalo Soldiers* (Norman: Universityof Oklahoma Press, 1967), pp. 135–39. Howard, *Nez Perce Joseph*, p. 44: ". . . wide intervening rivers, wooded buttes, and precipitous ravines, conditions of which Indians take advantage against even the best Gatlings."

15. See Robert M. Utley, *Fronter Regulars* (New York: Macmillan, 1973), pp. 45–57, and *The Contribution of the Frontier to the American Military Tradition* (Colorado Springs: U.S. Air Force Academy, 1977). The same points are made even more strongly in Neil B. Thompson, *Crazy Horse Called them Walk-a-Heaps* (Saint Cloud, Minn.: North Star Press, 1979). Stephen E. Ambrose, *Upton and the Army* (Baton Rouge: Louisiana State University Press, 1964); Russell F. Weigley, *Towards an American Army* (New York: Columbia University Press, 1962), pp. 100–26, 137–61.

16. Randolph B. Marcy, *The Prairie Traveler* (New York: Harper, 1859), especially pp. 173–205, is a good summary of the campaigning methods used after 1865; see also Marcy's recommendation of permanent Indian scouts in 1852, in Grant Foreman, ed., *Adventure on Red River* (Norman: University of Oklahoma Press, 1937), pp. 55–56. An exception to the lack of professional interest before 1860 was the Corps of Topographical Engineers, which was primarily concerned with exploration; see William H. Goetzmann, *Army Exploration in the American West, 1803–1863* (New Haven: Yale University Press, 1959); William P. Clark, *The Indian Sign-Language* (Philadelphia: L. R. Hamersley, 1885).

17. Robert G. Carter, *On the Border with Mackenzie* (Washington, D.C.: Eynon, 1935), p. 537; James H. Bradley, *The March of the Montana Column*, ed. Edgar I. Stewart (Norman: University of Oklahoma Press, 1961), p. 105; Ben Innis, *Bloody Knife* (Fort Collins, Colo.: Old Army Press, 1973), p. 89.

18. Carter, *On the Border*, p. 536; Thrapp, ed., *Dateline Fort Bowie*, pp. 120–21; DeCost Smith, *Indian Experiences* (Caldwell, Ida.: Caxton, 1943), p. 142: "Just as the white man considered himself 'smarter' than the Indian, the Indian regarded the white man as far below him in wilderness craft."

19. Smith, *Indian Experiences*, p. 142.

20. Thomas Cruse, *Apache Days and After* (Caldwell, Ida.: Caxton, 1971), p. 58; Charles B. Gatewood, "Campaigning against Victorio in 1879," *The Great Divide*, April 1894, pp. 102–4; Dan L. Thrapp, *Victorio and the Mimbres Apaches* (Norman: University of Oklahoma Press, 1974), pp. 237–51. Morrow himself concluded that 150 Apache scouts unaccompanied by troops would probably have had better results (Thrapp, *Victorio*, pp. 367–68). See also S. G. Fisher, "Journal of S. G. Fisher, Chief of Scouts to General O. O. Howard during the Campaign against the Nez Perce Indians, 1877," *Contributions to the Historical Society of Montana* 2 (Helena, 1896):75: "the truth is that Uncle Sam's boys are too slow for this business."

21. Harry H. Turney-High, *Primitive War* (Columbia: University of South Carolina Press, 1971), pp. 40, 109, 117; Ran-

dolph B. Marcy, *Thirty Years of Army Life on the Border*
(New York: Harper, 1866), p. 252 (note that these admonitions are in Marcy's memoirs, not in an official publication); Hutchins, "Mounted Riflemen," pp. 87–90;
George Crook, *General George Crook: His Autobiography*
(Norman: University of Oklahoma Press, 1946), pp. 10,
268.

22. With the possible exception of Eugene A. Carr; see James
T. King, *War Eagle* (Lincoln: University of Nebraska
Press, 1963). Sheridan saw some Indian fighting in the
1850s.

23. John Bigelow, *On the Bloody Trail of Geronimo*, ed.
Arthur Woodward (Los Angeles: Westernlore, 1958), p. 44.
See also William H. Carter, *From Yorktown to Santiago
with the Sixth U.S. Cavalry* (Baltimore: Lord Baltimore
Press, 1900), p. 251. Bigelow's *Principles of Strategy*
(Philadelphia: Lippincott, 1894) takes some notice of In-
dian wars practice.

24. Wesley Merritt, *Merritt and the Indian Wars*, ed. Barry C.
Johnson (London: Johnson-Taunton Military Press, 1972),
p. 13.

25. Clark, *Indian Sign-Language*, pp. 330–32; Turney-High,
Primitive War, pp. 108–9; Red Wing's comment is in
Thomas H. Leforge, *Memoirs of a White Crow Indian*
(1928; rpt. Lincoln: University of Nebraska Press, 1974),
p. 297.

26. Callwell, *Small Wars*, pp. 43–56, expounds on the special
problems of intelligence in such wars.

27. Luther H. North, *Man of the Plains*, ed. Donald F.
Danker (Lincoln: University of Nebraska Press, 1961),
p. 121.

28. Shannon's account is reprinted in full in H. B. Wharfield,
Apache Indian Scouts (El Cajon, Calif.: privately printed,
1964), p. 81. Farrow, *Mountain Scouting*, pp. 228–37,
goes into detail on the subject, but doubts that most
whites can acquire the art.

29. Trobriand, *Army Life in Dakota*, p. 348. The rider lay low
against the horse's neck, with a buffalo robe draped over
both. From a distance, in profile, the silhouette resembled
a buffalo well enough to allow time for observation.

30. C. C. Augur to Ranald Mackenzie, August 28, 1874, in Ernest Wallace, ed., "Ranald Mackenzie's Official Correspondence Relating to Texas, 1873–1879," *Museum Journal* 10 (1966):81; Callwell, *Small Wars*, p. 294: "it is never safe to assume that there is no enemy because there is no enemy to be seen."

31. Thrapp, *Victorio*, p. 237. The Pawnees had no acquaintance with the Wyoming Shoshones until they both scouted for Crook in 1876; see Alfred Sorenson, "A Quarter of a Century on the Frontier, or the Adventures of Major Frank North . . . ," NSHS, p. 182.

32. Karen D. Petersen, *Plains Indian Art from Fort Marion* (Norman: University of Oklahoma Press, 1971), pp. 54–55, and drawings, pp. 289–92; Thomas B. Marquis, *Wooden Leg* (1931; rpt. Lincoln: University of Nebraska Press, 1961), p. 262.

33. Ernest Wallace and E. Adamson Hoebel, *The Comanches* (Norman: University of Oklahoma Press, 1952), pp. 18–19. Turney-High, *Primitive War*, pp. 107–8: "The American Indian was a marvelous scout because his life depended on it, both as a hunter and a warrior. Craft acuteness of this order is common enough in civilized life."

34. Philip Sheridan, *Personal Memoirs of P. H. Sheridan*, 2 vols. (New York: Charles L. Webster, 1888), 2:299; Thrapp, ed., *Dateline Fort Bowie*, p. 155.

35. George Crook, *General George Crook: His Autobiography*, ed. Martin H. Schmitt (Norman: University of Oklahoma Press, 1946), pp. 147–50; James H. Cook, *Fifty Years on the Old Frontier* (New Haven: Yale University Press, 1923), pp. 194–98.

36. John Gibbon, *Gibbon on the Sioux Campaign of 1876* (Bellevue, Nebr.: Old Army Press, 1970), p. 41.

37. Everett V. Stonequist, *The Marginal Man* (New York: Scribner's, 1937).

38. Clark, *Indian Sign-Language*; Garrick Mallery, *Sign Language among North American Indians* (Washington, D.C.: Smithsonian Institution, 1881).

39. Arthur L. Wagner, *The Service of Security and Information* (Washington, D.C.: James J. Chapman, 1893), pp. 221–28.

40. These points pervade the literature. See especially Tro-
    briand, *Army Life in Dakota*, pp. 54–55; Richard I. Dodge,
    Our Wild Indians (Hartford: Worthington, 1882), pp. 490–
    91; Farrow, *Mountain Scouting*, pp. 239–42.

41. Luther North, "The Fighting Norths and Pawnee Scouts,"
    Motor Travel, April 1931, p. 16: "About the most diffi-
    cult thing in Indian warfare is to *surprise* any good-sized
    hostile band."

42. There are numerous firsthand accounts of this campaign.
    See John Gregory Bourke, *Mackenzie's Last Fight with
    the Cheyennes* (Bellevue, Nebr.: Old Army Press, 1970);
    Frank North's version in Sorenson, "Quarter of a Cen-
    tury," pp. 180–96; Luther North's in *Motor Travel*, April,
    May, and June 1931, and in North, *Man of the Plains*, pp.
    194–236; and Homer K. Wheeler, *Buffalo Days* (New
    York: A. L. Burt, 1925), pp. 123–47. An invaluable un-
    published account by William Garnett, interpreter with
    the Sioux scouts, is in the Eli S. Ricker Interviews,
    Tablets 1 and 2, NSHS; see also Bourke, Diaries, vol. 14.
    Rush Roberts, a Pawnee scout, left a brief account many
    years later (courtesy of Don Rickey, Denver). For the
    Cheyenne version, see George Bird Grinnell, *The Fighting
    Cheyennes* (Norman: University of Oklahoma Press,
    1955), pp. 359–82; John Stands-in-Timber and Margot
    Liberty, with Robert M. Utley, *Cheyenne Memories* (New
    Haven: Yale University Press, 1967), pp. 214–19; George
    Bird Grinnell, *Pawnee Hero Stories and Folk Tales* (1889;
    rpt. Lincoln: University of Nebraska Press, 1961), pp. 74–75.

43. See the sources cited in note 42 and Peter J. Powell,
    "Ox'zem: Box Elder and His Sacred Wheel Lance," *Mon-
    tana* 20 (Spring 1970):14–20. See also Karl N. Llewellyn
    and E. Adamson Hoebel, *The Cheyenne Way* (Norman:
    University of Oklahoma Press, 1941), pp. 117–21, 265–66.

44. See the sources cited in note 42, especially Wheeler, *Buf-
    falo Days*, pp. 131–36; Garnett narrative, Ricker inter-
    views, Tablet 2, pp. 9–10.

45. Garnett narrative, Ricker interviews, pp. 9–10; Wheeler,
    Buffalo Days, pp. 130–32.

46. Wheeler, *Buffalo Days*, pp. 135–36.

47. Bourke, *Mackenzie's Last Fight*, pp. 28–32; North, *Man of*

the *Plains*, pp 217n–18n; John Gregory Bourke, *On the Border with Crook* (1891; rpt. Lincoln: University of Nebraska Press, 1971), p. 407.

48. Dodge, *Our Wild Indians*, pp. 493, 499–500; Dodge commanded the infantry in this campaign.
49. Anson Mills, "The Battle of the Rosebud," in *POIW*, p. 9; H. R. Lemly, "The Fight on the Rosebud," in ibid., p. 18; Crook's report is in U.S. Congress, House, Secretary of War, *Annual Report, 1876*, 1:498.
50. Stanley Vestal [Walter S. Campbell], *Warpath* (Boston: Houghton Mifflin, 1934), pp. 188–89, and *Warpath and Council Fire* (New York: Random House, 1948), p. 230.
51. Gibbon, *Gibbon on the Sioux Campaign*, p. 7; Bradley, *March of the Montana Column*, pp. 39–47. Gibbon did not quite understand why the Crows wanted him to swear to believe what they told him and to take their advice, but Bradley did. Bourke, Diaries, 7:796; Parker, *Old Army Memories*, p. 156; George Armstrong Custer, *My Life on the Plains* (Norman: University of Oklahoma Press, 1962), pp. 235–36.
52. John C. Ewers, *The Horse in Blackfoot Indian Culture, with Comparative Material from Other Western Tribes* (Washington, D.C.: Smithsonian Institution, 1955); Frank G. Roe, *The Indian and the Horse* (Norman: University of Oklahoma Press, 1955).
53. Edmund Carpenter, *Oh, What a Blow That Phantom Gave Me!* (New York: Holt, Rinehart & Winston, 1973), pp. 151–53, presents the theory that nonliterates cannot be marksmen, because literacy develops the coordination necessary to close just one eye.
54. John S. Gray, *Centennial Campaign* (Fort Collins, Colo.: Old Army Press, 1976), p. 291; George Crook, "The Apache Problem," *Journal of the Military Service Institution of the United States* 7 (1886):262–69; Crook's annual report, in Secretary of War, *Annual Report, 1883*, vol. 1. See also General Alfred Terry's reflections in ibid., *1887*, 1:120–21; Terry argued that breechloading rifles had revived the need to emphasize individual skill with weapons, neglected since the invention of firearms in favor of concerted, precise movement at command.

55. Dodge, *Our Wild Indians*, pp. 442–44; Dodge to Augur, August 18, 1867; Frank North to Dodge, August 18, 1867; James Murie to Dodge, August 18, 1867; Dodge to Augur, August 19, 1867, all in Letters Received, Department of the Platte, RG 500, NARS; Sorenson, "Quarter of a Century," p. 123. The carrying of overcoats into the field in Nebraska in August sounds implausible; William F. Cody, *The Life of Hon. William F. Cody, Known as Buffalo Bill, the Famous Hunter, Scout, and Guide* (Hartford: Bliss, 1879), p. 250, notes Pawnee scouts parading in overcoats in the summer of 1869; see also Sorenson, "Quarter of a Century," p. 134, possibly copied from Cody. George E. Hyde, *Life of George Bent*, ed. Savoie Lottinville (Norman: University of Oklahoma Press, 1968), pp. 277–78, credits the Pawnee victory to their Spencer repeating carbines; when he notes that the Pawnees "soon got rid of most of their uniforms," he may be referring to the overcoat ruse.

56. John F. Finerty, *War-Path and Bivouac* (Norman: University of Oklahoma Press, 1961), pp. 265, 285.

57. John Gregory Bourke, *With General Crook in the Indian Wars* (Palo Alto: Lewis Osborne, 1968), p. 56; Bourke, *Mackenzie's Last Fight*, p. 27; probably rather free translations in both cases.

58. William C. Brown, "The Sheepeater Campaign," *Tenth Annual Report of the Board of Trustees of the State Historical Society of Idaho* (Boise, 1926), pp. 27–51; C. B. Hardin, "The Sheepeater Campaign," *Journal of the Military Service Institution of the United States* 47 (July-August 1910):25–40; Oliver O. Howard, *My Life and Experiences among Our Hostile Indians* (Hartford: Worthington, 1907), pp. 421–33 (the experience is reflected in many places in Farrow, *Mountain Scouting*, especially pp. 235–36); Joan Corbett Quinn, "A Mountain Charade: the Sheepeater Campaign of 1879," *Montana* 28 (January 1978):16–27. See also Robert H. Ruby and John A. Brown, *The Cayuse Indians* (Norman: University of Oklahoma Press, 1972), pp. 286–87.

59. Thrapp, ed., *Dateline Fort Bowie*, p. 120.

60. George E. Hyde, *Spotted Tail's Folk* (Norman: University

of Oklahoma Press, 1961), pp. 243–46; James C. Olson,
Red Cloud and the Sioux Problem (Lincoln: University of
Nebraska Press, 1965), pp. 238–39.

61. Mark H. Brown, *The Flight of the Nez Perce* (New York:
Putnam, 1967), pp. 389–90; Stands-in-Timber and Liberty,
Cheyenne Memories, pp. 227–28, credit this exploit to
High Wolf.

62. The Ute leader Tse-ne-gat was acquitted of all charges.
Scott's account is in Hugh L. Scott, *Some Memories of a
Soldier* (New York: Century, 1928), pp. 533–41; Forbes
Parkhill, *The Last of the Indian Wars* (New York:
Crowell, 1961). Bi-joshii's earlier troubles resulted from
an Indian agent's attempts to stamp out Navajo polygamy
in 1913; see Scott, *Some Memories*, pp. 487–95; Frank
McNitt, *The Indian Traders* (Norman: University of Okla-
homa Press, 1962), pp. 347–58.

6. "Indian Thinking": White
Leadership and Indian Scouts

1. Frederic Remington, "How an Apache War Was Won,"
in Harold McCracken, ed., *Frederic Remington's Own
West* (New York: Dial, 1960), p. 49. The officer in question may have been James Watson.

2. Gary L. Roberts, "The Shame of Little Wolf," *Montana*
28 (July 1978):36–47; Karl N. Llewellyn and E. Adamson
Hoebel, *The Cheyenne Way* (Norman: University of Oklahoma Press, 1941), pp. 81–86, 105–6; Bernard Mishkin,
Rank and Warfare among the Plains Indians (Seattle: University of Washington Press, 1973), especially pp. 32–34.
Little Wolf and Starving Elk were both scouts at Fort
Keogh at the time of the incident; the army let the Cheyennes settle the matter in their own way.

3. See Edward S. Farrow, *Mountain Scouting* (New York: privately printed, 1881), pp. 213–27; Hugh L. Scott, *Some
Memories of a Soldier* (New York: Century, 1928), pp. 95–
96, on the number of experienced officers in the
Seventh Cavalry, ca. 1878, who were "first-rate garrison
soldiers" but "blind on the prairie." Frank E. Vandiver,

Black Jack, 2 vols. (College Station: Texas A&M University Press, 1977), 1:99–101, on John J. Pershing's experiences commanding Sioux scouts; Grenville Goodwin, *Western Apache Raiding and Warfare*, ed. Keith Basso (Tucson: University of Arizona Press, 1971), pp. 105–7.

4. Farrow, *Mountain Scouting*, p. 227.
5. James W. Watson, "Scouting in Arizona, 1890," *Journal of the U.S. Cavalry Association* 10 (June 1908):134; Farrow, *Mountain Scouting*, pp. 239–48, implicitly accepts this concept.
6. O. G. Libby, ed., *The Arikara Narrative of the Campaign against the Hostile Dakotas, June 1876* (New York: Sol Lewis, 1973), p. 77. The contrast between Red Star's assessment and the popular image of Custer hardly requires comment.
7. Goodwin, *Western Apache Raiding*, pp. 154 (John Rope narrative) and 312 (note by Basso). See also Otto L. Hein, *Memories of Long Ago, By an Old Army Officer* (New York: Putnam, 1925), p. 89, for an occasion when Crook "suggested" that some junior officers join a victory dance by Apache scouts.
8. Captain Lee P. Gillette, commanding officer, Fort Philip Kearny, Nebraska Territory, to North, February 25, 1865; North to Gillette, February 23, 1865, both in Record Books, Omaha and Pawnee Scouts, OAG, RG 500, NARS; Alfred Sorenson, "A Quarter of a Century on the Frontier," p. 72.
9. Thomas H. Leforge, *Memoirs of a White Crow Indian* (1928; rpt. Lincoln: University of Nebraska Press, 1974), pp. 210–11, Augustus Tassin, "Reminiscences of Indian Scouting," *Overland Monthly* 14 (August 1889):152–53, tells how he held roll call for his Apaches in Arizona Territory, but he had to use numbers—in Apache—rather than their lengthy names.
10. Goodwin, *Western Apache Raiding*, pp. 183 (John Rope narrative) and 314 (Goodwin's note).
11. C. S. Roberts to W. E. Shipp, August 14, 1885, in John Bigelow, *On the Bloody Trail of Geronimo*, ed. Arthur Woodward (Los Angeles: Westernlore, 1958), pp. 43–44.

12. Bigelow, *On the Bloody Trail*. George Crook, *General George Crook: His Autobiography*, ed. Martin F. Schmitt (Norman: University of Oklahoma Press, 1946): "I never believed in that mode of discipline which consisted in trying to break down men's self-respect and make a mere machine of them instead of appealing to their better feelings and judgment."

13. Narrative by William Garnett in Eli S. Ricker Interviews, Tablet 1, p. 122, NSHS; John Gregory Bourke, Diaries, U.S. Military Academy Library, West Point, N.Y., 5:390: "Knowing the unfailing accuracy of an *Indian's* judgement in matters of this kind, *General Crook* told the [Crow and Shoshone] chiefs to arrange the plan of march according to their own ideas." John S. Gray, *Centennial Campaign* (Fort Collins, Colo.: Old Army Press, 1976), pp. 200–201, criticizes Crook for relying too much on Washakie's information and advice. See Thomas Cruse, *Apache Days and After* (Caldwell, Ida.: Caxton, 1941), pp. 55–56, on Charles Gatewood's methods of command with his Apache scouts.

14. Robert G. Carter, *On the Border with Mackenzie* (Washington, D.C.: Eynon, 1935), pp. 197–98. Ernest Wallace, "Ranald Mackenzie's Official Correspondence Relative to Texas . . . ," *Museum Journal* 9 (1965) and 10 (1966), has innumerable references to the value of the scouts.

15. George Crook, "The Apache Problem," *Journal of the United Military Service Institution of the United States* 7 (1886):263–64.

16. Robert M. Utley, *Frontier Regulars* (New York: Macmillan, 1973), pp. 20–23. The army finally instituted compulsory retirement at age sixty-two in 1882. See Timothy K. Nenninger, *The Leavenworth Schools and the Old Army* (Westport, Conn.: Greenwood Press, 1978), p. 31; George W. Cullum, *Biographical Register of the Officers and Graduates of the U.S. Military Academy* . . . (Cambridge, Mass.: Riverside Press, 1901), 4:281. See also James H. Wilson, *The Life and Services of Brevet Brigadier General Andrew Jonathan Alexander, United States Army* (New York, 1887), pp. 111–13, for Alexander's reflections.

17. Edward M. Coffman, *The Young Officer in the Old Army* (Colorado Springs: U.S. Air Force Academy, 1976); Scott, *Some Memories*, pp. 31–32; Britton Davis, *The Truth about Geronimo* (1929; rpt. Lincoln: University of Nebraska Press, 1976), p. 195.

18. Donald F. Danker, "The North Brothers and the Pawnee Scouts," *Nebraska History* 42 (September 1961):162.

19. Orrin H. Bonney and Lorraine Bonney, eds., *Battle Drums and Geysers* (Chicago: Swallow Press, 1970), pp. 3–142. William White, *Custer, Cavalry, and Crows* (Fort Collins, Colo.: Old Army Press, 1975), describes many of Doane's activities as a participant. See also Leforge, *Memoirs of a White Crow Indian*, pp. 280–81; Mary Allen Phinney, *Jirah Isham Allen, Montana Pioneer* (Rutland, Vt.: Tuttle, 1929), pp. 80–100.

20. Thomas C. Leonard, "Red, White, and the Army Blue: Empathy and Anger in the American West," *American Quarterly* 26 (May 1974):176–90; William B. Skelton, "Army Officers' Attitudes toward Indians, 1830–1860," *Pacific Northwest Quarterly* 67 (July 1976):113–24. Richard I. Dodge, *Our Wild Indians* (Hartford: Worthington, 1882), and Farrow, *Mountain Scouting*, pp. 213–27, are prime examples of such ambivalence.

21. Cullum, *Biographical Register*, 4:188, notes that Bourke was president of the American Folklore Society. On Matthews and Mallery, see *DAB*, 12:240, 222–23. Mallery's book was *Sign Language among North American Indians* (Washington, D.C.: Smithsonian Institution, 1881).

22. William P. Clark, *The Indian Sign-Language* (Philadelphia: L. R. Hamersley, 1885), pp. 5–6; Bourke, Diaries, 7:848, 14:1416; John Gregory Bourke, *On the Border with Crook* (1981; rpt. Lincoln: University of Nebraska Press, 1971), pp. 356, 361, 371; Clark's report in J. N. G. Whistler, commanding officer, Fort Keogh, Montana Territory, to Assistant Adjutant General, Department of Dakota, April 2, 1879, OAG, Letters Received, RG 94, NARS (microfilm NSHS); "How the Wary Wolf Was Wired," *Bismarck Tribune*, April 19, 1879; Thomas B. Marquis, *Wooden Leg* (1931; rpt. Lincoln: University of Nebraska Press, 1962), pp. 304–6; Phinney, *Jirah Isham*

Allen, pp. 105-9, 116; John F. Finerty, *War-Path and Bivouac* (Norman: University of Oklahoma Press, 1961), especially pp. 252-58, 279, 296-97; Mark H. Brown and W. R. Felton, *The Frontier Years* (New York: Holt, Rinehart & Winston, 1955), p. 41, quoting L. A. Huffman; Gary L. Roberts, "The Shame of Little Wolf," *Montana* 28 (July 1978):41-43; ACP file on W. P. Clark, RG 94, NARS.

23. Richard H. Pratt, *Battlefield and Classroom*, ed. Robert M. Utley (New Haven: Yale University Press, 1964); Elaine G. Eastman, *Pratt* (Norman: University of Oklahoma Press, 1935). Pratt's authoritarian methods are severely criticized in George E. Hyde, *Spotted Tail's Folk* (Norman: University of Oklahoma Press, 1961), pp. 289-93, and James L. Haley, *The Buffalo War* (New York: Doubleday, 1976), pp. 213-21. For a balanced assessment, see Francis Paul Prucha, *American Indian Policy in Crisis* (Norman: University of Oklahoma Press, 1976), pp. 271-83.

24. Pratt, *Battlefield and Classroom*, pp. 5-6, 79; Karen D. Petersen, *Plains Indian Art from Fort Marion* (Norman: University of Oklahoma Press, 1971), on Pratt's relations with Indian prisoners at Fort Marion, Fla.; Jason Betzinez, with W. S. Nye, *I Fought with Geronimo* (Harrisburg, Pa.: Stackpole, 1959), pp. 149-59, 174, 202-3; Luther Standing Bear, *My People, the Sioux* (Boston: Houghton Mifflin, 1928), pp. 123-90.

25. Katherine M. Weist, "Ned Casey and His Cheyenne Scouts: A Noble Experiment in an Atmosphere of Tension," *Montana* 27 (January 1977): 26-39; Maurice Frink, with Casey Barthelmess, *Photographer on an Army Mule* (Norman: University of Oklahoma Press, 1965), pp. 99-123; Thomas B. Marquis, *Cheyenne and Sioux* (Stockton, Calif.: Pacific Center for Western Historical Studies, 1973), pp. 38-59; George Bird Grinnell, *The Fighting Cheyennes* (Norman: University of Oklahoma Press, 1955), pp. 397, 433-34; Marquis, *Wooden Leg*, pp. 333-45; Frederic Remington, "Chasing a Major-General," *Pony Tracks* (Norman: University of Oklahoma Press, 1961), pp. 3-16; Hamlin Garland, "A Typical Indian Scare: The Cheyenne Trouble," in Lonnie E. Underhill

and Daniel F. Littlefield, eds., *Hamlin Garland's Observations on the American Indian, 1895-1905* (Tucson: University of Arizona Press, 1976), pp. 145–57.

26. See the sources in note 25 and Frederic Remington, "Lieutenant Casey's Last Scout," *Pony Tracks*, pp. 17–34; Robert M. Utley, "The Ordeal of Plenty Horses," *American Heritage* 26 (December 1974):15–19, 82–89. Plenty Horses was one of the less successful products of Pratt's Carlisle school; he killed Casey to gain status as a warrior.

27. See Dan L. Thrapp, *The Conquest of Apacheria* (Norman: University of Oklahoma Press, 1967), pp. 303–5, 364–65; Angie Debo, *Geronimo* (Norman: University of Oklahoma Press, 1976), p. 280. My conclusions are based on the Charles B. Gatewood Collection, Arizona Historical Society, Tucson, including Gatewood's fragmentary memoirs and Gatewood to wife, June 25, 1886, and on Gatewood, "Campaigning against Victorio in 1879," *The Great Divide*, April 1894, pp. 102–4. Gatewood's accusations against the Chiricahuas are printed in full in Herbert Welsh, *The Apache Prisoners in Fort Marion, St. Augustine, Florida* (Philadelphia: Office of the Indian Rights Association, 1887), pp. 50–54. Ace Daklugie, a Chiricahua who had little good to say about whites, compliments Gatewood's courage and integrity in Eve Ball, with Nora Henn and Lynda Sanchez, *Indeh* (Provo, Utah: Brigham Young University Press, 1980), pp. 82, 110–12.

28. Tassin, "Recollections of Indian Scouting," p. 152.

29. Robert Bruce, *The Fighting Norths and Pawnee Scouts* (Lincoln: University of Nebraska Press, 1932), p. 24.

30. Davis, *Truth about Geronimo*, especially pp. 35–36, 49–50, 148; Dan L. Thrapp, *Al Sieber, Chief of Scouts* (Norman: University of Oklahoma Press, 1964). Remington characterizes Sieber as "a stern, modest man who had been in a hundred fights, but who was an Indian-thinker besides" (How an Apache War Was Won," p. 49).

31. Parker to Hatch, May 26, 1880, in U.S. Congress, House, Secretary of War, *Annual Report, 1880*, 1:99; *Record of Engagements with Hostile Indians within the Military Division of the Missouri, from 1868 to 1882, Lieutenant-General P. H. Sheridan, Commanding* (Washington, D.C.: Government Printing Office, 1882), p. 95; *Chronological*

List of Actions, etc., with Indians, from January 1, 1866, to January 1891 (Washington, D.C.: OAG, n.d.), p. 50; Dan L. Thrapp, *Victorio and the Mimbres Apaches* (Norman: University of Oklahoma Press, 1967), pp. 277–81. My assessment follows Thrapp.

32. James Parker, *The Old Army Memories, 1872–1918* (Philadelphia: Dorrance, 1929), p. 41. A waggish officer once pointed out the unmilitary Gatewood to an unsuspecting tourist as a typical example of the Arizona "bad man" (G. J. Fiebeger, "General Crook's Campaign in Old Mexico . . . ," *POIW*, p. 198). T. E. Lawrence, *Seven Pillars of Wisdom* (London: Chatto & Windus, 1935), p. 30: "Easily was a man made an infidel, but hardly might he be converted to another faith . . . and then madness was very near, as I believe it would be near the man who could see things through the veils at once of two customs, two educations, two environments."

33. Rudolph Friedrich Kurz, *Journal of Rudolph Friedrich Kurz*, ed. J. N. B. Hewitt (Washington, D.C.: Government Printing Office, p. 205; Farrow, *Mountain Scouting*, p. 277.

34. Sorenson, "Quarter of a Century," pp. 60, 65–66; Bruce, *Fighting Norths*, p. 24.

35. On Murie, see Luther H. North, *Man of the Plains*, ed. Donald F. Danker (Lincoln: University of Nebraska Press, 1961), pp. 32, 37–38, 49, 52, 59.

36. William McKay, "William McKay's Journal, 1866–67: Indian Scouts," ed. Keith and Donna Clark, *Oregon Historical Quarterly* 79 (Summer–Fall 1978):120–71, 269–83; Thrapp, *Conquest of Apacheria*, p. 34n; Austin N. Leiby, "The Marmon Battalion and the Apache Campaign of 1885," in Albert H. Schroeder, ed., *The Changing Ways of Southwestern Indians* (Glorieta, N.M.: Rio Grande Press, 1973), pp. 211–29.

37. "Company Descriptive Book, Co. F, Indian Scouts," Item 2053, RG 391, NARS; only three officers were involved, but Lieutenant J. A. Rucker served two terms.

38. Walter S. Schuyler to Robert Bruce, n.d., in Bruce, *Fighting Norths*, p. 6; Luther North in ibid., pp. 32–48.

39. Thomas Cruse to C. B. Gatewood, Jr., February 9, 1926, and Gatewood's reminiscences, both in Gatewood Collection; Gatewood, "Campaigning against Victorio."

40. Daniel F. Littlefield, *Africans and Seminoles* (Westport, Conn.: Greenwood Press, 1977); Kenneth W. Porter, "The Seminole in Mexico, 1850–1861," *Hispanic American Historical Review* 31 (February 1951):1–36; Kenneth W. Porter, "The Seminole-Negro Indian Scouts, 1870–1881," *Southwestern Historical Quarterly* 55 (January 1952):358–77.

41. See the sources in note 40 and Edward S. Wallace, "John Lapham Bullis, the Thunderbolt of the Texas Frontier," *Southwestern Historical Quarterly* 54 (April 1951):452–61, 55 (July 1951):77–85; *Outline Descriptions of the Posts in the Military Division of the Missouri* (Chicago: Military Division of the Missouri, 1876), p. 203; *The Medal of Honor of the United States Army* (Washington, D.C., 1948), pp. 222–23; Parker, *Old Army Memories*, p. 100; Frank D. Reeve, ed., "Frederick E. Phelps: A Soldier's Memoirs," *New Mexico Historical Review* 25 (July 1950):202–16; Thrapp, *Al Sieber*, pp. 361, 363–73.

42. Carl C. Rister, *Fort Griffin on the Texas Frontier* (Norman: University of Oklahoma Press, 1956), pp. 72, 109, 129, 208; U.S. Congress, House, *Tonkawa Indians at Fort Griffin, Texas*, 44th Cong., 1st sess., House Executive Document no. 102 (1875); Pratt, *Battlefield and Classroom*, pp. 54–64; Secretary of War, *Annual Report, 1879*, 1:74; Marquis, *Wooden Leg*, p. 327; Alfred W. Bowers, *Hidatsa Social and Ceremonial Organization* (Washington, D.C.: Smithsonian Institution, 1965), pp. 30, 44–45, 77, 251; "Gen'l Correspondence Book of Detachment of Indian Scouts, 1874–76," Item 1340, RG 393, pt. 1, NARS; H. B. Wharfield, *With Scouts and Cavalry at Fort Apache* (Tucson: Arizona Pioneers' Historical Society, 1965) (Wharfield commanded the scout detachment at Fort Apache in 1918); "Descriptive Book for a Detachment of Seminole Indian Scouts, 1889–93," Item 2060, RG 391, NARS.

7. Renegades, Patriots, and Pragmatists

1. John F. Finerty, *War-Path and Bivouac*, (Norman: University of Oklahoma Press, 1961), p. 279.

2. The Kiowas regarded their Comanche allies as friendly, outgoing folk who would go to a great deal of trouble to help people in distress. Such a view of the Comanches would have been incomprehensible to the citizens of Texas and Northern Mexico. See Wilbur S. Nye, *Bad Medicine and Good* (Norman: University of Oklahoma Press, 1962), pp. 43–44.

3. William P. Clark, *The Indian Sign Language* (Philadelphia: L. R. Hamersley, 1885), p. 223. William Tomkins, *Universal Indian Sign Language of the Plains of North America* (San Diego: William Tomkins, 1926), p. 31, gives a sign referring to the same skin color as the speaker.

4. Stanley Vestal, *New Sources of Indian History, 1850–1891* (Norman: University of Oklahoma Press, 1934), pp. 236–44; Hugh A. Dempsey, *Crowfoot* (Norman: University of Oklahoma Press, 1972), pp. 88–92, 123.

5. John C. Ewers, "Intertribal Warfare as the Precursor of Indian-white Warfare on the Northern Great Plains," *Western Historical Quarterly* 6 (October 1975):402; Anthony McGinnis, "Intertribal Conflict on the Northern Plains and Its Suppression," *Journal of the West* 18 (April 1979):49–61.

6. Harry H. Turney-High, *Primitive War* (Columbia: University of South Carolina Press, 1971), pp. 104, 134, and Bernard Mishkin, *Rank and Warfare among the Plains Indians* (Seattle: University of Washington Press, 1966), emphasize the "game" and status aspects. See also Anthony McGinnis, "Economic Warfare on the Northern Plains," *Annals of Wyoming* 44 (Spring 1972); W. W. Newcomb, "A Reexamination of the Causes of Plains Warfare," *American Anthropologist* 52 (July–September 1950):317–30.

7. Washington Irving, *The Adventures of Captain Bonneville, U.S.A., in the Rocky Mountains and the Far West*, ed. Edgeley W. Todd (Norman: University of Oklahoma Press, 1961), especially pp. 80–89; Osborne Russell, *Journal of a Trapper*, ed. Aubrey L. Haines (Lincoln: University of Nebraska Press, 1965), pp. 58–60, 114–15; Warren A. Ferris, *Life in the Rocky Mountains*, ed. Paul C. Phillips (Denver: Old West, 1940).

8. McGinnis, "Economic Warfare"; Richard White, "The

Winning of the West: The Expansion of the Western
Sioux in the Eighteenth and Nineteenth Centuries," *Journal of American History* 65 (September 1978): 319–43;
Matthew C. Field, *Prairie and Mountain Sketches*, ed.
Kate L. Gregg (Norman: University of Oklahoma Press,
1957), pp. 138–39; Ewers, "Intertribal Warfare," pp. 407–
9; Preston Holder, *The Hoe and the Horse on the Plains*
(Lincoln: University of Nebraska Press, 1970), p. 20.

9. Edwin T. Denig, *Five Indian Tribes of the Upper Missouri*, ed. John C. Ewers (Norman: University of Oklahoma Press, 1961), pp. 60–62; Holder, *Hoe and the Horse*,
pp. 86–87, 133–34; Philip Régis de Trobriand, *Army Life
in Dakota*, ed. Milo M. Quaife (Chicago: Donnelly, 1941),
p. 59; O. G. Libby, ed., *The Arikara Narrative of the Campaign against the Hostile Dakotas, June 1876* (New York:
Sol Lewis, 1973), pp. 37, 44–45, 51, 52. Red Star tells
how, after a number of other Arikaras had enlisted for the
1876 campaign, he ran into Son of the Star, who remarked, "I see you have not gone." Red Star thought it
over and decided to enlist. A great many young men have
had similar experiences.

10. McGinnis, "Economic Warfare"; Denig, *Five Indian
Tribes*, p. 204; Robert Lowie, *The Crow Indians* (New
York: Farrar & Reinhart, 1935).

11. Baptiste Pourier interview, in Eli S. Ricker Interviews,
NSHS, ser. 2, Tablet 15, p. 29. "Big Bat" Pourier was in a
position to know, having served as a scout at Fort C. F.
Smith.

12. See Finerty, *War-Path and Bivouac*, pp. 262–63, and Peter
Koch, "Life at Musselshell in 1869 and 1870," *Contributions to the Historical Society of Montana* 2:300–301, for
differing views on the Crows. In the early 1870s Fort
Ellis, Montana Territory, and the nearby Bozeman area
found the Crows the best protection against Sioux raids;
see Earl of Dunraven, *The Great Divide* (London: Chatto
& Windus, 1876), pp. 56–57. Peter Nabokov, *Two Leggings* (New York: Crowell, 1967), records many instances
in which the Crow chiefs restrained the young men.

13. James H. Bradley, *The March of the Montana Column*,
ed. Edgar I. Stewart (Norman: University of Oklahoma

Press, 1961), pp. 40–47. Blackfoot's speech is in W. A. Graham, *The Custer Myth* (Harrisburg, Pa.: Stackpole, 1952), p. 5. Mark H. Brown, "A New Focus on the Sioux War," *Montana* 11 (October 1961):76–85, argues that the raids on the Crows, whom the government was obliged to protect, were a major cause of the 1876 war. Most historians have been reluctant to accept this thesis.

14. "Proceedings of a Council of the Principal Chiefs of the Mountain and River Crow Tribes, Held in Camp on the Big Horn River, June 10, 1877 . . . ," in Gustavus Cheney Doane Papers, courtesy Merrill G. Burlingame, Bozeman, Mont.; John Gregory Bourke, Diaries, 5:391, U.S. Military Academy Library, West Point, N.Y.; Denig, *Five Indian Tribes*, pp. 148–49; Lewis H. Morgan, *Indian Journals, 1859–62*, ed. Leslie A. White (Ann Arbor: University of Michigan Press, 1959), p. 170.

15. Bradley, *March of the Montana Column*, p. 42.

16. Frank B. Linderman, *Plenty-coups, Chief of the Crows* (1930; rpt. Lincoln: University of Nebraska Press, 1962), pp. 77–78, 153–54; see Nabokov, *Two Leggings*, p. 187, for a less positive assessment. See the recollections of the Crow scouts with Custer in Joseph K. Dixon, *The Vanishing Race* (New York: Rodman Wanamaker, 1913); Graham, *Custer Myth*; Walter Camp, comp., *Custer in 76*, ed. Kenneth Hammer (Provo: Brigham Young University Press, 1976).

17. George E. Hyde, *Indians of the High Plains* (Norman: University of Oklahoma Press, 1959), pp. 155–56, 180–81; James S. Brown, *Life of a Pioneer* (Salt Lake City: Cannon, 1900), pp. 316–19, 338–41, 353–59; William T. Hamilton, *My Sixty Years on the Plains* (Norman: University of Oklahoma Press, 1960), pp. 40–75, 135–52; Percival G. Lowe, *Five Years a Dragoon ('49 to '54) and Other Adventures on the Great Plains* (Norman: University of Oklahoma Press, 1965), p. 66; Robert D. Evans, *A Sailor's Log* (New York: Appleton, 1911), pp. 21–24; Dale L. Morgan, ed., "Washakie and the Shoshoni: A Selection of Documents from the Records of the Utah Superintendency of Indian Affairs," *Annals of Wyoming* 25–30 (July 1953–April 1958); Grace R. Hebard, *Washakie* (Cleveland:

Arthur H. Clark, 1930); Virginia C. Trenhold and Maurine Carley, *The Shoshonis* (Norman: University of Oklahoma Press, 1964).

18. Trenholm and Carley, *Shoshonis*, pp. 163–74, 223–43; Hebard, *Washakie*, pp. 119–68; Robert R. David, *Finn Burnett, Frontiersman* (Glendale, Calif.: Arthur H. Clark, 1937); pp. 251–52, 254–76; Morgan, ed., "Washakie and the Shoshoni," 30:83, 86; E. S. Topping, *The Chronicles of the Yellowstone* (St. Paul: Pioneer Press, 1883), pp. 79–80; James Chisholm, *South Pass 1868*, ed. Lola M. Homsher (Lincoln: University of Nebraska Press, 1960), pp. 83, 110, 124, 179, 182–83; Charles Lindsay, ed., "The Diary of Dr. Thomas G. Maghee," *Nebraska History* 12 (July–September 1929):247–304; Theophilus F. Rodenbough, comp., *From Everglade to Cañon with the Second Dragoons* (New York: Van Nostrand, 1875), pp. 396–99; Frank U. Robinson, "The Battle of Snake Mountain," *POIW*, pp. 185–90.

19. This is the thesis of McGinnis, "Intertribal Conflict."

20. Bourke, Diaries, 5:384–90; Linderman, *Plenty-coups*, pp. 159–60; Hebard, *Washakie*, pp. 174–205; Joe DeBarthe, *Life and Adventures of Frank Grouard*, ed. Edgar I. Stewart (Norman: University of Oklahoma Press, 1958), p. 115. Trenholm and Carley, *Shoshonis*, pp. 252–53, assert that Washakie was not present at the Rosebud battle, as earlier historians had assumed; Lemly, "Fight on the Rosebud," *POIW*, p. 13, mentions his presence in a letter written three days after the battle.

21. Lemly, "Fight on the Rosebud," pp. 13–18; Anson Mills, "The Battle of the Rosebud," *POIW*, pp. 3–12; Bourke, *Diaries*, 5:384–422, 6:581–607; Linderman, *Plenty-coups*, pp. 153–72; George Crook, *General George Crook: His Autobiography*, ed. Martin F. Schmitt (Norman: University of Oklahoma Press, 1946), pp. 194–95; Hebard, *Washakie*, pp. 174–204; Finerty, *War-Path and Bivouac*, pp. 64–72, 82–98; for the hostile side, Thomas B. Marquis, *Wooden Leg* (1931; rpt. Lincoln: University of Nebraska Press, 1962), pp. 193–207; Stanley Vestal, *Warpath* (Boston: Houghton Mifflin, 1934), pp. 187–89, and *Warpath and Council Fire* (New York: Random House,

1948), p. 230; John Stands-in-Timber and Margot Liberty, *Cheyenne Memories* (New Haven: Yale University Press, 1967), pp. 181–90; George Bird Grinnell, *The Fighting Cheyennes* (Norman: University of Oklahoma Press, 1955), pp. 328–44; He Dog's comment in Camp, *Custer in '76*, p. 205. Jesse W. Vaughn, *With Crook at the Rosebud* (Harrisburg, Pa.: Stackpole, 1956), does his best to make sense of this affair; he reprints most of the official reports. Jesse W. Vaughn, *Indian Fights* (Norman: University of Oklahoma Press, 1966), p. 139: "[Crook] would have suffered a disastrous defeat except for the support of the Crows and Snakes at critical times."

22. Bourke, *Diaries* 5:422: "the friendly Indians will strike many a blow against the *Sioux* before snow falls."

23. Richard H. Pratt, *Battlefield and Classroom*, ed. Robert M. Utley (New Haven: Yale University Press, 1964), pp. 9–10, 67, 70–72; Pratt to Acting Assistant Adjutant General, Fort Sill Column, November 29, 1874, in Joe F. Taylor, ed., "The Indian Campaign on the Staked Plains, 1874–75: Military Correspondence from War Department Adjutant General's Office, File 2815–1874," *Panhandle-Plains Historical Review* 34 (1961):121.

24. Ernest Wallace and E. Adamson Hoebel, *The Comanches* (Norman: University of Oklahoma Press, 1952), p. 70, consider the Comanche attitude toward the Tonkawas to be largely a rationalization. See U.S. Department of War, *The War of the Rebellion: A Compilation of the Official Records of the Union and Confederate Armies*, 53 vols. (Washington, D.C.: Government Printing Office, 1880–1900), ser. 1, 13:918–21; James Mooney, "Our Last Cannibal Tribe," *Harper's Monthly* 103 (September 1901):550–55; James B. Barry, *A Texas Ranger and Frontiersman*, ed. James K. Greer (Dallas: Southwest Press, 1932), pp. 157–65.

25. Governor J. W. Throckmorton to General James Oakes, March 11, 1867; Oakes to commanding officer, U.S. forces, Waco, March 11, 1867; S. H. Starr to Oakes, April 20, 1867; S. D. Sturgis to Assistant Adjutant General, District of Texas, March 18, 1868; enlistment papers, 1870–77; Assistant Adjutant General, Department of Texas, to

Commanding Officer, Fort Griffin, September 11, 1873,
all in Post Records, Fort Griffin, Tex., RG 393, NARS;
H. H. McConnell, *Five Years a Cavalryman* (Freeport,
N.Y.: Books for Libraries Press, 1970), pp. 59–60; Charles
A. Messiter, *Sport and Adventures among the North
American Indians* (London: R. H. Porter, 1890), pp. 211–
13; U.S. Congress, House, *Tonkawa Indians at Fort
Griffin, Texas*, 44th Cong., 1st sess., House Executive
Document no. 102 (1875).

26. Tabular Statements of Expeditions and Scouts; John Lee
to Acting Assistant Adjutant General, 5th Military District, June 12, 1869; Mackenzie to Commanding Officer,
Fort Griffin, July 24, 1872, all in Post Records, Fort Griffin; Robert G. Carter, *On the Border with Mackenzie*
(Washington, D.C.: Eynon, 1935), pp. 135, 137, 178–80,
191; James B. Gillette, *Six Years with the Texas Rangers*
(New Haven: Yale University Press, 1925), pp. 64–66.

27. Berta Hart Nance, "D. A. Nance and the Tonkawa Indians," *West Texas Historical Association Yearbook* 28
(1952):91–92; Llerena B. Friend, ed., *M. K. Kellogg's
Texas Journal, 1872* (Austin: University of Texas Press,
1967), pp. 123–28; Sallie R. Matthews, *Interwoven* (Austin: University of Texas Press, n.d.), pp. 46–47, 111–13,
158; Carl C. Rister, *Fort Griffin on the Texas Frontier*
(Norman: University of Oklahoma Press, 1956), pp. 72–
76, 208; Robert G. Carter, *The Old Sergeant's Story* (New
York: F. H. Hitchcock, 1926), pp. 90, 93, 103–7; H.
Sweeney to Post Adjutant, Fort Griffin, March 25, 1872;
"Circular," Headquarters, Fort Griffin, September 14,
1873; enlistment papers; all in Post Records, Fort Griffin.

28. Pratt, *Battlefield and Classroom*, pp. 55–58; General Or-
ders no. 5, November 28, 1874, Post Records, Fort Griffin;
Michael L. Tate, "Indian Scouting Detachments in the
Red River War, 1874–75," *Red River Valley Historical Re-
view* 3 (Spring 1978):202–26; William H. Leckie, "Buell's
Campaign," *Red River Valley Historical Review* 3 (Spring
1978):186–93; U.S. Congress, House, *Tonkawa Indians at
Fort Griffin*, pp. 2–4; Friend, ed., *M. K. Kellogg's Texas
Journal*, pp. 123–28; Assistant Adjutant General, Depart-
ment of Texas, to commanding officer, Fort Griffin,

August 16, 1872; Commissioner of Indian Affairs E. P. Smith to Secretary of Interior, June 23, 1873; Secretary of the Interior C. Delano to Secretary of War, June 14, 1873; Muster Roll, Tonkawa Indian Scouts, April 30–July 30, 1875, all in Post Records, Fort Griffin.

29. U.S. Congress, House, *Tonkawa Indians at Fort Griffin*, pp. 2–4; Lieutenant Elias Chandler, Acting Agent, to Commissioner of Indian Affairs, January 18, 1882, Letters Received, Office of Indian Affairs, RG 75, NARS; Berlin B. Chapman, "Establishment of the Iowa Reservation," *Chronicles of Oklahoma* 21 (December 1943):312–17; Harry Hoijer, *Tonkawa, an Indian Language of Texas* (New York: Columbia University Press, 1933), p. x; Elizabeth A. H. John, *Storms Brewed in Other Men's Worlds* (College Station: Texas A & M Press, 1975), p. 772.

30. Robert Ignatius Burns, *The Jesuits and the Indian Wars of the Northwest* (New Haven: Yale University Press, 1966), pp. 4–11, 391–400; Alvin M. Josephy, *The Nez Perce Indians and the Opening of the Northwest* (New Haven: Yale University Press, 1965), p. 21.

31. Brigham D. Madsen, *The Bannock of Idaho* (Caldwell, Ida.: Caxton, 1958); Oliver O. Howard, *My Life and Experiences among Our Hostile Indians* (Hartford: Worthington, 1907), pp. 365–70, and *Nez Perce Joseph* (Boston: Lee & Shepard, 1881), pp. 210–11, 243–44, 251; Stanton G. Fisher, "Journal of S. G. Fisher, Chief of Scouts, to General O. O. Howard during the Campaign against the Nez Perce Indians, 1877," in *Contributions to the Historical Society of Montana* (Helena: State Publishing Co., 1896), 2:269–82; Omer C. Stewart, "The Question of Bannock Territory," in Earl H. Swanson, ed., *Languages and Cultures of Western North America* (Pocatello: Idaho State University Press, 1970), pp. 201–31.

32. Burns, *Jesuits and the Indian Wars*, pp. 427–28; John Fahey, *The Flathead Indians* (Norman: University of Oklahoma Press, 1974), pp. 188–98.

33. Fisher, "Journal," pp. 277, 279–81; Howard, *My Life and Experiences*, pp. 443–47, accuses the Crows of being secretly in league with the Nez Perces; Thomas H. Leforge, *Memoirs of a White Crow Indian* (1928; rpt.

Lincoln: University of Nebraska Press, 1974), pp. 128–30; Mary Allen Phinney, *Jirah Isham Allen, Montana Pioneer* (Rutland, Vt.: Tuttle, 1929), pp. 95–97; Hugh L. Scott, *Some Memories of a Soldier* (New York: Century, 1928), pp. 60–69; Mark H. Brown, *The Flight of the Nez Perce* (New York: Putnam, 1967), pp. 346–47.

34. George F. Brimlow, *The Bannock War of 1878* (Caldwell, Ida.: Caxton, 1938); Sarah Winnemucca Hopkins, *Life among the Piutes* (Bishop, Calif.: Sierra Media, 1969), pp. 137–202, the account of Sarah Winnemucca, who served as guide and scout for Howard; U.S. Congress, House, Secretary of War, *Annual Report, 1878,* 1:212 (Howard's report), 224–26 (Captain Evan Miles's report on a fight at Umatilla agency); Howard, *My Life and Experiences,* pp. 377–420; Crook, *General George Crook,* pp. 221–23; Luther S. Kelly, *"Yellowstone Kelly"* (New Haven: Yale University Press, 1926), pp. 167–72, on Buffalo Horn; Clarence Hines, ed., "Indian Agent's Letter-Book: I. The Piute-Bannock Raid of July, 1878," *Oregon Historical Quarterly* 39 (March 1938):8–15.

35. Nelson A. Miles, *Personal Recollections and Observations of General Nelson A. Miles* (Chicago: Werner, 1896), pp. 295–300.

36. Ibid.; Phinney, *Jirah Isham Allen,* pp. 95–96.

37. Alfred Sorenson, "Quarter of a Century on the Frontier," p. 189, NSHS; Ernest Wallace, ed., "Ranald Mackenzie's Correspondence relative to Texas . . . ," *Museum Journal* 10 (1966):146–47, 157, 164. For an Indian superintendent's objections, see William McKay, "William McKay's Journal, 1866–67," ed. Keith Clark and Donna Clark, *Oregon Historical Quarterly* 79 (Fall 1978):302.

38. Frank Gilbert Roe, *The Indian and the Horse* (Norman: University of Oklahoma Press, 1955), pp. 123–26, 227–28; John C. Ewers, *The Horse in Blackfoot Indian Culture* (Washington, D.C.: Smithsonian Institution, 1955), pp. 171–215; Mishkin, *Rank and Warfare,* pp. 5–29, 28–34; John Keegan, *The Face of Battle* (New York: Viking, 1976), pp. 180–81.

39. Eve Ball, *In the Days of Victorio* (Tucson: University of Arizona Press, 1970), p. 80; William B. White, "The Mili-

tary and the Melting Pot," Ph.D. dissertation, University of Wisconsin, 1968, pp. 29–30.

40. W. R. Parnell, "Operations against Hostile Indians with General George Crook, 1867–'68," *United Service* n.s. 1 (June 1889):634–35.

41. See especially Nabokov, *Two Leggings;* Two Leggings ended his life story with the end of intertribal warfare; after that, "we just lived" (p. 197); Royal B. Hassrick, *The Sioux* (Norman: University of Oklahoma Press, 1964), especially pp. 76–100; Mishkin, *Rank and Warfare.*

42. Peter Farb, *Man's Rise to Civilization* (New York: Dutton, 1978), pp. 92–93, 292–93; Turney-High, *Primitive War*, pp. 103–4, 220–22. Francis Jennings, *The Invasion of America* (Chapel Hill: University of North Carolina Press, 1975), pp. 150–52, denounces the widespread assertion that a young Indian man could not marry until he had killed and scalped someone; he points out that such a practice would rapidly lead to total extinction.

43. Lawrence Kelly, ed., *Navajo Roundup* (Boulder: Pruett, 1970), pp. 52, 76; Finerty, *War-Path and Bivouac*, pp. 249–50, 256.

8. The Other Good Indians: The Intratribal Conflict

1. Lawrie Tatum, *Our Red Brothers and the Peace Policy of President Ulysses S. Grant* (Philadelphia: John C. Winston, 1899), pp. 74–75.

2. John Bigelow, *On the Bloody Trail of Geronimo*, ed. Arthur Woodward (Los Angeles: Westernlore, 1958), p. 40: "The gentleman . . . was moved by the sight of my two [Apache] Indians to impart to me his distrust of Indian allies, observing, 'If only Uncle Sam would enlist some of our American mountaineers!' I thought I should as lief trust to friendly Indians in a tight place as to his 'American mountaineers.'"

3. Crook and Bourke, despite their relative sophistication, exhibit the former tendency. See George Crook, *General George Crook: His Autobiography*, ed. Martin F. Schmitt (Norman: University of Oklahoma Press, 1946), p. 190;

John G. Bourke, *On the Border with Crook* (1891; rpt. Lincoln: University of Nebraska Press, 1971), pp. 398–401, 414–15; Wesley Merritt, *Merritt on the Indian Wars*, ed. Barry C. Johnson (London: Johnson-Taunton Military Press, 1975), pp. 19–22, refers to hostile Apaches as "red murderers," "snakes," and "cowardly assassins," while Apache scouts are "gallant and faithful." See Louise K. Barnett, *The Ignoble Savage* (Westport, Conn.: Greenwood Press, 1975), pp. 80–96, on the same dichotomy in fiction. See also Alvin M. Josephy, *The Patriot Chiefs* (New York: Viking, 1958) and *The Nez Perce Indians and the Opening of the Northwest* (New Haven: Yale University Press, 1965); Mari Sandoz, *Crazy Horse* (New York: Hastings House, 1942).

4. Francis Jennings, *The Invasion of America* (Chapel Hill: University of North Carolina Press, 1975), attributes almost satanic calculation and hypocrisy to the Puritans in their relations with Indians.

5. P. Richard Metcalf, "Who Should Rule at Home?: Native American Politics and Indian-White Relations," *Journal of American History* 61 (December 1974):651–65; Robert F. Berkhofer, "The Political Context of a New Indian History," *Pacific Historical Review* 40 (August 1971):357–82; Calvin Martin, "Ethnohistory: A Better Way to Write Indian History," *Western Historical Quarterly* 9 (January 1978):41–56.

6. Ross E. Dunn, *Resistance in the Desert* (Madison: University of Wisconsin Press, 1977), p. 19; Iliffe quoted in ibid., p. 20.

7. Crook, *General George Crook*, pp. 222–23.

8. Crook's annual report in U.S. Congress, House, Secretary of War, *Annual Report, 1883*, 1:167.

9. See Francis Parkman, *The Conspiracy of Pontiac and the Indian War after the Conquest of Canada* (Boston: Little, Brown, 1910), pp. 47–48, for the Indian hewn from a rock; Jennings, *Invasion of America*, p. 41. George Armstrong Custer, *My Life on the Plains* (Norman: University of Oklahoma Press, 1962), pp. 19–23, finds "the Indian" incapable of accepting civilization, except at the cost of "health, vigor, and courage."

10. Berkhofer, "Political Context," p. 363.
11. Wilbur S. Nye, *Bad Medicine and Good* (Norman: University of Oklahoma Press, 1962), p. xiii; Ernest Wallace and E. Adamson Hoebel, *The Comanches* (Norman: University of Oklahoma Press, 1952), pp. 25–26; T. R. Fehrenbach, *Comanches* (New York: Alfred A. Knopf, 1974), pp. 382–83.
12. Nye, *Bad Medicine*, pp. xvii–xviii, 129–31, 222–23; Mildred P. Mayhall, *The Kiowas* (Norman: University of Oklahoma Press, 1962), pp. 297–98; Tatum, *Our Red Brothers*, pp. 114–80; Thomas C. Battey, *Life and Adventures of a Quaker among the Indians* (Norman: University of Oklahoma Press, 1968), has an extended account of Kicking Bird.
13. Nye, *Bad Medicine*, pp. 82–90; Mayhall, *Kiowas*, p. 297.
14. See Martin, "Ethnohistory," pp. 52–55; Calvin Martin, *Keepers of the Game* (Berkeley: University of California Press, 1978); Robert F. Berkhofer, *Salvation and the Savage* (New York: Atheneum, 1972), especially pp. 125–51; none of these writers specifically considers Indian scouts.
15. Berkhofer, *Salvation and the Savage*, pp. 107–24; for the variety of individual experiences, see Karen D. Petersen, *Plains Indian Art from Fort Marion* (Norman: University of Oklahoma Press, 1971); Nye, *Bad Medicine*, pp. 267–75.
16. Berkhofer, *Salvation and the Savage*, pp. 89–106; Robert Ignatius Burns, *The Jesuits and the Indian Wars of the Northwest* (New Haven: Yale University Press, 1966); Lawrence Kip, *Army Life on the Pacific* (New York: Redfield, 1859), pp. 34–35.
17. Bourke, *On the Border*, p. 391; Luther S. Kelly, *"Yellowstone Kelly"* (New Haven: Yale University Press, 1926), pp. 232–39.
18. Garnett narrative, in Eli S. Ricker Interviews, NSHS, Tablet 1, pp. 119–22; John Gregory Bourke, Diaries, 14:1409, U.S. Military Academy Library, West Point, N.Y.; George Crook, *Résumé of Operations against Apache Indians, 1882 to 1886* (Omaha: privately published, 1886), p. 4; Britton Davis, *The Truth about Geronimo* (1929; rpt. Lincoln: University of Nebraska Press, 1976), p. 123; Eve

Ball, *In the Days of Victorio* (Tucson: University of Arizona Press, 1970), pp. 162–63.

19. Dan L. Thrapp, ed., *Dateline Fort Bowie* (Norman: University of Oklahoma Press, 1979), p. 120; Berkhofer, "Political Context," pp. 378–79; Edward Spicer, *Cycles of Conquest* (Tucson: University of Arizona Press, 1962), p. 492.

20. Edwin T. Denig, *Five Indian Tribes of the Upper Missouri*, ed. John C. Ewers (Norman: University of Oklahoma Press, 1961), especially pp. 23–24, 36–39; Royal B. Hassrick, *The Sioux* (Norman: University of Oklahoma Press, 1964), pp. 3–31; Richard White, "The Winning of the West: The Expansion of the Western Sioux in the Eighteenth and Nineteenth Centuries," *Journal of American History* 65 (September 1978):326.

21. George E. Hyde, *Life of George Bent*, ed. Savoie Lottinville (Norman: University of Oklahoma Press, 1968), pp. 17, 21–22; Virginia Cole Trenholm, *The Arapahos, Our People* (Norman: University of Oklahoma Press, 1970), p. 34; Donald J. Berthrong, *The Southern Cheyennes* (Norman: University of Oklahoma Press, 1964), pp. 3–26.

22. George E. Hyde, *Spotted Tail's Folk* (Norman: University of Oklahoma Press, 1961), pp. 99–129.

23. Dodge to Assistant Adjutant General, May 15, 1867, Letters Received, Department of the Platte, RG 94, NARS; Custer, *My Life on the Plains*, pp. 178–201; Hyde, *Red Cloud's Folk*, p. 155.

24. U.S. Congress, Senate, *Papers Relative to Indian Operations on the Plains*, 50th Cong., 1st sess., Senate Executive Document no. 33 (1877), pp. 10–11; Hyde, *Red Cloud's Folk*, pp. 142–43; Stan Hoig, *The Peace Chiefs of the Cheyennes*, (Norman: University of Oklahoma Press, 1980), pp. 126–27.

25. On this complex period, see James C. Olson, *Red Cloud and the Sioux Problems* (Lincoln: University of Nebraska Press, 1965); Edgar I. Stewart, *Custer's Luck* (Norman: University of Oklahoma Press, 1955); John S. Gray, *Centennial Campaign* (Fort Collins, Colo.: Old Army Press, 1976). The terms "winter roamers" and "summer roamers" are Gray's. Gray makes the point that the automatic

designation of the winter roamers as "hostile" was rather arbitrary.

26. Hyde, *Red Cloud's Folk*, pp. 220–23; Olson, *Red Cloud*, pp. 169–70. On the Crawford–Three Bears friendship, see William T. Corbusier, *Verde to San Carlos* (Tucson: Dale Stuart King, 1968), p. 173, quoting Dr. William H. Corbusier.

27. George A. Woodward, "The Northern Cheyennes at Fort Fetterman," ed. John E. Parsons, in Michael S. Kennedy, ed., *The Red Man's West* (New York: Hastings House, 1965), pp. 290–300.

28. Hyde, *Life of George Bent*, p. 197; George Bird Grinnell, *The Cheyenne Indians* (New Haven: Yale University Press, 1923), 1:131–32; Erik H. Erikson, *Childhood and Society*, rev. ed. (New York: Norton, 1964), p. 143; Thomas B. Marquis, *Wooden Leg* (1931; rpt. Lincoln: University of Nebraska Press, 1962), p. 249.

29. Bourke, *Diaries*, 4:228–44; Hyde, *Red Cloud's Folk*, pp. 259–60.

30. Narratives of Left Hand and Waterman, as told to Tim McCoy, in W. A. Graham, *The Custer Myth* (Harrisburg, Pa.: Stackpole, 1952), pp. 109–12. Bourke, *On the Border*, p. 392, indicates that an Arapaho named Left Hand was a scout for Crook later in the same year.

31. Marquis, *Wooden Leg*, pp. 248–51.

32. O. G. Libby, ed., *The Arikara Narrative of the Campaign against the Hostile Dakotas, June 1876* (New York: Sol Lewis, 1973), pp. 139, 191; Walter Camp, comp., *Custer in '76*, ed. Kenneth Hammer (Provo: Brigham Young University Press, 1976), p. 287; Ben Innis, *Bloody Knife!* (Fort Collins, Colo.: Old Army Press, 1973), pp. 18–28; Elizabeth B. Custer, *Boots and Saddles* (New York: Harper, 1885), pp. 131–37. Among Custer's Sioux scouts was the unfortunate soul named Broken Penis. The famous Arikara scout Bloody Knife was raised among the Hunkpapas, his father being Sioux.

33. Bowen to W. S. Campbell, in Stanley Vestal, ed., *New Sources of Indian History, 1850–1891* (Norman: University of Oklahoma Press, 1934), p. 131; Campbell (Vestal) remarks on the Sioux's scrupulosity about their word in

ibid., pp. 122–23. See also William P. Clark, *The Indian Sign Language* (Philadelphia: L. R. Hamersley, 1885), p. 234. For Left Hand, see Camp, *Custer in '76*, p. 284.

34. Bourke, Diaries, 14:1367, gives 90 Araphaoes, 5 Cheyennes, and 60 Sioux.

35. William Garnett narrative, Ricker interviews, Tablet 1, pp. 85–87, 99–103; Bourke, Diaries, 14:1367–87. Arapaho historian Tom Shakespeare, relying apparently on tribal tradition, says that the Araphaoes were also motivated by a desire to avert removal to Indian Territory; see Tom Shakespeare, *The Sky People* (New York: Vantage Press, 1971), p. 100.

36. Garnett narrative, Ricker interviews, Tablet 1, pp. 85–87; Corbusier, *Verde to San Carlos*, p. 173; Crook to Assistant Adjutant General, Military Division of the Missouri, May 18, 1877, Letters Received, OAG, 1871–80, Indian Scouts Correspondence, 1876–78, roll 259, RG 500, NARS, notes that the Sioux scouts include "some of the most influential men . . . and their retention in service . . . is of paramount importance." On Three Bears, see John Gregory Bourke, *MacKenzie's Last Fight with the Cheyennes* (Belleview, Nebr.: Old Army Press, 1970), p. 12, and *On the Border*, p. 407; Clark, *Indian Sign Language*, p. 82.

37. Bourke, Diaries, 14:1386–92.

38. George Washington Manypenny, *Our Indian Wards* (Cincinnati: R. Clarke, 1880), p. 330. Garnett narrative, Ricker interviews, Tablet 1, p. 119, and Bourke, Diaries, 14:1383, use the term "Northern Indians" with specific reference to the hostile Sioux.

39. George Bird Grinnell, *The Fighting Cheyennes* (Norman: University of Oklahoma Press, 1955), pp. 383–427; Nelson A. Miles, Personal Recollections and Observations of General Nelson A. Miles (Chicago: Werner, 1896), pp. 241–51.

40. George P. Ahern, "The Experience of Major Mauck in Disarming a Band of Cheyennes on the North Fork of the Canadian River in 1878," *POIW*, pp. 89–92; Crook's annual report in Secretary of War, *Annual Report, 1879*, 1:77; Mari Sandoz, *Cheyenne Autumn* (New York: Hastings House, 1953); John Stands-in-Timber and Margot Lib-

erty, *Cheyenne Memories* (New Haven: Yale University Press, 1967), pp. 237–39. See Thomas B. Marquis, *Cheyenne and Sioux* (Stockton, Calif.: Pacific Center for Western Historical Studies, 1973), p. 39, for Tangled Yellow Hair's comment.

41. Marquis, *Wooden Leg*, pp. 297, 325, 333. But Wooden Leg always retained the greatest respect and affection for Little Wolf, despite the chief's service as a scout; see ibid., pp. 16–17.

42. Bourke, *On the Boulder*, pp. 394–95; John F. Finerty, *War-Path and Bivouac* (Norman: University of Oklahoma Press, 1961), p. 249; Marquis, *Wooden Leg*, pp. 287–88; Grinnell, *Fighting Cheyennes*, p. 382.

43. James H. Cook, *Fifty Years on the Old Frontier* (New Haven: Yale University Press, 1923), p. 191.

44. Bourke, Diaries, 14:1386.

9. The Pawnee Wolves

1. William P. Clark, *The Indian Sign Language* (Philadelphia: L. R. Hamersley, 1885), pp. 279–80; Harry H. Turney-High, *Primitive War* (Columbia: University of South Carolina Press, 1971), pp. 108–9; George Bird Grinnell, *Pawnee Hero Stories and Folk Tales* (1889; rpt. Lincoln: University of Nebraska Press, 1961), pp. 243–48.

2. George E. Hyde, *The Pawnee Indians* (Norman: University of Oklahoma Press, 1974), pp. 7–164; Gene Weltfish, *The Lost Universe* (1965; rpt. Lincoln: University of Nebraska Press, 1977); Preston Holder, *The Hoe and the Horse on the Plains* (Lincoln: University of Nebraska Press, 1970); Grinnell, *Pawnee Hero Stories*; David J. Wishart, "The Dispossession of the Pawnee," *Annals of the Association of American Geographers* 69 (September 1979):382–401.

3. Hyde, *Pawnee Indians*, pp. 165–238; Holder, *Hoe and the Horse*, pp. 89–126; Wishart, "Dispossession of the Pawnee," pp. 385, 387–94. On the Pawnees' bad reputation in the 1830s, see Washington Irving, *A Tour on the Prairies* (Norman: University of Oklahoma Press, 1956), pp. 75–78. See also Harold D. Langley, ed., *To Utah with*

the *Dragoons and Glimpses of Life in Arizona and California* (Salt Lake City: University of Utah Press, 1974), pp. 32–33, 36–37.

4. Hyde, *Pawnee Indians*, pp. 165–238; Holder, *Hoe and the Horse*, pp. 89–126; Wishart, "Dispossession of the Pawnee," pp. 390–98.

5. Confusion exists primarily because of Eugene F. Ware's account in *The Indian War of 1864* (Lincoln: University of Nebraska Press, 1960), in which he gives a most unflattering description of a Pawnee contingent under Frank North accompanying a column under General Robert Mitchell in the summer of 1864. Almost all other evidence indicates that the first Pawnee scout unit was the one led by Joseph McFadden and authorized by General Curtis. Donald F. Danker, "The North Brothers and the Pawnee Scouts," *Nebraska History* 42 (September 1961):163–64, concludes that Ware must have telescoped events in his memory; it is hard to see when Ware encountered the McFadden company to create his confusion. George E. Hyde, *Life of George Bent*, ed. Savoie Lottinville (Norman: University of Oklahoma Press, 1968), p. 138, seems to confirm part of Ware's account, but Bent was not present, and he was familiar with Ware's book. Ware was acutely prejudiced against all Indians, and used his account to demonstrate the worthlessness of the race. Agent Lushbaugh's annual report for 1864 (see note 6) makes specific and prominent mention of the enlistment of the McFadden company and says nothing about an earlier enlistment.

6. Alfred Sorenson, "A Quarter of a Century on the Frontier," NSHS, pp. 60–71; Luther H. North, *Man of the Plains*, ed. Donald F. Danker (Lincoln: University of Nebraska Press, 1961), pp. 29–32; B. F. Lushbaugh's report in U.S. Congress, House, Commissioner of Indian Affairs, *Annual Report, 1864*, pp. 526–27. Elsewhere Lushbaugh claims that the enlistment of the Pawnees was his idea, and that he suggested it to Curtis; Lushbaugh to Commissioner Dole, February 11, 1865, Letters Received, OIA, Pawnee Agency, 1858–80, RG 75, NARS (microfilm, NSHS). Some Pawnees acted as guides and scouts for the army in 1857, but their services were judged unsatis-

factory; see Henry B. McClellan, *I Rode with Jeb Stuart*
(1885; Bloomington: Indiana University Press, 1958),
pp. 22–24; Robert M. Peck, "Recollections of Early Times in
Kansas Territory," *Kansas State Historical Society Collections* 8 (1903–4):494, 499.

7. Sorenson, "Quarter of a Century," pp. 60–71; North, *Man
of the Plains*, pp. 29–32.

8. Sorenson, "Quarter of a Century," pp. 10–15; L. H. North
to G. B. Grinnell, February 14, 1877, Luther H. North
Papers, NSHS, ser. 1, folder 2.

9. Holder, *Hoe and the Horse*, pp. 36–47, 108–9; Weltfish,
Lost Universe, p. 7, emphasizes that the chiefs were fully
cognizant of public opinion and did not risk purely arbitrary decisions.

10. Luther North interview, *Omaha World-Herald*, October 2,
1910; Richard I. Dodge, *Our Wild Indians* (Hartford:
Worthington, 1882), p. 464, on the face-striking incident,
which neither of the Norths mentions; North, *Man of the
Plains*, pp. 210–11.

11. Sorenson, "Quarter of a Century," p. 86; North, *Man of
the Plains*, pp. 45–47.

12. Wishart, "Dispossession of the Pawnee," p. 393.

13. Weltfish, *Lost Universe*, pp. 19, 93; Holder, *Hoe and the
Horse*, pp. 53–56, 109, 133–34.

14. Hyde, *Pawnee Indians*, p. 302.

15. Superintendent S. M. Janney to Commissioner E. S.
Parker, February 17, 1870, and Agent C. H. Whaley to
Superintendent Dennis, March 22, 1869, both in Letters
Received, Pawnee Agency, 1859–80, RG 75, NARS (micro-
film, NSHS).

16. See Holder, *Hoe and the Horse*, pp. 133–34, on the Boys
as a disturbing element; Roy W. Meyer, *The Village Indians of the Upper Missouri* (Lincoln: University of
Nebraska Press, 1977), p. 127, on the problems created
among the Arikaras by scouts.

17. O. G. Hammond, General Superintendent, Union Pacific
Railroad, to Representative Oakes Ames, n.d.; and E. D.
Townsend, Adjutant General, to Commissioner Parker,
June 24, 1870, both in Letters Received, Pawnee Agency.
Ames is remembered chiefly as the principal figure in the

Crédit Mobilier scandal, connected with the federal subsidization of the Union Pacific. Hyde, *Pawnee Indians*, p. 281, notes how delighted the Pawnees were to be paid for killing Sioux and Cheyennes, and how this arrangement contradicted the agents' admonitions against intertribal war. Neither of the Norths mentions anything about the episode.

18. Sorenson, "Quarter of a Century," pp. 117–26; North, *Man of the Plains*, pp. 48–64; L. H. North to Grinnell, March 11, 1928, Luther H. North Papers, ser. 1, folder 5; Henry M. Stanley, *My Early Travels and Adventures in America and Asia*, 2 vols. (New York: Scribner's 1895), 1: 196; *Chronological List of Actions, etc., with Indians, from January 1, 1886, to January, 1891* (Washington, D.C.: OAG, n.d.), pp. 6–7; Luther North quoted in Robert Bruce, *The Fighting Norths and Pawnee Scouts* (Lincoln: NSHS, 1932), pp. 26–31.

19. Augur's report in U.S. Congress, House, Secretary of War, *Annual Report, 1867*, 1:59–60.

20. Danker, "North Brothers and the Pawnee Scouts," p. 171. This is another incident that neither of the North brothers chooses to mention.

21. Ibid., p. 172; Sorenson, "Quarter of a Century," pp. 126–29; North, *Man of the Plains*, pp. 66–68; J. J. Aldrich, "Diary of a Twenty Days' Sport Buffalo Hunting on the Plains with the Pawnee . . . ," *Omaha Weekly Herald*, August 19 and August 26, 1868; "Major Frank North and the Pawnees," *Omaha Weekly Herald*, September 2, 1868; North to Assistant Adjutant General, August 8, 1868, Letters Received, Department of the Platte, RG 94, NARS. As Danker notes in "North Brothers and the Pawnee Scouts," the Pawnees suffered heavily from an attack in the same area in 1873, when North was not present.

22. James T. King, "The Republican River Expedition, June–July, 1869," M.A. thesis, University of Nebraska, 1957, pp. 20–60, and *War Eagle* (Lincoln: University of Nebraska Press, 1963), pp. 94–106.

23. King, "Republican River Expedition," pp. 50–103, and *War Eagle*, pp. 103–13; Sorenson, "Quarter of a Century,"

pp. 137–45; North, *Man of the Plains*, pp. 103–20; Donald Danker, ed., "Journal of an Indian Fighter: The 1869 Diary of Major Frank J. North," *Nebraska History* 23 (June 1958):87–177. For the Cheyenne view, see Hyde, *Life of George Bent*, pp. 328–40; Grinnell, *Fighting Cheyennes*, pp. 310–18. See also William F. Cody, *The Life of Hon. William F. Cody, Known as Buffalo Bill, the Famous Hunter, Scout, and Guide* (Hartford: Bliss, 1879), pp. 249–62.

24. Carr to Assistant Adjutant General, July 20, 1869, Letters Received, Department of the Platte.

25. Sorenson, "Quarter of a Century" pp. 146–48; North's copy of the resolution in Frank J. North Papers; *The Medal of Honor of the United States Army* (Washington, D.C.: Government Printing Office, 1946), p. 211; Luther North in Bruce, *Fighting Norths*, p. 19.

26. Sorenson, "Quarter of a Century," pp. 149–55; *Record of Engagements with Hostile Indians within the Military Division of the Missouri, from 1868 to 1882, Lieutenant-General P. H. Sheridan, Commanding* (Washington, D.C.: Government Printing Office, 1882) devotes less than two pages (pp. 30–31) to 1871. *Chronological List* shows the bulk of engagements until 1875 shifting to Texas and the Southwest, especially Arizona Territory.

27. Hyde, *Pawnee Indians*, pp. 279–301; Wishart, "Dispossession of the Pawnee," pp. 369–99; Grinnell, *Pawnee Hero Stories*, pp. 389–91.

28. Hyde, *Pawnee Indians*, pp. 289–301, 303–11; Grinnell, *Pawnee Hero Stories*, pp. 391–97; Wishart, "Disposssession of the Pawnee," pp. 399–401. John Gregory Bourke, *Mackenzie's Last Fight with the Cheyennes* (Bellevue, Nebr.: Old Army Press, 1970), pp. 10, 12, and Luther North in Bruce, *Fighting Norths*, p. 19, describe Frank White.

29. Hyde, *Pawnee Indians*, pp. 311–28; many documents relating to the 1873 battle were published in *Nebraska History* 16 (July–September 1936); Luther North in Bruce, *Fighting Norths*, p. 19.

30. Hyde, *Pawnee Indians*, pp. 329–49; Grinnell, *Pawnee*

Hero Stories, pp. 397–408; Richard H. Pratt, *Battlefield and Classroom*, ed. Robert M. Utley (New Haven: Yale University Press, 1964), pp. 79–80, 99.

31. Special Orders no. 82, Sidney Barracks, Nebr., August 15, 1876, and Orders, Headquarters, Military Division of the Missouri, Chicago, August 15, 1876, both in Frank J. North Papers; Sorenson, "Quarter of a Century," pp. 161–65; North, *Man of the Plains*, pp. 194–97.

32. Muster Roll, 1876, Frank J. North Papers; Sorenson, "Quarter of a Century," pp. 165–66; North, *Man of the Plains*, pp. 197–98; Will Marpin, "Nebraska's Famous Pawnee Indian Scouts" (interview with Luther North), *Niobrara Tribune*, 1926?, Luther H. North Papers.

33. Sorenson, "Quarter of a Century," pp. 167–77; North, *Man of the Plains*, pp. 202–4; Addison E. Sheldon, record of conference of Luther North and Oglala Sioux at Chadron, Nebr., June 21, 1933, and L. H. North to G. B. Grinnell, August 24, 1933, both in Luther H. North Papers; William Garnett narrative, in Ricker interviews, NSHS, Tablet 1, pp. 42–57. Both conference and Garnett narrative are published in *Nebraska History* 15 (October–December 1934):279–91. Philip Wells interview, in Ricker interviews, ser. 2, Tablet 3, pp. 34–36, notes that the Cheyennes did not speak of whites as "enemies"; there was no particular honor in scalping a white man.

34. Frank North Journal, Frank North Papers, very brief and factual; North, *Man of the Plains*, pp. 210–19; Bourke, *Mackenzie's Last Fight*, p. 27; L. H. North to G. B. Grinnell, March 23, 1877, Luther H. North Papers. Luther was more broad-minded in later years.

35. Bruce, *Fighting Norths*, pp. 44–45; F. J. North to Sheridan, April 13, 1877, and Crook to North, April 19, 1877, both in Frank J. North Papers; Crook to Sheridan, April 16, 1877, Letters Received, OAG, 1871–80, roll 259, RG 500, NARS.

36. North, *Man of the Plains*, pp. 237–79; Bruce, *Fighting Norths*, pp. 64, 68; unidentified clipping,? *Tribune*, probably 1879, Frank J. North Papers; Grinnell, *Pawnee Hero Stories*, pp. 70–73, 79–82, on Pawnee scouting against the Utes in Colorado.

37. Hyde, *Pawnee Indians*, pp. 342–48, 365.
38. Ibid., pp. 272–73.

10. "More Formidable Indians": The Apache Scouts

1. See Keith Basso's introduction to Grenville Goodwin, *Western Apache Raiding and Warfare*, ed. Basso (Tucson: University of Arizona Press, 1971), p. 9; George Crook, "The Apache Problem," *Journal of the United Military Service Institution of the United States* 7 (1886):269.
2. This expedition follows Goodwin, *Western Apache Raiding*; Grenville Goodwin, *The Social Organization of the Western Apache* (Tucson: University of Arizona Press, 1969); Morris E. Opler, *An Apache Life-Way* (Chicago: University of Chicago Press, 1941).
3. See the works cited in note 2 and Eve Ball, *In the Days of Victorio* (Tucson: University of Arizona Press, 1970), p. 80. The Lone Ranger's faithful Indian companion probably received his name from some writer ignorant of Spanish who thought the name sounded "Indian."
4. See the works cited in note 2 and Francis Jennings, *The Invasion of America* (Chapel Hill: University of North Carolina Press, 1975), p. 111; Robert H. Lowie, *Primitive Society* (New York: Liveright, 1920), pp. 397–406, points out that custom, social pressures, and religious sanctions go far to prevent anarchy in such cases.
5. Max L. Moorhead, *The Apache Frontier* (Norman: University of Oklahoma Press, 1968), pp. 188–89. James Kaywaykla, the narrator in Ball, *Days of Victorio*, p. 80, was not aware of this precedent when he expressed indignation at the fact that Chiricahuas had scouted for the United States against other Chiricahuas.
6. Goodwin, *Western Apache Raiding*, pp. 191–93, 219, 314.
7. See John Morgan Gates, "General Crook's First Apache Campaign," *Journal of the West* 6 (April 1967):310–20; Joyce Evelyn Mason, "The Use of Indian Scouts in the Apache Wars, 1870–1886," Ph.D. dissertation, Indiana University, 1970, pp. 22–64; John G. Bourke, "Bourke on

the Southwest," *New Mexico Historical Review* 9 (October 1934).

8. See the works cited in note 7 and John Gregory Bourke, *With Crook in the Indian Wars* (Palo Alto: Lewis Osborne, 1968), pp. 47–56; "Notes of Scout from Camp Verde to McDowell and Return, Dec. 1, 1873, to Jan. 18, 1874," and muster roll of scouts, in Walter S. Schuyler Papers, Huntington Library, San Marino, Calif.; *The Medal of Honor of the United States Army* (Washington, D.C.: Government Printing Office, 1946), pp. 218–19; *Chronological List of Actions, etc., with Indians, from January 1, 1866, to January, 1891* (Washington, D.C.: OAG, n.d.), p. 35.

9. Dan L. Thrapp, *Al Sieber* (Norman: University of Oklahoma Press, 1964), p. 214. Thrapp does not separate the two types on the basis of time.

10. John Rope narrative in Goodwin, *Western Apache Raiding*, pp. 116, 130; Ball, *In the Days of Victorio*, p. 80.

11. Rope narrative in Goodwin, *Western Apache Raiding*, pp. 128, 156.

12. Augustus Tassin, "Reminiscences of Indian Scouting," *Overland Monthly* 14 (August 1889):167–69. As a traditional Apache would not tell his true name to another, white nicknames were convenient and acceptable. Tizwin had so named himself, humorously.

13. The account of Ace Daklugie, a Chiricahua Apache, is in Eve Ball, "Cibicu, an Apache Interpretation," in Ray Brandes, ed., *Troopers West* (San Diego: Frontier Heritage Press, 1970), pp. 121–33. Thomas Cruse's account in *Apache Days and After* (Caldwell, Ida.: Caxton, 1941), pp. 97–99, agrees in most respects.

14. Cruse, *Apache Days*, pp. 99–101.

15. Thomas Cruse to C. B. Gatewood, Jr., January 19, 1926, and March 3, 1926, both in Charles B. Gatewood Collection, Arizona Historical Society, Tucson: James T. King, *War Eagle* (Lincoln: University of Nebraska Press, 1963), pp. 206–12; Daklugie in Ball, "Cibicu," p. 129, says that his father, Juh, was present but did not know who had fired the first shot. He blames Cruse for accusing the

scouts of firing first; Cruse made no such accusation in either his letters or his published memoirs. See Cruse, *Apache Days*, pp. 111–12, 112–23.

16. Daklugie claims that Mose had warned the medicine man of the impending arrest; see Eve Ball, *Indeh* (Provo, Utah: Brigham Young University Press, 1980), p. 54; Cruse to C. B. Gatewood, Jr., January 19, February 9, and March 3, 1926, all in Gatewood Collection; Cruse, *Apache Days*, pp. 117–18, 138–39; *Chronological List*, p. 52. Crook was later told that Skippy, the clown of the company, had not participated in the shooting, and that "his life was sworn away by heated, ignorant or mendacious witnesses" (Crook to J. W. Zabrieskie, October 8, 1882, cited in Mason, "Use of Indian Scouts," p. 203).

17. Mason, "Use of Indian Scouts," p. 206.

18. "Company Descriptive Book of Co. A, Indian Scouts, 1872–1877," item 2053, RG 391, NARS, shows Alchise's first enlistment on December 2, 1872; Cruse to C. B. Gatewood, Jr., January 19 and February 9, 1926, Gatewood Collection; *Medal of Honor*, p. 218; Agent J. C. Tiffany to Commissioner of Indian Affairs, December 6, 1881, Letters Received, OIA, RG 75, NARS, makes accusations against Alchise. See "Company Descriptive Book of Co. A, Indian Scouts, 1877–1882," for personnel of the unit; H. B. Wharfield, *Alchesay* (El Cajon, Calif.: Apache Press, 1969). Alchise's name is still honored on the Fort Apache Reservation; see Irene Burlison, *Yesterday and Today in the Life of the Apaches* (Philadelphia: Dorrance, 1973), pp. 22–23.

19. See Tiffany to Commissioner, December 6, 1881, Letters Received, OIA, RG 75, NARS, for military attacks on reservation Apaches; John Gregory Bourke, *On the Border with Crook* (1891; rpt. Lincoln: University of Nebraska Press, 1971), pp. 436–37. Ball, *In the Days of Victorio*, p. 155: "Some of the officers were hard on us, but they were not thieves."

20. Mason, "Use of Indian Scouts," pp. 214–17; Cruse to C. B. Gatewood, Jr., January 19, 1926, and Gatewood MS, both in Gatewood Collection.

21. Dan L. Thrapp, *General Crook and the Sierra Madre Adventure* (Norman: University of Oklahoma Press, 1974), pp. 48-90; Thrapp, *Al Sieber*, pp. 225-43; Ball, *In the Days of Victorio*, pp. 136-45; Jason Betzinez, *I Fought with Geronimo* (Harrisburg, Pa.: Stackpole, 1959), pp. 56-80. See Angie Debo, *Geronimo* (Norman: University of Oklahoma Press, 1976), pp. 137-38, on the question of how willingly the reservation Indians fled.

22. Cruse to C. B. Gatewood, Jr., February 9, 1926, Gatewood Collection; Mason, "Use of Indian Scouts," p. 203, citing Crook to Zabrieskie, October 8, 1882; Crook's report in U.S. Congress, House, Secretary of War, *Annual Report, 1883*; General Orders no. 42, October 5, 1882, in Bourke, *On the Border*, p. 443, admonishing officers about the fear the Indians now had of the soldiers, and the need for great care in deciding to use force, to avoid becoming "instruments of oppression."

23. John G. Bourke, *An Apache Campaign in the Sierra Madre* New York: Scribner's, 1958). Rope's account and that of scout David Longstreet are in Goodwin, *Western Apache Raiding*, pp. 153-72, 197-200. See also Gustav Fiebeger, "General Crook's Campaign in Old Mexico in 1883," *POIW*, pp. 193-201; Thrapp, *General Crook*; Betzinez, *I Fought with Geronimo*; Ball, *In the Days of Victorio* and *Indeh*.

24. See the works in note 23 and Britton Davis, *The Truth about Geronimo* (1929; rpt. Lincoln: University of Nebraska Press, 1976), pp. 77-101. Some of those who came in immediately were enlisted as scouts to wait at the border for the rest, in part to protect them from civil law-enforcement officials who might try to arrest them. See Crook to Adjutant General, August 7, 1883; Z. L. Tidball, U.S. Marshal, Arizona Territory, to Crook, November 25, 1883, and endorsements, both in Letters Received, OIA, RG 75, NARS.

25. Ball, *In the Days of Victorio*, pp. 156-57, 162-68, 175-77; Eve Ball, "The Apache Scouts: A Chiricahua Appraisal," *Arizona and the West* 7 (Winter 1967):315-28. The reservation was under military control at this time; see Crook, *Résumé of Operations*, pp. 4-5; Gatewood MS., Gatewood Collection. Geronimo's son did enlist as a scout; see

"Warm Springs and Chiricahua Indians," item 2059, RG 391, NARS.

26. Ball, *In the Days of Victorio*, pp. 162–67, 175–76, and "Apache Scouts," pp. 323–26.

27. Morris E. Opler, "A Chiricahua Apache's Account of the Geronimo Campaign of 1886," *New Mexico Historical Review* 13 (October 1938):260–86, and *Apache Odyssey* (New York: Holt, Rinehart & Winston, 1969). Betzinez, *I Fought with Geronimo*, pp. 129–30, reports an incident discreditable to Chato, but does not connect him with any of the troubles on the reservation.

28. George Crook, *Résumé of Operations against Apache Indians, 1882–1886* (Omaha, 1886), p. 6; Davis, *Truth about Geronimo*, pp. 151–52.

29. Ball, *In the Days of Victorio*, pp. 168, 175–77, and "Apache Scouts," pp. 325–26; Opler, "Chiricahua Apache's Account," p. 367; Davis, *Truth about Geronimo*, pp. 142–48.

30. Opler, *Apache Odyssey*, p. 48. Betzinez, *I Fought with Geronimo*, pp. 54–55, thinks that the Chiricahua scouts were simply happy to get away from the reservation and do something interesting.

31. See Crook's interview with Charles Lummis in Dan L. Thrapp, ed., *Dateline Fort Bowie* (Norman: University of Oklahoma Press, 1979), pp. 119–23; Crook, "Apache Problem," pp. 26–65, and *Résumé of Operations*, pp. 19–21. Scouts enlisted at San Carlos, June 10, 1885, are listed in "Descriptive Book of Indian Scouts, 1885," item 2058c, RG 391, NARS.

32. Reports of Endicott and Sheridan in U.S. Congress, House, Secretary of War, *Annual Report, 1886*, 1:7, 71.

33. *Chronological List*, p. 54; Crawford's dispatch, June 25, 1885, in Herbert Welsh, *The Apache Prisoners in Fort Marion, St. Augustine, Florida* (Philadelphia: Office of the Indian Rights Association, 1887), pp. 55–56. Crawford is praised in romantic terms in Davis, *Truth about Geronimo*, pp. 345–46. W. E. Shipp, "Captain Crawford's Last Expedition," *Journal of the U.S. Cavalry Association* 5 (December 1892):345–46, also praises him as an "Indian thinker." Shipp notes that Crawford enlisted Chiricahua and White Mountain Apaches because they were less

"civilized" than other Apaches. Among Crawford's scouts was Dutchy, who had an especially bad reputation. Crook had protected him from arrest for acts committed while he was hostile. Crawford put him in irons on one occasion, but later made him his orderly, thus showing both trust and lack of fear. See Shipp, "Captain Crawford's Last Expedition," p. 347; Davis, *Truth about Geronimo*, pp. 115–16; Tidball to Crook, November 25, 1883, Letters Received, OIA, RG 75, NARS.

34. For this expedition, see Shipp, "Captain Crawford's Last Expedition"; Marion P. Maus's version in Nelson A. Miles, *The Personal Recollections and Observations of General Nelson A. Miles* (Chicago: Werner, 1896), pp. 450–71; Tom Horn, *Life of Tom Horn, Government Scout and Interpreter* (Denver: Couthon, 1904), pp. 195–231 (to be used with caution).

35. See the works in note 34 and Thrapp, ed., *Dateline Fort Bowie*, pp. 163–84. Henry W. Daly, chief packer, in "Scouts—Good and Bad," *American Legion Monthly* 2 (August 1928):24–25, 66, 68–70, and "The Geronimo Campaign," *Arizona Historical Review* 3 (1930):26–44, maintained that Dutchy shot Crawford; no one actually present at the fight makes such a suggestion. See also Charles P. Elliott, "The Geronimo Campaign of 1885–6," *Journal of the U.S. Cavalry Association* 21 (September 1910):211–35; Robert Hanna, "With Crawford in Mexico," *Arizona Historical Review* 6 (April 1935):56–65. Ironically, the Mexican troops were Tarahumara Indians, specially enlisted to fight Apaches.

36. Davis, *Truth about Geronimo*, pp. 200–212 (transcript of conference); Bourke, *On the Border*, pp. 474–79; Ball, *In the Days of Victorio*, pp. 190, 200. Note that Kaywaykla credits his stepfather with working with the whites for the good of his people, but does not extend similar credit to others.

37. Crook and Sheridan's correspondence is in Crook, *Résumé of Operations*, pp. 8–19. See Sheridan's report in Secretary of War, *Annual Report, 1886*, 1:72.

38. Miles's report in Secretary of War, *Annual Report, 1886*, 1:170–71. Crook's opinions on disarming Indians are in ibid., *1883*, 1:14–15.

39. Miles, *Personal Recollections*, pp. 485–88, including his "General Field Orders No. 7," April 20, 1886; Gatewood to wife, June 25, 1886, Gatewood Collection.

40. A graphic depiction from the viewpoint of Leonard Wood is his *Chasing Geronimo*, ed. Jack C. Lane (Albuquerque: University of New Mexico Press, 1970). Many items of Miles's and Lawton's correspondence of the period are in the Gatewood Collection. Charles B. Gatewood, "The Surrender of Geronimo," *POIW*, pp. 106–13; James Parker, "The Surrender of Geronimo," *POIW*, pp. 95–102; Thomas J. Clay, "Some Unwritten Incidents of the Geronimo Campaign," *POIW*, pp. 114–23, including a sample of the acrimonious correspondence still being generated over forty years later. For Chiricahua views, see Opler, "Chiricahua Apache's Account," pp. 372, 275–77; Ball, *In the Days of Victorio*, pp. 184–89, and *Indeh*, pp. 106–19, including Martine and Kayitah's account; another version of their account is in the Gatewood Collection. A balanced assessment is Robert M. Utley, *Frontier Regulars* (New York: Macmillan, 1973), pp. 401–3.

41. Miles, *Personal Recollections*, pp. 494–505 (Miles describes Chato unfavorably, without even mentioning his service as a scout); Betzinez, *I Fought with Geronimo*, pp. 140–48; Ball, *In The Days of Victorio*, pp. 190–94, and "Apache Scouts," p. 327; Parker, "Surrender of Geronimo," p. 95.

42. Sheridan's report in Secretary of War, *Annual Report, 1886*, 1:72; Crook, *Résumé of Operations*, pp. 21–23. *Chronological List*, p. 54, credits four dead hostiles to regular troops, none of them to Lawton's command. See Crook's report in Secretary of War, *Annual Report, 1883*, 1:167: "With all the interest at stake we cannot afford to fight them; we are too culpable, as a nation, for the existing condition of affairs." The difference in Crook's and Sheridan's viewpoints is evident in their reflections on the Northern Cheyenne troubles in Secretary of War, *Annual Report, 1879*, 1:43, 77; Sheridan's report indicates a desire to simplify a morally ambiguous situation.

43. Shipp, "Captain Crawford's Last Expedition," p. 354; Opler, "Chiricahua Apache's Account," pp. 375–76, and *Apache Odyssey*, p. 48.

44. Maus's charge in Miles, *Personal Recollections*, p. 465;
Gatewood's letter in full in Welsh, *Apache Prisoners*,
pp. 50–53. Daly, "Geronimo Campaign," pp. 31, 35, charges
mutinous conduct. Ball, *In the Days of Victorio*, p. 181,
and "Apache Scouts," p. 326. Lawton charged that a
scout named Chimney deserted to the enemy (Lawton to
Assistant Adjutant General, Department of Arizona, May
13, 1886, Gatewood Collection). Another officer involved,
H. C. Benson, says Chimney turned up at Fort Huachuca
in a few days; see H. C. Benson, "The Geronimo Campaign," *Army and Navy Journal* (July 3, 1909):1240. In
any case, Chimney was a White Mountain Apache, not a
Chiricahua.

45. Crook's correspondence with John G. Bourke in Bourke
Papers, NSHS, demonstrates his attempts to work behind
the scenes for the Chiricahuas' release. Despite his
previous association with the Indian Rights group, he was
reluctant to join them publicly in this matter, in part perhaps because he knew such action would appear to be an
attack on Miles. He assured Bourke that the latter, no longer
on his staff, could help out without his connection becoming known—that is, without damaging Bourke's
chances of promotion. Welsh, *Apache Prisoners*, is the
Indian Rights Association's major piece of propaganda on
the matter.

46. Much has been written on this controversy. See Odie B.
Faulk, *The Geronimo Campaign* (New York: Oxford University Press, 1969), pp. 184–204; George Crook, *General
George Crook: His Autobiography*, ed. Martin F. Schmitt
(Norman: University of Oklahoma Press, 1946), pp. 289–
300; Miles, *Personal Recollections*, p. 497: "I was of the
opinion that a removal to the Indian Territory would be
the most advisable."

47. U.S. Congress, Senate, *Message from the President of the
United States Transmitting Letter of the Secretary of War
and Reoprts Touching the Apache Indians at Governor's
Island*, 51st Cong., 1st sess., Senate Executive Document
no. 35 (1890), pp. 3–4. Crook did not suggest that the
Chiricahuas be returned to Arizona. "Trouble might
ensue"—whether started by whites or Indians he did not

say—and if they did again break out, they would never surrender. Secretary of War Endicott, July 30, 1886, in Welsh, *Apache Prisoners*, p. 42: "President Cleveland has assured him [Chato] that so long as he shall keep faith with the government his interest shall be looked after"; Chato's discharge, signed by Crawford, October 23, 1885, gives his character as "good" (Welsh, *Apache Prisoners*, p. 43).

48. W. C. Brown, Diary, April 20, 1898, in Gatewood Collection; Betzinez, *I Fought with Geronimo*, p. 182; Debo, *Geronimo*, pp. 358–454; Ball, *Indeh*, pp. 122–276.

49. Frederic Remington, "How an Apache War Was Won," in Harold McCracken, ed., *Frederic Remington's Own West* (New York: Dial, 1960); Powhatan Clarke, "A Hot Trail," *Cosmopolitan* 17 (October 1894):706–16; Thrapp, *Al Sieber*, pp. 314–50; Goodwin, *Western Apache Raiding*, pp. 137–40, 175–85. Masai and the Apache Kid have been described as typical Apaches, but in fact they were cut off from Apache society in a way that was most abnormal.

50. James A. Shannon, "With the Apache Scouts in Mexico," in H. B. Wharfield, *Apache Indian Scouts* (El Cajon, Calif., 1964), pp. 70–84; John No-Sey, "Must Buy Their Own Coffins," *Winners of the West*, June 30, 1934; it is noteworthy that more than one Indian scout wrote to this publication, published for veterans of the Indian wars. H. B. Wharfield, *With Scouts and Cavalry at Fort Apache* (Tucson: Arizona Pioneers Historical Society, 1965); Rita Doerner, "Sinew Riley, Apache Scout," *Journal of Arizona History* 14 (Winter 1973):271–80.

11. The White Man's Road

1. The characterization of Crook is in Robert M. Utley, *The Contribution of the Frontier to the American Military Tradition* (Colorado Springs: U.S. Air Force Academy, 1977), p. 7; Crook's recommendations are in George Crook, *General George Crook: His Autobiography*, ed. Martin F. Schmitt (Norman: University of Oklahoma Press, 1946), p. 214; Crook to Commissioner J. R. C.

Atkins, November 28, 1887, Letters Received OIA, RG 75,
NARS; Augur's and McDowell's reports in U.S. Congress,
House, Secretary of War, *Annual Report, 1867*, 1:59,
126-27.

2. See, for instance, Crook's complaints in Secretary of War,
Annual Report, 1883, 1:169: ". . . friendly and peaceable
Indians like the Hualpais are allowed to actually starve . . .
we are constantly offering inducements for them to mis-
behave." Luther Standing Bear, a Sioux, recalls being en-
rolled as a scout at the age of ten, in 1877; this must have
been a means of issuing rations and pay to the family
(Luther Standing Bear, *My People, the Sioux* [Boston:
Houghton Mifflin, 1928], pp. 89-90).

3. Crook, *General George Crook*, p. 214; Roy W. Meyer, *The
Village Indians of the Upper Missouri* (Lincoln: University
of Nebraska Press, 1977), p. 127; Saul M. Janney to Ely
Parker, February 17, 1870, Letters Received, Pawnee
Agency, RG 75, NARS.

4. Mark H. Brown and W. R. Felton, *The Frontier Years*
(New York: Holt, Rinehart & Winston, 1955), p. 117;
Ralph H. Ogle, *Federal Control of the Western Apaches,
1848-1886* (Albuquerque: University of New Mexico
Press, 1970), pp. 150-59; Michael L. Tate, "Apache
Scouts, Police, and Judges as Agents of Acculturation,
1865-1920," Ph.D. dissertation, University of Toledo,
1974, pp. 93-95.

5. Joyce Evelyn Mason, "The Use of Indian Scouts in the
Apache Wars, 1870-1886," Ph.D. dissertation, Indiana
University, 1970), p. 206; H. B. Wharfield, *Alchesay* (El
Cajon, Calif.: Apache Press, 1969), pp. 10-11.

6. George Bird Grinnell, *The Fighting Cheyennes* (Norman:
University of Oklahoma Press, 1955), pp. 412, 428; Wil-
liam White, *Custer, Cavalry, and Crows* (Fort Collins,
Colo.: Old Army Press, 1975), pp. 123-24; Nelson A.
Miles, *Personal Recollections and Observations of General
Nelson A. Miles* (Chicago: Werner, 1896), pp. 248, 267-
68, 277-78.

7. For the assimilation movement, see Francis Paul Prucha,
American Indian Policy in Crisis (Norman: University of

Oklahoma Press, 1976); Henry A. Fritz, *Movement for
Indian Assimilation* (Philadelphia: University of Pennsylvania Press, 1963). A. C. Greene, ed., *The Last Captive*
(Austin: Encino Press, 1972), p. 21, suggests that Indian
methods of assimilating captives were very effective
brainwashing.

8. Richard H. Pratt, *Battlefield and Classroom*, ed. Robert M.
Utley (New Haven: Yale University Press, 1964), pp. 100–
154; Karen D. Petersen, *Plains Indian Art from Fort
Marion* (Norman: University of Oklahoma Press, 1971);
James F. Downs, *Cultures in Crisis* (Beverly Hills, Calif.:
Glencoe Press, 1971), pp. 163–64.

9. John Gregory Bourke, *On the Border with Crook* (1891;
rpt. Lincoln: University of Nebraska Press, 1971), p. 338;
H. C. Cushing, "Military Colonization of Indians,"
United Service 3 (September 1880):370–75; George S.
Wilson, "How Shall the American Savage Be Civilized?,"
Atlantic Monthly 50 (November 1882):596–607; William
H. Powell, "The Indian as a Soldier," *United Service*
n.s. 3 (March 1890):229–38; Ezra P. Ewers, "The Military
Service of Indians," *Journal of the United Military Service
Institution of the United States* 15 (November 1894):
1188–92; Frederic Remington, "Indians as Irregular Cav-
alry," *Harper's Weekly*, December 27, 1890, pp. 1005–6.
Wilson's proposal was a relatively conventional one for
making yeomen farmers out of a specific tribe, the Pimas,
but it was to be carried out under military control.

10. Cushing, "Military Colonization."

11. Crook to John D. C. Atkins, November 28, 1887, Letters
Received, OIA, RG 75, NARS.

12. Cushing, "Military Colonization," p. 371.

13. U.S. Congress, House, Commissioner of Indian Affairs,
Annual Report, 1878, p. 5.

14. U.S. Congress, House, *Tonkawa Indians at Fort Griffin,
Texas*, 44th Cong., 1st sess., House Executive Document
no. 102 (1875); Kenneth W. Porter, "The Seminole-Negro
Indian Scouts, 1870–1881," *Southwestern Historical
Quarterly* 55 (January 1952):357–77; Thomas B. Marquis,
Wooden Leg (1931; rpt. Lincoln: University of Nebraska

Press, 1962), p. 327; U.S. Congress, Senate, *Walapai Papers*, 74th Cong., 2d sess. (1890), Senate Executive Document no. 273; James B. Barry, *A Texas Ranger and Frontiersman*, ed. James K. Greer (Dallas: Southwest Press, 1932), p. 111; James Chisholm, *South Pass*, ed. Lola M. Homsher (Lincoln: University of Nebraska Press, 1960), pp. 83, 110; Gatewood to Indian Agent, San Carlos, Arizona Territory, February 8, 1883, Letters Received, OIA, RG 75, NARS; Homer W. Wheeler, *Buffalo Days* (New York: A. L. Burt, 1925), pp. 211–12.

15. Francis Paul Prucha, ed., *Americanizing the American Indians* (Cambridge: Harvard University Press, 1973); Bourke, *On the Border*, pp. 458–59.

16. Fritz, *Movement for Indian Assimilation*, pp. 132–33.

17. General Orders no. 28, in Secretary of War, *Annual Report, 1891*, 1:102.

18. Don Rickey, Jr., "Warrior-Soldiers: The All-Indian 'L' Troop, 6th U.S. Cavalry, in the Early 1890s," in Ray Brandes, ed., *Troopers West* (San Diego: Frontier Heritage Press, 1970), pp. 42–43.

19. John M. Schofield, *Forty-six Years in the Army* (New York: Century, 1897), pp. 485–89; Rickey, "Warrior-Soldiers," pp. 56–57; Hugh L. Scott, *Some Memories of a Soldier* (New York: Century, 1928), pp. 169–70. The rise and decline of the Indian companies can be traced in Secretary of War, *Annual Reports, 1891 to 1897*. See also Wheeler, *Buffalo Days*, pp. 284–303, on Wheeler's Southern Cheyenne and Arapaho company of the Fifth Cavalry; William Bruce White, "The Military and the Melting Pot," Ph.D. dissertation, University of Wisconsin, 1968. See also Michael L. Tate, "Soldiers of the Line: Apache Companies in the U.S. Army, 1891–1897," *Arizona and the West* 16 (Winter 1974):343–64.

20. John Morgan Gates, *Schoolbooks and Krags* (Westport, Conn.: Greenwood Press, 1973), pp. 85, 174–75, 212–13, 233. For a proposal to enlist a troop of Sioux cavalry at Cheyenne River reservation, South Dakota, for the Spanish-American War, see Fremont Stewart to Alfred Lee, June 10, 1898, Richardson Collection, South Dakota Historical Society, Pierre (courtesy Terence Lindell).

12. Conclusion

1. U.S. Congress, House, Commissioner of Indian Affairs, *Annual Report, 1878*, pp. x–xii; Robert M. Utley, *Frontier Regulars* (New York: Macmillan, 1973), p. 57. For a particularly interesting example in which General Sheridan intervened on the Southern Cheyenne and Arapaho reservation, removing the agent and enlisting a number of the younger men as scouts, see U.S. Congress, House, Secretary of War, *Annual Report, 1885*, 1:66–70; Donald J. Berthrong, *The Cheyenne and Arapaho Ordeal* (Norman: University of Oklahoma Press, 1976), pp. 109–15.

2. On torture, see George Bird Grinnell to W. S. Campbell, May 6, 1929, in Stanley Vestal, ed., *New Sources of Indian History, 1850–1891* (Norman: University of Oklahoma Press, 1934), p. 157; Stanley Vestal, *Warpath* (Boston: Houghton Mifflin, 1934), p. 69. In Grant Foreman, ed., *Adventure on Red River* (Norman: University of Oklahoma Press, 1937), p. 169, Marcy asserts, ". . . the prairie Indians do not put their prisoners to death by prolonged tortures." On Apache torture, see Grenville Goodwin, *The Social Organization of the Western Apache* (Tucson: University of Arizona Press, 1969), p. 554. The mythology of the subject undoubtedly owes much to experience with eastern tribes, some of which certainly did torture prisoners; see Francis Jennings, *The Invasion of America* (Chapel Hill: University of North Carolina Press, 1975), pp. 160–64.

3. On volunteers taking scalps, see LeRoy R. Hafen and Anne W. Hafen, eds., *Powder River Campaigns and Sawyers Expedition of 1865* (Glendale, Calif.: Arthur H. Clark, 1961), p. 128; George E. Hyde, *Life of George Bent*, ed. Savoie Lottinville (Norman: University of Oklahoma Press, 1968), p. 154; James S. Brisbin, *Belden, the White Chief* (Cincinnati: C. F. Vent, 1870), pp. 365, 370; Charles H. Springer, *Soldiering in Sioux Country, 1865*, ed. Benjamin F. Cooling (San Diego: Frontier Heritage Press, 1971), pp. 44–45; Frederic Remington, "How the Law Got into the Chaparral," in Harold McCracken, ed., *Frederic Remington's Own West* (New York: Dial, 1960), p. 116. Dan L.

Thrapp, "Where Was the Battle of Turret Peak Fought?," in Brandes, ed., *Troopers West*, p. 108, implies torture by Apache scouts to gain information, without citing evidence.

4. John F. Finerty, *War-path and Bivouac* (Norman: University of Oklahoma Press, 1971), p. 262; John Gregory Bourke, Diaries, 5:415, U.S. Military Academy Library, West Point, N.Y.

5. Miles to Assistant Adjutant General, Department of Dakota, December 24, 1877, in Frank D. Baldwin, Letters and Diaries, W. C. Brown Papers, Western Historical Collections, University of Colorado, Boulder. Miles does not mention the incident in his memoirs. Thomas H. Leforge, *Memoirs of a White Crow Indian* (1928; rpt. Lincoln: University of Nebraska Press, 1974), pp. 269–70, claims the Crows were unaware they were attacking a truce party, and were both shamed and frightened when they found out; this was a violation of their own rules of war, and the Sioux would single them out for vengeance.

6. Luther North insisted that Frank and he never permitted torture by the Pawnee scouts; scalping was permitted (interview in *Omaha World-Herald*, October 2, 1910; L. H. North to G. B. Grinnell, February 2, 1877, both in Luther H. North Papers, NSHS). Frank North once invited reporter Henry Stanley to view the Cheyenne scalps his men had just taken at Plum Creek in 1867 (Henry M. Stanley, *My Early Travels and Adventures in America and Asia*, 2 vols. [New York: Scribner's, 1895], 1:196).

7. William P. Clark, *The Indian Sign-Language* (Philadelphia: L. R. Hamersley, 1885), pp. 395–97. Clark observes: "In all our Indian wars it has *seemed* necessary to use Indian allies"; the wording seems to imply doubt about the necessity. Such a statement from a man of his experience cannot be disregarded, although there is abundant evidence to the contrary. Clark also notes that a chief serving as a scout (Little Wolf?) told him that his people killed women and children to terrorize the enemy—the same reason given by many white advocates of a similar policy.

8. See William White's account of the killing of Blackfoot prisoners by cavalry under orders, in William White, *Custer, Cavalry, and Crows* (Fort Collins, Colo.: Old Army Press, 1975), p. 33. This is a secondhand account, but White knew these men and believed the story.

9. Jennings, *Invasion of America*, pp. 146–70; William B. Skelton, "Army Officers' Attitudes toward Indians, 1830–1860," *Pacific Northwest Quarterly* 67 (July 1976):120–23; Louise K. Barnett, *The Ignoble Savage* (Westport, Conn.: Greenwood Press, 1975), p. 98.

10. Crook's statement in Dan L. Thrapp, ed., *Dateline Fort Bowie* (Norman: University of Oklahoma Press, 1979), p. 111. Oliver O. Howard, *Nez Perce Joseph* (Boston: Lee & Shepard, 1881), pp. 251–52, wrestles with the moral problems, but arrives only at the conventional dichotomy of civilized and savage warfare. Thomas C. Leonard, *Above the Battle* (New York: Oxford University Press, 1978), examines American attitudes toward war in this period, and the yearning for a "worthy opponent."

11. George Crook, *General George Crook: His Autobiography*, ed. Martin F. Schmitt (Norman: University of Oklahoma Press, 1946), p. 214.

12. Frank B. Linderman, *Plenty-coups, Chief of the Crows* (Lincoln: University of Nebraska Press, 1962), pp. 78, 154; Peter Nabokov, *Two Leggings* (New York: Crowell, 1967), p. 187.

13. It can be argued that it was the fear of further resistance, in the case of the Sioux and Cheyennes, that prevented removal.

14. The military did not always appreciate the parallel, however. A colonel asked Captain Charley, a Tonkawa leader, why the tribe did not farm and build houses. Charley asked the colonel why he did not do the same. The colonel explained that as a soldier and an officer, he was not supposed to work. Charley then observed that "me and you all the same; you soldier, you no work; me warrior, me not work" (H. H. McConnell, *Five Years a Cavalryman* [Freeport, N.Y.: Books for Libraries Press, 1970], p. 60).

15. Philip Régis de Trobriand, *Army Life in Dakota*, ed. Milo M. Quaif (Chicago: Donnelly, 1941), pp. 170–74, 223.
16. Carl C. Rister, *Fort Griffin on the Texas Frontier* (Norman: University of Oklahoma Press, 1956), pp. 72, 129, 208; Thomas B. Marquis, *Wooden Leg* (1931; rpt. Lincoln: University of Nebraska Press, 1962), p. 334, and *Cheyenne and Sioux* (Stockton, Calif.: Pacific Center for Western Historical Studies, 1973), p. 39.
17. Michael L. Tate, "John P. Clum and the Origins of an Apache Constabulary, 1874–77," *American Indian Quarterly* 3 (Summer 1977):115.

Bibliographical Essay

Fuller references are given in the notes. For a more complete bibliography, see Thomas W. Dunlay, "Indian Scouts and Auxiliaries with the U.S. Army in the Trans-Mississippi West, 1860–1890," Ph.D. dissertation, University of Nebraska–Lincoln, 1980.

The most significant source of unpublished archival materials has been the Nebraska State Historical Society, Lincoln. The Papers of Frank J. North and Luther H. North are, of course, indispensable sources on the history of the Pawnee scouts, and offer many useful insights into the Plains conflicts and Indian-white relations. The John G. Bourke Papers are also part of the society archives, along with microfilms of Bourke's diaries, the originals of which are in the U.S. Military Academy Library, West Point, New York. Also in the society collections are the transcribed interviews conducted by Eli S. Ricker early in this century, with various early frontiersmen, Indians, mixed-bloods, and veterans of the Indians wars. Although Ricker seems to have interjected his own conclusions on occasion and put things in his own words, this is nonetheless an invaluable source of oral history, which has been exploited by only a few scholars.

Part of the Frank J. North Collection is Alfred Sorenson, "A Quarter of a Century on the Frontier, or the Adventures of Major Frank North, the 'White Chief of the Pawnee,' The Story of His Life as Told by Himself and Written by Alfred Sorenson," a manuscript apparently prepared with North's help before his death in 1885; page references are to a typed transcript.

The Charles B. Gatewood Collection in the Arizona Historical Society, Tucson, consists of material collected by C. B. Gatewood, Jr., apparently with the intention of writing a life of his father. It does include fragmentary memoirs by C. B. Gatewood, Sr., along with his correspondence. There is also valuable correspondence between C. B. Gatewood, Jr., and various veterans of the Indian wars, and copies of official correspondence, chiefly from the last Geronimo campaign, 1885–86.

Dr. Merrill G. Burlingame, of Bozeman, Montana, made available portions of the Gustavus C. Doane Papers, dealing with Doane's service with Crow scouts; these papers will eventually be deposited with the library of the University of Montana, Bozeman.

I consulted many of the materials from the National Archives and Record Service in microfilm at the Nebraska State Historical Society. These materials include Record Group 75, Letters Received, Office of Indian Affairs, Pawnee Agency, 1859–1880; Record Group 500 (special designation), Company muster rolls and records of events, Omaha and Pawnee Scouts, 1865–66; U.S. War Department, Records of U.S. Army Commands, Selected Documents, Headquarters, Department of the Platte, 1866–67; Letters Received, Office of Adjutant General, 1871–1880, Roll 259—Indian Scouts Correspondence, 1876–78. The last is extremely revealing and has never been cited by historians before.

At the National Archives in Washington, I consulted various records, including a number of company records for Indian scout detachments, primarily from Arizona. These are interesting and provide some useful insights, but the fact that Indians often enlisted under various names at various times creates problems with their use. I also consulted personnel files on various officers and the post records of Fort Griffin, Texas (Record Group 393, Part III), which contain the records of the Tonkawa scouts.

Among government publications, of particular value have been *Record of Engagements with Hostile Indians within the Military Division of the Missouri, 1868 to 1882,* and *Chronological List of Actions, etc., with Indians, from January 1, 1866, to January, 1891.* The first has been reprinted by the Old Army Press, and both are included in Joseph P. Peters, comp., *Indian*

Battles and Skirmishes on the American Frontier (New York: Argonaut Press, 1966).

The annual reports of the secretaries of war and of the commissioners of Indian affairs include innumerable reports of officers and Indian agents. These reports were published annually as House executive documents, the latter as part of the report of the secretary of the interior. Among other Congressional documents, special notice should be given to *Tonkawa Indians at Fort Griffin, Texas* (44th Cong., 1st sess., House Executive Document no. 102 [1875]); *Papers Relative to Indian Operations on the Plains* (50th Cong., 1st sess., Senate Executive Document no. 33 [1887]); *Reports Touching the Apache Indians at Governor's Island* (51st Cong., 1st sess., Senate Executive Document no. 35 [1890]).

The indispensable work for anyone studying any Civil War military operation is *War of the Rebellion: A Compilation of the Official Records of the Union and Confederate Armies*, 53 vols. (Washington, D.C.: Government Printing Office, 1880–1900).

Published Primary Material

The popularity of the Old West and the Indian Wars has ensured that a wealth of primary material has been published, and in many cases reprinted over the years. Naturally these materials have received attention from historians, but since few historians were specifically interested in Indian scouts or in Indian-white cooperation and the motives behind it, the same materials might well repay further examination.

As mentioned earlier, few professional historians made any attempt to gather the recollections of Indian participants in the wars of the nineteenth century while those people were still alive. Such materials as we have we owe to the efforts of anthropologists and amateurs of varying degrees of competence. Most of these researchers were not specifically interested in Indian scouts as such, with the exception of Custer's scouts in 1876. For this material, see O. G. Libby, ed., *The Arikara Narrative of the Campaign against the Hostile Dakotas, June 1876* (New York: Sol Lewis, 1973); Walter Camp, comp., *Custer in '76*

(Provo: Brigham Young University Press, 1976); W. A. Graham, comp., *The Custer Myth* (Harrisburg, Pa.: Stackpole, 1952). Frank B. Linderman, *Plenty-coups, Chief of the Crows* (1930; reprinted Lincoln: University of Nebraska Press, 1962), is also significant.

Recollections by Apache scouts are scarce, but a very good one is that of John Rope, in Grenville Goodwin, *Western Apache Raiding and Warfare*, ed. Keith H. Basso (Tucson: University of Arizona Press, 1970); a shorter memoir by the scout David Longstreet is in the same volume. Significant observations by sons of scouts may be found in Morris Opler, "A Chiricahua Apache's Account of the Geronimo Campaign of 1886," *New Mexico Historical Review* 13 (October 1938):360–86, and Opler's *Apache Odyssey: A Journey between Two Worlds* (New York: Holt, Rinehart & Winston, 1969). George Bird Grinnell recorded some useful material on Pawnee and Cheyenne scouts in his *Pawnee Hero Stories and Folk Tales* (1889; reprinted Lincoln: University of Nebraska Press, 1961), and *The Fighting Cheyennes* (Norman: University of Oklahoma Press, 1955).

Recollections from the "hostile" side are often significant for an understanding of the scouts' effectiveness, motives, and cultural background. Stanley Vestal's *Warpath* (Boston: Houghton Mifflin, 1934), the recollections of Chief White Bull, is valuable. George E. Hyde, *The Life of George Bent, Written from His Letters*, ed. Savoie Lottinville (Norman: University of Oklahoma Press, 1968), is a uniquely valuable source for the Plains wars of the 1860s.

Jason Betzinez, *I Fought with Geronimo*, with W. S. Nye (Harrisburg, Pa.: Stackpole, 1959), is of value, although it is certainly colored by the author's thorough assimilation into white society. In spite of certain strictures in the text, Eve Ball's collections of Apache reminiscences are of immense value; see *In the Days of Victorio: Recollections of a Warm Springs Apache* (Tucson: University of Arizona Press, 1970); *Indeh: An Apache Odyssey* (Provo, Utah: Brigham Young University Press, 1980); and "The Apache Scouts: A Chiricahua Appraisal," *Arizona and the West* 7 (Winter 1967):315–28.

Thomas B. Marquis also collected valuable material from Indians and whites in Montana. The most helpful include *Wooden*

Leg: A Warrior Who Fought Custer (1931; reprinted Lincoln: University of Nebraska Press, 1962) and *Cheyenne and Sioux* (Stockton, Calif.: Pacific Center for Western Historical Studies, 1973); and, with Thomas H. Leforge, *Memoirs of a White Crow Indian* (1928; reprinted Lincoln: University of Nebraska Press, 1974).

Certain collections of documents have had special value: Leroy R. Hafen and Ann W. Hafen, eds., *Powder River Campaigns and Sawyers Expedition* (Glendale, Calif.: Arthur H. Clark, 1961); Ernest Wallace, ed., "Ranald Mackenzie's Official Correspondence Relative to Texas . . . ," *Museum Journal* 9 (1965) and 10 (1966); Joe F. Taylor, ed., "The Indian Campaign on the Staked Plains, 1874–75: Military Correspondence . . . ," *Panhandle-Plains Historical Review* 34 (1961) and 35 (1962). The papers presented by veterans at meetings of the Order of Indian Wars have been edited by John M. Carroll and published as *Papers of the Order of Indian Wars* (Fort Collins, Colo.: Old Army Press, 1975).

Memoirs and reminiscences by whites have their recognized limitations, especially in understanding of Indians, but are indispensable nevertheless. Among those that give insight into the important Texas frontier experience are Noah Smithwick, *The Evolution of a State* (Austin: Gammel, 1900); John S. Ford, *Rip Ford's Texas*, ed. Stephen B. Oates (Austin: University of Texas Press, 1963); James Pike, *Scout and Ranger* (Princeton: Princeton University Press, 1932); John Henry Brown, *Indian Wars and Pioneers of Texas* (Austin: L. E. Daniel, n.d.); Raymond Estep, ed., "Lieutenant Wm. E. Burnett Letters . . . ," *Chronicles of Oklahoma* 38 (Autumn and Winter 1960):274–309, 369–96, and 39 (Spring 1961):15–41.

Army reminiscences vary greatly in quality, and most represent officers' viewpoints. Among the very best are those of John G. Bourke: *On the Border with Crook* (1891; reprinted Lincoln: University of Nebraska Press, 1971); *An Apache Campaign in the Sierra Madre* (New York: Scribner's, 1958); and *Mackenzie's Last Fight with the Cheyennes: With General Crook in the Indian Wars* (Palo Alto: Lewis Osborne, 1968). Also very good are Britton Davis, *The Truth about Geronimo* (1929; reprinted Lincoln: University of Nebraska Press, 1976), and Thomas Cruse,

Apache Days and After (Caldwell, Ida.: Caxton Printers, 1940). Robert G. Carter, *On the Border with Mackenzie* (Washington, D.C.: Eynon, 1935), does not display the same sympathy for Indians, but is immensely informative about Plains campaigning and about the Tonkawa scouts in particular. Hugh L. Scott, *Some Memories of a Soldier* (New York: Century, 1928), and Homer W. Wheeler, *Buffalo Days* (New York: A. L. Burt, 1925), are of great interest. James H. Bradley, *The March of the Montana Column*, ed. Edgar I. Stewart (Norman: University of Oklahoma Press, 1961), has the value of having been written soon after the events. Charles B. Gatewood, "Campaigning against Victorio in 1879," *The Great Divide* (April 1894):102–4; W. E. Shipp, "Captain Crawford's Last Campaign," *Journal of the U.S. Cavalry Association* 5 (December 1892):343–61; Stanton G. Fisher, "Journal of S. G. Fisher, Chief of Scouts to General O. O. Howard during the Campaign against the Nez Perce Indians, 1877," *Contributions to the Historical Society of Montana* 2 (Helena: State Publishing Co., 1896):269–82; and John Bigelow, *On the Bloody Trail of Geronimo* (Los Angeles: Westernlore, 1958), are all close to the events and offer special insights.

General George Crook: His Autobiography, ed. Martin F. Schmitt (Norman: University of Oklahoma Press, 1946), offers surprisingly little on scouts, but much on the general's very positive opinions on other matters.

In a class by themselves are W. P. Clark, *The Indian Sign Language* (Philadelphia: L. R. Hamersly, 1885), and Edward S. Farrow, *Mountain Scouting* (New York: privately printed, 1881), as they offer not just reminiscence, but analysis applied to the frontier military experience, in a form intended to be of use to fellow officers. The same is true of George Crook, "The Apache Problem," *Journal of the Military Service Institution of the United States* 7 (1886):257–69, and Crook's *Résumé of Operations against Apache Indians, 1882 to 1886* (Omaha: privately printed, 1886), though they also constitute a defense of Crook's policies.

Luther North, brother of Frank, reminisced frequently and at length about his brother and the Pawnee Scouts; see Robert Bruce, *The Fighting Norths and Pawnee Scouts* (Lincoln: Nebraska State Historical Society, 1932), and Luther H. North,

Man of the Plains, ed. Donald Danker (Lincoln: University of Nebraska Press, 1961).

Secondary Sources

Certain theses and dissertations have been particularly helpful, among them Joyce Evelyn Mason, "The Use of Indian Scouts in the Apache Wars, 1870-1886," Ph.D. dissertation, Indiana University, 1970, and Michael L. Tate, "Apache Scouts, Police and Judges as Agents of Acculturation, 1865-1920," Ph.D. dissertation, University of Toledo, 1974.

For the military background and history of the frontier, consult Francis P. Prucha, *The Sword of the Republic* (New York: Macmillan, 1969), and three works by Robert M. Utley: *Frontiersmen in Blue: The United States Army and the Indian, 1848-1865* (New York: Macmillan, 1967), *Frontier Regulars: The United States Army and the Indian, 1866-1891* (New York: Macmillan, 1973), and *The Contribution of the Frontier to the American Military Tradition* (Colorado Springs: U.S. Air Force Academy, 1977). A comparison with the experience of other armies can be found in C. E. Callwell, *Small Wars: Their Principles and Practice* (London: His Majesty's Stationery Office, 1906).

A number of valuable works on white attitudes toward Indians have been published, but they rely heavily on elite sources; see Roy Harvey Pearce, *Savagism and Civilization: A Study of the Indian and the American Mind* (Baltimore: Johns Hopkins Press, 1953, 1965); Robert F. Berkhofer, *The White Man's Indian* (New York: Alfred A. Knopf, 1978); Louise K. Barnett, *The Ignoble Savage* (Westport, Conn.: Greenwood Press, 1975). There are two valuable articles on military attitudes: William B. Skelton, "Army Officers' Attitudes toward Indians, 1830-1860," *Pacific Northwest Quarterly* 67 (July 1976):113-24, and Thomas C. Leonard, "Red, White, and the Army Blue: Empathy and Anger in the American West," *American Quarterly* 26 (May 1974): 176-90.

The Indian-army relationship and the frontier military experience have not been fully explored, despite all of the writing on the subject. Russell F. Weigley, *Towards an American Army* (New York: Columbia University Press, 1962), and Timothy K. Nenninger, *The Leavenworth Schools and the Old Army* (Westport, Conn.: Greenwood Press, 1978), both regard the frontier period as one of stagnation, making no intellectual demands on the officers. Neil B. Thompson, *Crazy Horse Called Them Walk-A-Heaps* (St. Cloud, Minn.: North Star Press, 1979), despite a misleading title, is a critical analysis of the frontier army.

Analyses of Indian military tactics are few. Harry H. Turney-High, *Primitive War: Its Practice and Concepts* (Columbia: University of South Carolina Press, 1949), is at least thought-provoking. See also Frank R. Secoy, *Changing Military Patterns on the Great Plains* (Seattle: University of Washington Press, 1971).

For the Spanish antecedents of the Indian scouts, see Philip Wayne Powell, *Soldiers, Indians, and Silver* (Tempe: Arizona State University Press, 1975), and Oakah L. Jones, *Pueblo Warriors and Spanish Conquest* (Norman: University of Oklahoma Press, 1966). A provocative study of the English colonial background is Francis Jennings, *The Invasion of America* (Chapel Hill: University of North Carolina Press, 1975).

The indispensable works on the Apache wars are those of Dan L. Thrapp: *Al Sieber, Chief of Scouts* (Norman: University of Oklahoma Press, 1964); *The Conquest of Apacheria* (Norman: University of Oklahoma Press, 1967); *General Crook and the Sierra Madre Adventure* (Norman: University of Oklahoma Press, 1972); *Victorio and the Mimbres Apaches* (Norman: University of Oklahoma Press, 1973).

The field of Indian wars history has produced much second-rate writing, but among many excellent studies these should be mentioned: Robert I. Burns, *The Jesuits and the Indian Wars of the Northwest* (New Haven: Yale University Press, 1966); Mark H. Brown, *The Flight of the Nez Perce* (New York: Putnam, 1967); Frank McNitt, *Navajo Wars* (Albuquerque: University of New Mexico Press, 1972); T. R. Fehrenbach, *Comanches* (New York: Alfred A. Knopf, 1974); Jesse W. Vaughn, *Indian Fights* (Norman: University of Oklahoma Press, 1966); and James L. Haley, *The Buffalo War* (New York: Doubleday, 1976).

Anthropological studies have been invaluable, even if the historian cannot always resist a pointed comment. Among those of particular value, see Preston Holder, *The Hoe and the Horse on the Plains* (Lincoln: University of Nebraska Press, 1970); Gene Weltfish, *The Lost Universe* (1965; reprinted Lincoln: University of Nebraska Press, 1977); Royal B. Hassrick, *The Sioux: Life and Customs of a Warrior Society* (Norman: University of Oklahoma Press, 1964); William K. Jones, *Notes on the History and Material Culture of the Tonkawa Indians* (Washington, D.C.: Smithsonian Institution, 1969); and W. W. Newcomb, *The Indians of Texas* (Austin: University of Texas Press, 1961).

Ethnohistorical studies of particular value include Richard White, "The Winning of the West: The Expansion of the Western Sioux in the Eighteenth and Nineteenth Centuries," *Journal of American History* 69 (September 1979):319–43; W. W. Newcomb, "A Re-examination of the Causes of Plains Warfare," *American Anthropologist* 52 (July–September 1950):317–30; P. Richard Metcalf, "Who Should Rule at Home?: Native American Politics and Indian-White Relations," *Journal of American History* 61 (December 1974):651–65.

Index